MOMENT BY MOMENT

*One moment of a man's life is a fact so stupen-
dous as to take the lustre out of all fiction.*
RALPH WALDO EMERSON, 1803-1882

God creates the world anew in each moment.
JAN VAN RUYSBROECK, 1293-1381

The sacrament of the present moment.
JEAN PIERRE DE CAUSSADE, 1676-1751

MOMENT BY MOMENT

by Margaret T. Applegarth

author of *Men as Trees Walking,*
Right Here, Right Now, etc.

HARPER & BROTHERS PUBLISHERS

New York

CONTENTS

MOMENT BY MOMENT

1

THE YEAST IS RISING EVERYWHERE

For it is God which worketh in you both to will and to do of
His good pleasure.   GALATIANS 2:13

It must have been a memorable moment. It always is, when men
give recipes, and get them right! Other men trying not to look
too relieved. And women whispering to neighbors beside them:
"His mother's recipe, doubtless!" And doubtless it was. But
what wiser way to tease a listener into catching His real meaning? So? the Kingdom of heaven is like leaven? which a woman
took and hid in three measures of meal until the whole was
leavened? Everybody saw the drama—
  The Leaven nudging the Lump: "Come on and get up!"
  The Lump, lumpishly: "Let me alone! I don't want to! Stop
that shoving!"
  The Leaven, in a ferment of excitement, unable *not* to nudge:
"Get up! get up! get up! Can't you feel me pushing? prodding?"
  The Lump, resisting every inch of the way. But, moment by
moment, slowly rising. Then lo! *The Loaf!* All in order that a
family may be fed.
  But no matter how many women—from Palestine to the present moment—have considered this drama domestic, a chemist in
the congregation could create a sensation by whispering to the
worshiper beside him: "Listen, lady! What a text that was! Do
you realize what He was really saying? Do you know that one
spoonful of yeast, if allowed to increase under normal conditions,
with a food supply available, could expand in eleven months into
a mass equal to the size of the entire earth? Now *that's* the Kingdom of heaven at work in earnest!"

1

The lady knew enough not to laugh in church, but how could she help it, when a perfectly respectable stranger talked fairy tales: "Oh come now," she whispered back. "Not just *one* spoonful? And not in eleven months!"

"One spoonful! In eleven months! The church's most gigantic message, that!"

"Gigantic!" she gasped. "But equal to the entire earth?"

"The entire earth!"

She could hardly listen to the sermon from wondering about leaven. Safe little, tame little, quiet little leaven. Something she herself hid. And then forgot. Expecting it to do its duty, sight unseen.

She made a point of falling in step with the stranger walking down the aisle after church: "Just how do you know all those facts?"

"From being a chemist, madam. I kept wishing all through the sermon that that dominie of yours knew about Dr. van Veen of Holland. It would have been a jolly good footnote for him! Dr. van Veen spoke down at Atlantic City, at the convention of our American Chemical Society. Fantastic story he told. Seems he had been in a Japanese prison camp over in Java. The guards aimed to kill off the entire batch of 11,000 prisoners by a dreadful diet, sure to produce every known variety of deficiency diseases. So if you ever get interned, be sure to land in the same prison with a chemist! For what did Dr. van Veen do but start making yeast. Exposed a solution of sugar to the air. Trapped a few cells of it. Cultured them with more food—slices of putrid sweet potato, old rotten fish. Moment by moment those budding yeast cells began multiplying at their usual speed—lady, it's thrilling mathematics: each cell multiplying its own weight two thousand times every twenty-four hours! Those imprisoned chemists in Java just fed their yeast cells all sorts of stuff—sodden soybeans, poisoned fish. Until their yeast began providing plenty of palatable proteins and vitamins. And 11,000 listless prisoners began to feel like human beings again. Talk about feeding the five thousand! Don't ever doubt it, when yeast doubled that count in one prison camp in Java!"

The lady shook hands, with regret: "This is what you call thinking God's thoughts after Him, isn't it? Where is your Dr. van Veen now?"

"Right where a chemist with imagination belongs—in the United Nations! Expanding all over the earth!"

"And only eleven months to do it in, I suppose?"

"Exactly!"

The moment she reached home she hunted up a Baron von Hügel quotation which retold this same graphic story: "A Person came and lived and loved and did and taught and died and rose again, and lives on by His power and His spirit forever within us, and among us, so unspeakably rich and yet so simple, so sublime, and yet so homely, so divinely above us precisely in being so divinely near . . . to understand this Person there is needed all that all the races of civilization have to give in their experiments. None of them can understand the real workings of Christ until He has had His chance to stir everybody everywhere."

No wonder William James should say to the Lump: "Men habitually use only a small part of the powers which they actually possess, as low as 10 per cent; stating the thing broadly, the human being lives far below his limits. He energizes below his maximum, and he behaves below his optimum."

While Emerson addresses the Leaven: "Every great and commanding moment in the annals of the world is the triumph of some enthusiasm." ("*En–theos*": "*God in you.*")

In this little book, therefore, certain moments in the annals of the world are presented. To show that the Life within the Christian is timeless, dateless, ageless, raceless, as it expands all over the earth.

"The germ of love is the germ of prayer; the development and the perfection of love are the development and perfection of prayer. If you do not understand this, you have never yet loved and never prayed," old Nicholas Grou says to the Lump.

Within! within, O turn
Thy spirit's eyes, and learn
Thy wandering senses gently to control;
Thy dearest Friend dwells deep within Thy soul,
And asks thyself of thee,
That heart, and mind, and sense, He may make whole
In perfect harmony.

Gerhard Tersteegen

My God, my God! let me for once look on Thee
As though nought else existed; we alone.
And as creation crumbles, my soul's spark
Expands till I can say: "Even from myself
I need Thee, and I feel Thee, and I love Thee;
I do not plead my rapture in Thy works
For love of Thee—or that I feel as one
Who cannot die—but there is that in me
Which turns to Thee, which loves, or which should love."

Robert Browning

Stir up our hearts, O Lord, to make ready the way of
Thine Only-begotten Son, so that by His coming we may
be enabled to serve Thee with pure minds; through the
same Jesus Christ, Thy Son, our Lord, who liveth and
reigneth with Thee and the Holy Ghost, ever One God,
world without end. Amen.

Collect; *Lutheran Common Service Book*

2

THE DOXOLOGY OF THE DOUGH

Of the first of your dough ye shall give unto the Lord a heave
offering in your generation.   NUMBERS 15:21

Almost anybody would admit that this verse is antiquated. Hopelessly out of date. For who could follow such directions in our
generation? In our generation, with its sly sophisticated wise-
cracks—all more or less dirtbound, earthbound, skinbound, sex-
bound, scandalbound, drinkbound, fashionbound, gadgetbound,
noisebound, with radio blaring away by day and TV glaring
away by night—who would step forward and lift up dough and
wave it in church? Singing a doxology, too?

"People would think I was drunk!"

But as Emerson said in his sober New England way: "The eloquent man is no beautiful speaker, but one who is inwardly and
desperately drunk with a certain belief." *Drunk?*

To which that high brow from Harvard, William James, lent an
even more disturbing picture: "A Christian is an effective ferment
of goodness." *Ferment?*

Of course, on New Year's Eve, all sorts of people do get hopelessly spectacular. Perhaps that would be a suitable moment to
deal with Numbers 15, verse 21?

But Leon Bloy, the beloved French mystic, would stop any
such postponements: "It is to start right now to be a partaker in
Divinity, to be a child of God. Right now, and through all
eternity, continually rising upward, more and more moving, more
and more thunderous, not toward God, but in God, in the very
Essence of the Uncircumscribed."

"Now," said Emerson firmly, "now is the nick of time in matters
of eternity."

It hardly sounds like church. Not our good old First Church. But suppose the minister should announce a hymn. That always seems safe enough. So many well-bred people carried along by the thunder of the organ and the paid choir. But even the hymn is not safe as usual. By a woman. Not only unpredictable but too apt to write personally. Rather as Leon Bloy suggested Lucy Larcom wrote:

> Draw Thou my soul, O Christ,
> Closer to Thine;
> Breathe into every wish
> Thy will divine.
>
> Raised my low self above,
> Won by Thy deathless love,
> Ever, O Christ, through mine
> Let Thy life shine.

"The low self" certainly sounds like our generation! Sometimes in church, when the organ is playing and the pillars look especially superb, it comes over us that we are only half the persons we might be; but, how let God "breathe into every wish"? It is true that long centuries ago one of the earliest church fathers said in Latin something we found we could translate: *"Organum pulsatum a Spiritu sancto"*—"We are an organ played on by the Holy Spirit."

But how? And when?

"In the nick of time!" Emerson would say.

And although Mrs. James Hoover of Borneo had probably never heard of Gregory Nazianzen, she suddenly proved—in the nick of time—how right he was about the "organ." For once when her husband was away from their little jungle home in this tropical wilderness, she was terrified to see from her window that a group of fierce-looking head-hunters had completely surrounded the house. Here was ferment, surely! What to do? And how? Yet even while coming to the door, she saw their little cottage organ in the mission parlor. Quietly sitting down, as if led straight to the keyboard, she began playing hymns. The huge natives listened, fascinated, pleased by her friendliness. She played on and on. Wheezing out page after page of the familiar book. Always praying. Then, daring to turn her head away from the music, she saw a strange sight—all her dangerous warriors fast asleep, black elbows propped on black knees, black chins cupped in the palms of hands, massive headgear nodding; bliss on every face. And on hers!

For who else in all Borneo could have proved just then how truly Leon Bloy had spoken: "It is to start right now to be a partaker in Divinity, to be a child of God" . . . to be "an organ played on by the Holy Spirit."

The simplicity of it startles. Events never planned in any way turn out to be momentous when the things of God are lifted up and handled "in the very Essence of the Uncircumscribed." It is *"The Blessed Company of All True Believers"* come true in the twinkling of an eye. It is the enactment of the drama of the divine dough.

Somewhere Charles Péguy has said that one man reaches into his pocket and pulls out a word and uses it tamely. Whereas another man reaches into his pocket, but the word he pulls out is so electrifying that he tingles to his very fingertips, and shouts for joy, and is a new man forever after. This sounds like the doxology of the dough! Like "The Blessed Company of All True Believers" holding up bread and wine. But even these words take on extra quickening when pulled out of a pocket where a dictionary is—for *Blessed* is from the Old English "bledsian" meaning "to consecrate with blood"; and *Company* is from two Latin words meaning "bread together"; and *Believers* is Old English for "livers-by." Out of anybody's pocket these are electrifying words; ferment—in the nick of time!

At least that is the way it was one Good Friday in Italy when John Gualbert was riding on horseback along the narrow road from Porto Romano toward the Church of San Miniato. Suddenly he met his brother's murderer face to face. This was the eleventh century; and he had sworn that he would kill this man in revenge. So out came his sword in a flash. But then—the electrifying drama! For the adversary, unarmed, fell on his knees, and with arms outstretched in the form of the cross, implored him, for the sake of the Lord's holy passion on this very day, to spare his life.

Horrified at escaping such a crime on such a day, John Gualbert embraced the man in Christ's name, and let him go free. Then he humbly hastened to the Church of San Miniato, kneeling at the altar. We like to read in Butler's *Lives of the Saints* that the head of the Christ on the crucifix seemed to bow in approval! But the fact is that it was John Gualbert's own head that moved, and his own heart with it. For as Browning wrote: "A destiny disturbs our clod." And especially on the day when this upheaval of all old accepted plans had been offered up, and he could start becoming a "partaker in Divinity." No wonder John Gualbert became one of Italy's well-loved saints. The Bible disturbs our clod by saying that we are called to be saints, too. But not in a generation like ours! *We, with halos?* Too tame! But no word is more electrifying to pull out of Péguy's pocket: for "halo" means "threshing floor"! The place where chaff is gotten rid of; like a prologue for dough; like the discipline of climbing the steep ascent to heaven through peril, toil and pain. All of which seems too hard for church members? Of course the British really did it—blood and sweat and tears they called it, until they were a wonder to themselves; and in the nick of time it saved them all.

Nearly nine hundred years after John Gualbert knelt in San Miniato, an almost identical drama took place in New Zealand, at a Church of England Communion rail. Again we pull too tame a word from Péguy's pocket by simply saying "Converted" about the Maori tribes in New Zealand: a quarter of a century? Cannibals-into-church-members? But that minimizes the magnetism of "moving more and more toward God, of continually rising upward" which overcame one Maori chief named Tamati when he went to kneel at the Communion rail, to discover that he was beside Panapa, another Maori chief who had killed and eaten his father, only a few years before.

This was the first time they had met, and for a moment the old flaming spirit of revenge almost overwhelmed Tamati. He felt his muscles trembling from rage, his face contorted in fury; and he sprang to his feet determined to kill his enemy then and there, when suddenly all power passed straight out of his clenched fists. He opened them and looked at them in surprise. He came to himself, and walked down the long aisle to the door, then out into the churchyard. But in a few moments he returned. Very deliberately he knelt next to Panapa. Then sobs shook his whole body.

Later, the missionary asked him about this coming and going, this weeping. Tamati in New Zealand said almost what St. John Gualbert had said in Italy—for Tamati seemed to hear a voice telling him: "Hereby shall all men know that ye are my disciples, if ye love one another." Then he also saw a cross, and a man nailed on it, and he heard unforgettable words: "Father, forgive them."

Tamati then knew what Leon Bloy knew: "It is to start right now to be a partaker in Divinity." Precisely when it is hardest. Precisely when it is the custom in your generation to kill the man who killed your father. Right now, in the nick of time, to be an effective ferment of goodness. Right now, to be inwardly and desperately drunk with a new idea.

Until there is nothing tame about conversion. About turning completely around, and starting a fresh batch of more divine dough.

But how our generation needs to be reminded. The way General MacArthur reminded the Filipinos in three famous words: "I will return!" But while he was waiting down in Australia, the General fell to wondering about the Philippines—would the people remember? Very wisely, then, he went around collecting all the sugar and the chocolate available in Australia. He had these made into small chocolate bars. On the wrappers to be placed around the candy he had his own picture and his three words: "I will return!" Secretly this candy was sent into the Philippines; and whenever the friends faithful to his cause feared that the Filipinos were wavering in their loyalty, the chocolates were handed out. And there was the General's face, familiar to them because once he had governed their islands, and also his father before him. So, although the enemy seemed very powerful and permanent, they remembered all this past as they ate the chocolates; and remained true.

A greater than MacArthur also went away, and as He left He too said: "I will come back, and coming, will I find this faith on the earth?"

He has come back in Tamati and John Gualbert and Leon Bloy, who said so often: "The only sadness is not to be a saint."

But our Master, also, was none too sure we would stay faithful to His cause, when the enemy seemed permanent and powerful; so He gave us a meal to remind us. The Bread, made by the labor of men and women; the Wine, the greatest transfusion in history —since we belong to a new Ancestor now: "the very Essence of the Uncircumscribed."

No wonder it was written of that first communion: *"And they sang a hymn and went out."*

Went out to do what? To give. And forgive. To be an effective ferment of goodness in their generation. To be an organ played on by the Holy Spirit. Moment by moment. In the nick of time.

The characteristics of the executioner are to be found in nearly every modern man. . . . My hosanna has passed through whirlwinds of doubt.   Feodor Dostoevski

I wanted the address of someone who could do for Christianity what Franz Liszt did for the pianoforte—exemplify a technique.   Author unknown

Who would true Valour see,
Let him come hither;
One here will Constant be,
Come Wind, come Weather.
There's no Discouragement
Shall make him once Relent
His first avowed Intent,
*   To be a Pilgrim.*
Whoso beset him round

With dismal Storys,
Do but themselves confound;
His strength the more is,
No Lyon can him fright,
He'll with a Gyant fight,
But he will have a right
    To be a Pilgrim.
Hobgoblin, nor foul Fiend,
Can daunt his Spirit;
He knows he at the end
Shall Life inherit.
Then Fancies fly away,
He'll fear not what men say,
He'll labor night and day
    To be a Pilgrim.

John Bunyan, 1684

3

R.S.V.P.

Come, for all things are now ready.   LUKE 14:17

Have you never found yourself wondering how it would be on some Communion Sunday if the dramatic thing could happen in your church which used to happen at every Jewish Passover, when the youngest boy present was required to ask: "What mean ye by this service?" As in Exodus 12:26.

For the pity of it is that the most meaningful Sacrament of our Christian faith should ever have been allowed to grow so meaningless. Think how it would sharpen your own awareness of its loveliness, if your own small son were the one to be pushed forward some Sunday and prompted into asking: "What mean ye by this service?" For you, the parent, would then be the one to grope eagerly for words wonderful enough to make this ancient drama live once more for an innocent inquirer, looking up at you, brimful of curiosity. Hoping, of course, that it may be a story.

You cast around in your mind desperately. Good gracious, they ought to have a book for a man in this fix! Then you calm down. For of course there is a Book. And the Master Storyteller of all time told and retold this story. For He was forever wrapping up bread and beauty and brotherhood into a biography. This one would be about THE WHITEST TABLE IN THE WORLD: a sower went forth to sow . . . a seed fell into good ground . . . and sprang up . . . up against the law of gravity pushing it back . . . pounded by wind . . . pelted by rain . . . penetrated by sun . . . first the blade, then the ear, then the full grain in the ear . . . until this slender stalk swayed gracefully on its stem . . . so the farmer went forth once more, to cut down all this tender tallness, binding many similar stalks into sheaves . . . any previous private perfection lost now in this bundle of life . . . then, the threshing floor, the wheat flayed from the chaff . . . next, two women grinding at a millstone, until now no grain could ever boast again: "Once I belonged to such-and-such a stalk!" . . . and a housewife took three measures of this meal, hiding a little leaven in it until the lump was leavened . . . all so that He could say one day: "I am the bread of life" . . . and, on the night of the Last Supper: "This bread is my body, broken for you—take! Eat!"

For of course He had been describing the whole cycle of His own life: born in Bethlehem (the very word means "house of bread"); pursued by Herod; plagued by Pharisees; pestered by scribes; exasperated by His disciples; cut down by His foes in the prime of His manhood; stricken; smitten; afflicted. "This bread is my body, broken. For you. Take—eat!"

No wonder Evelyn Underhill could look at it and say: "The

awful power of that white eternity!" No wonder the Catholics
have a moving sentence: "Receive God!" No wonder the Episcopalians say: "Feed on Him in your heart!" No wonder it is the
White Host—Jesus Christ hidden in a piece of bread, in His
"prison of love."

When Alice Meynell looked at a congregation at communion
she wrote a poem about them:

> I saw this people like a field of flowers,
>   Each grown at such a price!
> The sum of unimaginable powers
>   Did no more than suffice.
> A thousand central daisies they,
>   A thousand of the one,
> For each, the entire monopoly of the day,
> For each the whole of the devoted sun.

A strange and stormy story for a small boy to grasp? Some of
it over his head, as a story should be; for he can grow up to digest
it! And now for the other side of this picture: THE REDDEST TABLE
IN THE WORLD. For it is written that after supper "He took the
cup, and after He had given thanks, He said: 'Drink ye all of it.'"
Actually the same story as before, for He who said: "I am the
vine, ye are the branches," knew how grapes and wheat grew up
the same way: the bleak branch, like a root out of dry ground,
no beauty . . . wind . . . rain . . . sun . . . more rain . . . more sun
. . . tender leaves budding . . . hard green noggins forming . . .
more rain . . . more sun . . . and once again the ancient annual
miracle of water-into-wine . . . then, luscious grapes torn from the
vine . . . thrown into the winepress . . . crushed . . . "Drink ye all
of it."

"I have trodden the winepress alone; and of the people there
was none to help me; I looked, and there was none to help;
therefore mine own arm brought salvation" . . . "As oft as ye
drink this cup, ye do show forth the Lord's death, till He come.
This do in remembrance of me."

Powerful pictures; but a small boy can put them away in his
memory and understand a little what an Italian gardener meant

when he said to Evelyn Underhill that he never planted grape-
vines too deep for them to hear the church bells ringing. Not
too deep for the "small rain" to reach, perhaps. Be sure to tell
your son that this is THE SADDEST TABLE IN THE WORLD—for the
Carpenter who must have carved many a table in His shop, knew
perfectly well that shedding blood had always been the symbol
of a covenant, an unbreakable promise. While sharing bread has
also stood for a sacrament of safety, no matter how savage the
people. Yet there He sat with His twelve dearest friends forced
to tell them: "One of you will betray me!" A sad echo sounded
all up and down this saddest of tables: "Lord, is it I?" "Is it I?"
"Is it I?"

Indeed, it comes echoing down to each congregation at each
communion. For of course they are remembering how Paul had to
write to the church in Corinth: "But let a man examine himself,
and so let him eat of that bread, and drink of that cup. For he
that eateth and drinketh unworthily, drinketh judgment to himself, not discerning the Lord's body. For this cause many are
weak and sickly among you, and many sleep" (1 Corinthians
11:28-30).

Surprise your son by suggesting now that this is THE SLEEPIEST
TABLE IN THE WORLD! Much too much like a dormitory. With far
too many sleep walkers who simply strolled in and sat down.
The place so quiet, however, that they took their forty winks, and
never even dreamed what they were missing.

Their names might be mentioned: Eutychus, in the front row.
He actually was the young man who fell asleep while the Apostle
Paul was preaching. Just as people often say today that young
people in church do not know what goes on. (But that is none
too true, for the chapter in this book called "O Yonge, Fresshe
Folkes, He or She" tells how wide-awake a thousand of them
are, every single summer! It could be, of course, that Eutychus
today copies his elders; and they often do seem drowsy about the
wonderful thing happening before their eyes.)

Behind the young man, an old, old man who has been asleep
a hundred years—Rip Van Winkle. When he does wake up, he
never wants anything to change from the way things were before

he slept; so his favorite expressions are, about any new suggestion: "No, we never *have* done that!" and: "No, we never *will* do that!" In spite of the thrilling things invented the past hundred years, he still lives back in horse-and-buggy days! Railroads and steamships, telegraphs and telephones, typewriters and sewing machines, submarines and airplanes, radio and TV—but he wants none of them. Of course, everything invented was made to increase a man's usefulness—machines to give him quicker fingers, railroads and airplanes to give him faster feet, telephones and radio to give him bigger ears and a louder voice; but what on earth can give him a kinder, larger heart, if he sleeps through Communion?

When somebody asked Henry Thoreau if he did not agree that the railroad was a decided improvement over the stagecoach, he answered: "Provided it carries better people; otherwise it's only meanness going faster!"

In the pew behind Rip Van Winkle slept the stylish *Sleeping Beauty*. She looks just exactly as advertisements look. Her hair just right. Her shoes just right. Her dress just right. Her pearls just right. It was about her and her sisters that Isaiah probably wrote his third chapter! It is definitely about her that every copywriter thinks twice as he plots his advertisements. For this little woman spends 80 per cent of the family's money. Therefore, make her uncomfortable with every stitch she wears, with every stick of furniture she owns, with every car in her garage. Advertisements are her undoing! So she sits in her pew not hearing the Lord of the Church saying: "Life does not consist in the abundance of the things that you possess."

Some day she will wake up in church, of course. Sorrow may come. Beauty may go. She may get tired of gadgets. Then the congregation will begin to notice something: "Sleeping Beauty has insomnia now!" Sleepless over catching up with undone, unremembered, unattempted acts. Above all, *this* act: of receiving the most beautiful benefit in life, absent-mindedly—she who loves beauty and fears she is losing it. Suddenly she will listen to the priestly words and echo them in her heart of hearts:

Almighty God, Father of our Lord Jesus Christ, Maker of all things, Judge of all men; we acknowledge and bewail our manifold sins and wickedness, which we, from time to time, most grievously have committed, by thought, word, and deed, against Thy Divine Majesty, provoking most justly Thy wrath and indignation against us. We do earnestly repent, and are heartily sorry for these our misdoings; the remembrance of them is grievous unto us; the burden of them is intolerable. Have mercy upon us, most merciful Father; for Thy Son our Lord Jesus Christ's sake, forgive us all that is past; and grant that we may hereafter serve Thee in newness of life.

Over in the Belgian Congo the usual African greeting is the word: *"Omwa?"* which means: "Are you awake?" Try teaching it to a little lad before Communion, that he may feel the mystery. Maybe certain verses from the ancient "Liturgy of St. James" can increase his awe:

> Let all mortal flesh keep silence,
> And with fear and trembling stand,
> Ponder nothing earthly-minded,
> For with blessing in His hand,
> Christ our God to earth descendeth,
> Our full homage to demand.

> King of kings, yet born of Mary,
> As of old on earth He stood,
> Lord of lords in earthly vesture—
> in the body and the blood—
> He will give to all the faithful
> His own self for heavenly food.

Perhaps learning to sing such words to the French traditional tune "Picardy" will bring any child to this Service with an understanding reverence.

For now he will begin to realize that this is the OLDEST TABLE IN ALL CHRISTENDOM—since it was over nineteen hundred years ago that The Carpenter first said to His friends: "Do this in remembrance of me." It is incredible, really, that when they were so careless about many other things He told them to do, this table and this meal they never stopped doing. Everybody everywhere still remembering. Year after year. Month after month.

Week after week. Moment after moment, somewhere on earth right now the same beloved words are being repeated, the same bread and the same wine distributed.

Not all of this can come before one celebration, of course! A single one of the capitalized sections will seem simpler. But be sure to point out sometime that this is THE RUDEST TABLE IN THE WORLD! For how impolite to receive a valuable gift and treat it lightly; or to be invited to a great dinner and make excuses; R.S.V.P. on the letter, which means "*Respondez s'il vous plait*": "Please reply." Imagine answering: "I have bought a farm and want to go out to look it over," "I have bought five yoke of oxen, and want to hitch them up and see how well they draw my wagon," "I have married a wife and I don't want to leave her yet."

Any boy can see how rude this would sound. Yet Jesus Himself said that was the way people answered. And consider this extra story: *Jacob,* falling asleep in a pew (behind *Sleeping Beauty,* who knows?) after bargaining in prayer: "If God will be with me, and will keep me in the way that I go, and will give me bread to eat, and raiment to put on, so that I come to my father's house in safety, then—*then!*—shall the Lord be my God, and of all that Thou shalt give me I will surely give the tenth unto Thee" (Genesis 28:20-22).

Another rudeness should enter this whole picture, too. For when the disciples came into the room where the Last Supper was ready, every one of them knew how hot and dusty his feet had become from walking on hot, dusty roads in sandals. In any other house some servant would always provide water to wash the feet of guests. But the twelve were alone with the Lord. And not a single disciple was willing to do such an embarrassing deed for any of the others. It was, therefore, the Lord who wrapped a towel around Him, who took a basin of water and humbled Himself and knelt before each of His twelve friends to perform this old hospitable custom. He who had called Himself "the water of life"! How conscience-stricken the disciples must have felt over their own particular rudeness; too vain to dare stoop! But the Gospel story says how Jesus, knowing that He came from God and was going to God, humbled Himself. Beautifully enough, all water follows this same cycle from God to God: the entire Atlantic and Pacific Ocean, all the seven seas, even the private mud puddle on our sidewalk, drawn upward by the sun into the clouds. Moment by moment. Century after century. Then descending in the small rain to refresh our dusty streets, our parched gardens. To enter into the wheat. To enter into the grape. To feed the hungry.

Think how rude to say roughly: "Not today. Too busy with my own affairs."

There is one extra wonder to be stressed: this is THE LONGEST TABLE ON EARTH—for it has literally bridged all the seven seas! Originally, there was only room for thirteen to sit down at it together. But now there is space for all 872,000,000 of us who bear the name of Christian. Each Communion table is, therefore, 25,000 miles long, and reaches around the entire circumference of the world. All because each Christian has one common Father, one shared Saviour, one Holy Book, one public Lord's Prayer, one private Lord's Prayer (in John Seventeen), one Holy Meal; one Hymnbook, too—in which men have loved to include old favorites written by all sorts of Christians in all sorts of places.

So that a little boy in Africa can whisper across to his opposite number in America: *"Omwa? Are you awake?"*

And young America can bow his head when Pastor Yamfu prays over in Kikongo: "Our Father God, we have come as one goes to a feast, bearing an empty plate, expecting it to be filled. . . . We have come into Thy house, happy with expectation. Now we wait for Thy Holy Spirit to come into our hungry hearts."

O Loving Father, quha be thy aith hes promisit vnto vs ane Saviour Iesus Christ, thy Sonne; thour hes not decevit vs, bot hes given him vnto vs, as thy Word hes declarit, and be thy Sacramentis thou hes confirmit. Yea, he hes further promisit vnto vs, that he will abyde with vs, vntill the consummation of the warlde. Thairfoir, deir Father, we beseik thee, gouerne vs, and replenish vs with

ioy. Let thy Crown and Kingdome abyde aboue vs, and preserve vs in peice, through the same Iesus Christ thy Sonne. So be it.

Ancient Scottish Collects; from Iona

For if this most Holy Sacrament were celebrated in one place only, and were consecrated by one priest in the whole world, with what great desire thinkest thou men would be drawn toward that place and toward such a priest of God, that they might behold the divine mysteries celebrated? But now are many men made priests, and in many places the Sacrament is celebrated; that the grace and love of God toward men might the more appear, the more widely the Holy Communion is spread abroad over all the world. Thomas à Kempis

We of the clergy make our bread and butter on the fact that Christ was crucified, yet very few of us are crucified with Him. Søren Kierkegaard

4

FIVE USELESS DAYS

I hate, I despise your feast days. Amos 5:21

If every man lives all of history in himself, as Emerson suggested, it seems high time for Americans to abandon ancient Aztec anniversary customs.

For when Cortez landed in Mexico he found that the Aztec astronomers had a religious calendar with eighteen months of twenty days each. This gave them three hundred and sixty days a year; but since their civic calendar had three hundred and sixty-five days, there were five days left over—religiously speaking. They called these "useless days." Nobody dreamed of starting anything important on any of these five days; why should he, since it was bound to amount to nothing? And a baby born on a useless day would come to no good end; how could he, poor little luckless one?

It seems absurd, however, for me to retain such a religious calendar, encircling five days in red, when the Child born on the first of these dates did not come to be labeled "useless."

Yet how does Christmas stand on my calendar? Angels once stated specifically that it was to bring *peace* and *goodwill*, wrapped up in a Baby. And this little breeze went blowing out of Bethlehem where it listed all over the earth, touching and refreshing every face in passing, if only men and women could have known what it was they were feeling; but of course in December they were too tied up in useless things—addressing five hundred cards and thinking, moment by moment: "How on earth did we ever get all these ridiculous people on our list? Surely if we put our minds to it we could cut out fully three hundred of them!" For men and women also go blowing around the globe, it seems, with their little useless ten-cent messages thought up by somebody whose business it is to think up ten-cent sentiments to be sent to someone who sent them ten-cent sentiments last year . . . so many little useless breezes blowing in useless eddies . . . When Christmas is a love affair. God so falling in love with me that . . . God so falling in love with my neighbor that . . . And with his neighbor. And with his, ad infinitum, to the end of the block, to the end of the town, to the end of the nation; then over the seven seas. The Bible says so. The preacher says so. Advertisements say so. And the square marked ⌐25⌐ on my calendar looks up, waiting.

But I feel it is useless. This year, anyhow. For who am I to cope with universal peace? I, a mere speck on the map? What a muddle peace is, everybody wanting it; but who can pin down whole populations in scattered places to make them sign on the dotted line? But the point is—populations are *people!* So I try pinning myself down: *"Will you or won't you give up all your hate this very moment,* to produce peace on the square foot of earth where you stand? Will you?" So then I remember that whole populations really have felt a breeze blowing on their faces until they pinned themselves down to sign on a dotted line. For no sooner was the war over in Europe than the World Council of Churches in Geneva received this eloquent appeal: "We, the Protestants of Holland, request Church World Service to divert a promised shipload of grain from us to our starving brothers in Germany. We grew a surplus of green vegetables in Holland, but were forbidden by our government to send this surplus to Germany. As Christians we cannot rest under this condition, hence our request that the grain, which we ourselves need, be sent to these brethren who have greater need."

Multiply such everlasting mercy, Christian by Christian, household by household, church by church, denomination by denomination, nation by nation, the whole world over, and think of the goodwill emerging. Useless no longer!

A few years ago a G.I. went grumbling to his pastor to say good-bye: "Here I am, demobilized from one war, I thought, only to find myself headed now for Korea! Where's the common sense or justice in that?" The pastor asked one penetrating question: "But you had these three or four free years, safe at home—what specific things did you do, flinging all your influence into producing peace?" And the soldier was speechless. But the pastor heard a voice saying to his city what was first said centuries ago: "O Jerusalem! Jerusalem! if thou hadst known, even thou, in this thy day, the things that make for thy peace."

A year ago a columnist from *The New Yorker* magazine visited a greeting-card establishment and found to his surprise that in 1953 enough money had been spent on friendship cards to pay for a battleship. And if these three and a half billion cards had been stacked one on top of the other, not even the Russians could invent a guided missile to go over the top, since it would soar 4,375 miles up in the air! The columnist began wondering how sensible it was to send such a staggering slice of love to *friends*

—why not to enemies? Picture their astonishment over finding you cared for them even ten-cents' worth!

A businessman has been looking for something which would cost ten cents to make, but could sell for a dollar, and be habit-forming! Gloriously enough, there is such a thing for a person like myself—eager for peace, but feeling futile. It costs ten cents provided I buy ten copies for a dollar, and it is bound to be habit-forming. I refer to that magnificent article in *The Christian Century:* "U.N.—Snare or Shield?" now reprinted, ten for a dollar, available at their office, 407 South Dearborn Street, Chicago 5, Illinois. Try rolling each copy, diplomalike, wrapping it in glamorous gold paper for ten unconvinced friends, with a tag reading something like this: "Thrilling, isn't it? Sixty nations sitting down together trying to create peace on earth, moment by moment?"

But when Christmas is useless, EASTER is, also. For when it means only new bonnets, spring suits, augmented choirs chanting lengthier anthems, the penetrating fragrance of lilies, mobs of presentable people parading on sidewalks, then I live on the wrong side of Easter—*if Christ be not risen, then is our preaching vain.*

"The great moments in life are not weddings or funerals or anniversaries or holidays," Emerson said, "but quiet afternoons when a new idea is born." And the only idea ever born into the world with power to shake the futile Christian out of his useless past is the moment-by-moment Presence of the Lord of life. In my garden, saying: "Mary!" By my fishing boat, saying: "Peter!" Beside my seat of custom, saying: "Levi!" Under my sycamore tree, saying: "Zacchaeus." At my supper table, saying "Cleopas!"

To remind me of all this afresh every seven days, God has given me SUNDAY! Often utterly useless. Although when John Ruskin sat in a meeting of Friends he experienced such an emotion that he wrote: "It causes a curling of the cheek, and is as good for one as a week at the seaside." And Bishop Gore noticed:

> No Sabbath means no church;
> no church means no worship;
> no worship means no religion;

no religion means no morals;
no morals means no society;
no society means no government;
no government means anarchy.

If I live to be threescore and ten, I shall have had more than
three thousand Sundays—like "rests" in the music of my life; each
such pause being an integral part of the score. *The Sabbath day
shall never cross the Mississippi!*" my godless ancestors boasted.
But John Mason Peck went west in his covered wagon—a hundred
and twenty-nine days from Litchfield, Connecticut, to St. Louis,
Missouri; and Sunday did cross the Mississippi. Wherever it
dawns, a day crowded with drama, dividing all worshipers into
"useful" or "useless" church members.

Back of the Old English word "worship" lies a picture of the
time when overlords owned Britain, and any fief desiring to
work certain fields in his lifetime, held some of this earth in his
clasped palms. Placing his hands between the hands of his over-
lord (the way children play Button-Button), this kneeling man
simply said: "Your worth-ship!"

So that it is in acknowledging and in receiving and in giving
that Sunday worship goes its full cycle. Exactly as in the recent
Coronation when the Queen's husband knelt before her throne
in Westminster Abbey, and placed his hands between her hands
in this same Old English ritual, as he said: "*I, Philip, Duke of
Edinburgh, do become your liege man of life and limb, and of
earthly worship; and faith and truth will I bear unto you, to live
and die, against all manner of folks. So help me God.*"

Whenever I say this in faith and truth on Sunday, all manner
of folks can see on Monday that my day of worship was not
useless. But only let me ask myself one question: "Would you
want heaven to be just like your church?" and my answer is a
crestfallen confession: "Not unless a breeze from Bethlehem
blows more freshly on all our poor dry bones! Not unless the
leaven stirs me and my neighbor into sharing our loaf with our
enemy. Not unless my hands and my neighbor's hands open like
tents to shield and shelter every lost soul in danger. Not unless

our clasped hands form a safe bridge of peace around the entire earth."

"Christ is risen!" the Russians used to say, when greeting one another.

"He is risen indeed!" the answer used to come. But something happened in Russia to make their old greeting useless. Let me never relive their godless page in history!

Which reminds me of MOTHER'S DAY—for is it not useless also? Ten-cent cards with ten-cent sentiments? Whistler's mother seen side view, looking tranquil; yet producing a son who could write —more venomously—a book entitled *The Gentle Art of Making Enemies,* in which one sentence says: "You cannot continually disappoint a continent."

The way my neighbor and I continually disappoint our continent. Perhaps because we each have *three mothers apiece*— which is two too many; and moment by moment we feel continually torn between them. In need of some modern Solomon to judge who is our real parent.

Mother Nature I know only too intimately. She gave me this definite body, set down on this definite street, amid all these definite uncles and aunts, with all these definite family customs and prejudices to adopt, and all these definite physical traits—this Johnson nose, this Cartwright accent in my speech, this Smith liver which makes me such a crosspatch at times. I read and re-read what Paul wrote to the Romans: "But I see another law in my members, warring against the law of my mind, and bringing me into captivity to the law of sin which is in my members. O wretched man that I am! Who shall deliver me from the body of this death? I thank God through Jesus Christ . . ." that there is His Spirit blowing where it lists, reviving even family bones like those I inherited.

But never underestimate the power of *Mother Tongue* over me! For ever since God let Adam name the animals in Eden, men have gone on naming everything else on earth, even deciding what should be called feminine: the moon, she; the sea, she; the ship, she; the state, she; the Church, she; peace, she; justice, she (blindfolded, holding impartial scales); hope, she; peace, she; purity, she; charity, she; et cetera. Not in any way a useless list; although men like to call attention to the fact that these are all flexible, adjustable and therefore more negative items: compared with the sun, the moon is only reflected light; the captain has to steer the ship if it is to land at any particular port; the churchmen have to govern the Church if it is to produce proper members. "Humility, she" has been bowing her head meekly enough throughout the years; but nobody on earth has ever stopped her from reflecting about flexibility and adjustability as compared with rigidity and adamantine authority:

> Our fathers have been churchmen
> Nineteen hundred years or so,
> And to every new suggestion
> They have always answered: NO!

In any case, considering the usual masculine make-up of any committee-of-seven in her church, a modern churchwoman finds it exhilarating to notice that even the early Scandinavians named two out of seven days in the week for women. *Monday: the Moon's Day!* For even if the moon is only reflected light, just look what she does twice a day out in the middle of the ocean—first lifting, then turning the tides!

Suppose this could become my memo for Monday: turn the tide today. The tide of prejudice. Of gossip. Of parochialism. Of Our Town-ism. "Even as Christ also loved the Church, that He might sanctify and cleanse it, and present it to Himself a glorious Church, not having spot or wrinkle or any such thing . . . holy, without blemish." (The Church, she? The woman, she? Even if I live to be threescore years and ten, I can see that I shall need all of my three thousand Mondays as washdays!)

With even deeper meaning, the early Eddas wrote about Friday: *Frigga's Day*. For Frigga was the wife of Odin, king of the gods; and because she worried about her baby, Baldur the Beautiful, she went to everything on land and sea, imploring it to protect Baldur from harm. Fire promised; Water promised; Air promised; Rocks promised. So that Baldur became an exciting plaything for the gods. They tossed him into the sea; he was returned to shore, dry! They threw him into the fire; not a hair was singed! They bounced him down precipices; not a bruise! But a certain woman went to Frigga privately, and her Mother Tongue led her to say: "Tell me in strict confidence, my dear, did you honestly ask everything to protect Baldur?"

"Yes, everything!"

"Every single, littlest thing?"

"Well, yes and no! For of course I did not go to the mistletoe —too little, really, to do any harm."

So that woman gathered armfuls of mistletoe to take to the gods the next morning: "Throw this at Baldur the Beautiful!"

"Too tame a game," they said.

But she insisted. So they threw the mistletoe at the son of god. And Baldur the Beautiful died. From little tame white berries on Friday, Frigga's Day. And I think how my present Good Friday was once Bad Friday, too; and how the Son of God was slain by little words of little men. By a little kiss from a little Judas. By three little denials from a little Peter. From little drops of water in which a little Pilate washed his hands. I see how it is possible on any Friday for my own Mother Tongue to "crucify the Son of God afresh, and put Him to open shame." Therefore I need all my Mondays: "For there is not a word in my tongue, but lo! O Lord, Thou knowest it altogether. . . . Wash me, and I shall be clean."

Then, and only then, can ten-cent sentiments about *Mother Love* on ten-cent cards come true in May, or in any other month. An instinctive, protective concern for every child everywhere. Especially a little brown baby from Bethlehem so easily slaughtered by inflexible men sending cablegrams to Yalta about the success of their Bomb: *"Babies Successfully Born,"* it read! But what it inflexibly led to would be *Babies Successfully Slain*, continually disappointing every continent. "You are my mother, and my sisters and my brothers if you hear the things I say, and do them!" The Church, she?

After which it is hard to choose my fifth useless day—should it be LINCOLN'S BIRTHDAY? (When I must stand before his statue in Washington, confessing that brown babies on this continent are still half slave and half free.) Should it be ARMISTICE DAY? (When at high noon I observe one moment of silence as my sole contribution toward peace.) Should it be LABOR DAY? (When moment by moment, year by year, Labor pays less and less attention to the Church of the Carpenter: "Come unto me, all ye who labor and are heavy-laden"?) Or would it not be more chastening to choose MY OWN BIRTHDAY? Acknowledging how many Christmases, Easters and Sundays I have observed uselessly. But fully determined now to adopt my Master's description of His own birthday: "To this end was I born, for this cause came I into the world, that I should bear witness to the truth. Everyone that is of the truth heareth my voice!"

Listen to the exhortation of the Dawn,
Look well to this day!
For it is Life; the very Life of Life.
In its brief course lies all the Virtues
And Realities of your existence:
    The bliss of growth,
    The glory of action,
    The splendor of beauty:
For yesterday is but a Dream,
And tomorrow is only a Vision;
But Today well lived
Makes every yesterday a dream of Happiness,
And every tomorrow a vision of Hope,
Look well, therefore, to this day!
Such is the Salutation of the Dawn.

                                    from the Sanscrit

God creates the world anew every moment.
                    Jan van Ruysbroeck, 1293-1381

5

SERMON TO THE SEVEN SITTERS

Even as Christ also loved the church, and gave Himself for it.
EPHESIANS 5:25

Clever people can always think up clever ways to get out of tight
situations. Like a certain traveling lecturer who boasted to the
local chairman during dinner that yes, by this time in his career,
he could talk on any subject whatsoever! The chairman, therefore, felt free to announce that our guest tonight will speak to
us about China; although he knew perfectly well that his man
had never set foot in that country.

But lecturers become accustomed to impossible introductions.
So he arose and began: "Ladies and gentlemen, there are only
two major things to stress about China, and they fall into the
categories of China Proper and China Improper. But if I should
bother to enumerate items about China Proper—its enormous
size, its vast population, its ancient history, its Oriental attitudes
—you would all be bored stiff and say to yourselves: 'But we
knew all that before this brash fellow was even born!' And, of
course, good friends, if I should dare dwell on China *Improper,*
on Ladies' Night! with so many wives present! you would all
be simply scandalized, turn sick at your stomachs, and need to
leave the dining room quickly. Therefore, in order that you may
sit comfortably for the next thirty minutes, permit me to share
with you a somewhat different matter . . ." And here followed
the lecture he intended to give in the first place.

This is hardly proper procedure for preachers. For only as
sermons present the improper do congregations sit up and take
notice. Only as Bible texts stab the saints and sinners can a
disturbance go trembling the length of a pew.

28

Modern novels usually waste a page near the front devoted to the author's innocent intention: "Any resemblance in this book to any living person is purely coincidental." But the Bible is quite different. Every resemblance to every living person is intentional. Purely! For as Søren Kierkegaard said: "I must say to myself, 'It is about me that this is written! This has my home address on it!'"

And in the book of Revelation where there are seven angels receiving seven letters to seven churches, with seven golden candlesticks to burn, seven stars to shine, seven seals to break, seven trumpets to blow, seven thunders to sound, seven vials full of seven last plagues, it would seem a decided letdown if the seven sitters in the modern church heard no least hint about their own improper motionlessness.

For any parent worries over sitters! Will they know what to do when trouble comes? How to turn off the gas, and call the police, and summon the fire department? Midway of almost any evening out you can overhear some parent phoning home to ask: "How are things?" reminding the sitter of That Letter of Instructions left on the hall table.

The preacher finds his Letter of Instructions left on his pulpit desk. When he reads in the book of Revelation about the Church Proper and Improper, he discovers that in no uncertain terms the Spirit describes a certain sickness of the stomach: "Because thou art neither hot nor cold, I will spew thee out of my mouth." The modern man of God is disturbed to go through the Bible finding who-sat-where, and what the Lord of the church said to such sitters through His preachers. For instance:

1. *The people sat down to eat and drink and rose up to play*—

This was Paul preaching to sitters in the church at Corinth, asking: "How are things?" Reminding them how Moses went up to receive from God the ten commandments, while Aaron stayed down in the valley, letting the people cast bracelets and earrings into a melting pot, then saying to Moses, later: "See what these silly people cast in! And just look what it turned into!"

The Jewish Talmud has a saying: "All of our miseries are a piece of the Golden Calf."

And those who sit down to eat and drink their chicken dinners at the church, often rise up to play the stock market, the Golden Calf they worship. The preacher would do well to remember the day when Jesus, too, was a sitter: sitting over against the treasury, beholding how the people cast money into the treasury. And many who were rich cast in much. It clanged down the brass tube of the temple collection receptacle with plenty of noise. But Mark tells us how Jesus called His disciples to notice the tiny tinkle of the widow's mite; for He who knew what was in man, knew what was left in safe-deposit vaults and on the stubs of checkbooks.

A short time ago, in Scotland, a Presbyterian church posted this notice on its bulletin board: "Will those of you who have been putting buttons in the collection plate, kindly put in your own buttons, and not buttons from the church upholstery."

Contributing only the heritage the sitter sat on; at no sacrifice. America has such sitters, also. For on a certain foreign mission offering Sunday, a certain sitter said to the usher who had reached his pew: "I'm not giving a red cent! I don't believe in missions!" The usher had the presence of mind to lean down and whisper: "Then do take a little out! This money is meant for the heathen."

At this point in the sermon to sitters who rise up to play, the Tenor sang that plaintive Appalachian spiritual which explains that he wonders as he wanders out under the sky, how Jesus our Saviour came for to die for poor onery sitters like you and like I.

2. *Blind Bartimaeus sat by the roadside,* begging—

Every preacher knows that all his sitters are beggars. Since every stitch they have on them as they sit before him, clothed and in their right minds, has been a handout from God: all God's sun and wind and rain to produce food for this beggar, all God's sheep and flax and silkworms to prepare raiment for this beggar, all God's herbs and plants and molds to help science cure the blindness of this sitter by the roadside begging; or this lame man sitting by the pool of Siloam, begging someone to get him into the water when an angel troubles it; or the mental state of some beggar sitting among the tombs, tearing his hair.

The preacher opens his book of Oriental proverbs and reads about himself in wisdom out of Japan: "It is hard for a physician to cure all the blind who pass by his door by leaning out the window and squeezing eyedrops down on everybody." One sermon can hardly hope to cure all sitters! Yet in this same Oriental book of wisdom he reads of the Arab beggar whose benefactor asked him to deliver a letter.

"Sir," the beggar complained, "I solicit alms; I do not run errands!"

To sit blindfolded in the pew, on the buttons of the past, with palms turned upward, receiving handouts from nineteen centuries of Christianity, is ingratitude personified. For the Church is the mother of the arts: music, drama, architecture, pictures, symbols —all begun to woo this sitter! Nursing homes and hospitals and doctors and nurses, first trained by Mother Church to help her helpless sitters. Libraries, the desire of Mother Church to collect the ancient wisdom of the past—patiently copying by hand Bibles, missals, history, biography, in order that illiterate sitters might be given all this priceless treasure.

Over in Paris, the past few years, Abbé Pierre has been teaching French beggars to help themselves by rummaging in dump heaps, salvaging something to sell to help support themselves. Meanwhile, during frigid winter weather, Abbé Pierre pestered the city government into providing shelters for his evicted "Sans-Toits"— his roofless ones, roomless and rootless. And to the rich, worshipers of the Golden Calf, this energetic little bearded priest became the conscience of Paris as he kept calling out a text from Lamentations: "See how the city sitteth solitary! Is it nothing to you all ye that pass by!"

"The poor," said Jesus, "ye have always with you." But when the Lord's satisfied sitters on Sunday turn into beggars from Monday through Saturday, then Paul preaches against such poaching: "That no one of you be puffed up one against the other; for who maketh you to differ from another? And what hast thou that thou didst not receive? And if thou didst receive it why dost thou glory, as if thou hast not received it? Now ye are full, now ye are rich, now ye have reigned as kings . . . a spectacle unto the world, and to angels, and to men" (I Corinthians 4:6-9).

There are even nine silent lepers sitting in the average church, healed, but silent moment by moment all week long, who should feel troubled by the Tenor's voice saying that he wonders as he wanders out under the sky, how Jesus our Saviour came for to die for poor onery sitters like you and like I.

3. *By the rivers of Babylon, there we sat down, yea, we wept; when we remembered Zion, how can we worship here—*

Jeremiah wrote these weeping sitters a stirring sermon: "Stuff and nonsense! You can worship God in Babylon exactly the way you used to in Jerusalem! Did you think God was only in His temple here! He is inside each of you, right now, right where you sit under the weeping willow trees, all so damp and dismal."

Elizabeth Barrett Browning was annoyed to find what a sighing sitter she was: "Why do we all praise God and sigh? Why should we sigh?"

Peter knew exactly why he sighed and wept: from sitting in a palace courtyard, warming himself, and letting the mocking voice of a maidservant humiliate him into denying three times that he had even known Jesus. Then there was that cock, crowing twice, and his remembrance that Jesus had foretold this very denial. Leaving Pilate's palace, hands tied as a prisoner, the Lord turned and looked at Peter. Who wept bitterly.

Ever since that day every weathervane in all Christendom has been set up on steeples and barns as a silent sermon to sitters. For in medieval days when men and women could not read, and yet wanted to know which way the wind was blowing, they could look up and be reminded of Peter—how mild a zephyr had blown the man over!

But the preacher longs to say to his own Weeping Willies and Calamity Janes: God is not a Complaint Department! The Customer Is *Not* Always Right! Sometimes he even longs to turn their attention toward the end of their pew: "Uncomfortably like a tombstone, isn't it?" If a shudder spreads among the sitters, well and good! For then he can read off the epitaphs which all began: SACRED TO THE MEMORY OF . . . For moment by moment all sitters are working their way toward the day when the family must select some headstone appropriate to this sitter's days on earth. But what weeping and wailing and gnashing of teeth if a waiter discovered that his customers had chipped in to carve over his grave:

BY AND BY
GOD CAUGHT HIS EYE.

And how comfortably can Lady O'Looney rest under her stone in Pewsy Churchyard:

HERE LIES THE BODY OF LADY O'LOONEY
GREAT NIECE OF BURKE COMMONLY CALLED THE DIVINE
SHE WAS BLAND, PASSIONATE AND DEEPLY RELIGIOUS
ALSO
SHE PAINTED IN WATER COLORS AND SENT SEVERAL
PICTURES TO THE EXHIBITION.
SHE WAS FIRST COUSIN OF LADY JONES;
AND OF SUCH IS THE KINGDOM OF GOD.

Even the Bishop of Worcester might weep over his epitaph, dated 1576:

HERE BORN, HERE BISHOP, BURIED HERE.
A BULLINGHAM BY NAME AND STOCK.
A PAINFUL PREACHER OF THE TRUTH.

Surely David Livingstone fared far better. For on that great black slab flat on the floor of Westminster Abbey, words in gold run around the outer margin, reading: "Other Sheep I Have Which Are Also Of This Fold, Them Also I Must Bring." While engraved in the center were his own words: "May Heaven's Richest Blessing Come Down On Everyone—American, English, Turk—Who Will Heal This Open Sore Of The World." So devoted had his days been to getting rid of the slave traffic.

George Meredith, too, was fortunate in having words from one of his books chosen for his epitaph: "Our Life Is But A Little

Holding Lent To Do A Mighty Labor." For this is like a holy
hint for any sitter to see on the end of his pew, especially when
the Tenor tells how he wonders as he wanders out under the sky,
how Jesus our Saviour came for to die for poor onery sitters like
you and like I.

4. *If ever I have sat silent indoors afraid to what the mob would
say—*

Of all poor onery people surely the most selfish sitters are those
who never speak up, who never stick their necks out, who never
go out on the end of a limb over any lost cause. The way Catherine
Breckovski went all out in Russia, to free the serfs, during seventy
of her eighty-four years; more than fifty of them in exile and
prison. The way Bishop Berggrav and Bishop Dibelius and
Pastor Niemoller spoke up against the Nazis—paying the penalty
of imprisonment and persecution by the police. The way Reinhold
von Thadden has become Germany's leading layman—by losing
all his possessions and his family business, seized by the Nazis;
through his daring to govern the occupied city of Louvain with
Christian courtesy, through protecting all Belgians and Jews with
compassion, until the Nazis imprisoned such an impossible
German; who *would* live at risk of his life! and sing with the
Baltic martyrs of old: "I do not know the way, but Thou dost
know!"

To all who weep over smaller woes than these, the Tenor then
tells why he wonders as he wanders out under the sky, how
Jesus our Saviour came for to die for poor onery sitters like you
and like I.

After which the poor parson would have preferred to hide
behind the pulpit desk, for he had reached that terrifying type
of sitter known as VIP:

5. *Those that sit in the seats of the mighty—*

For no matter where the poor onery parson wanders he wonders
at Beacon Street matrons who sat themselves down on the
historic red brick sidewalks of Boston, to prevent city employees
from ripping them up in order to replace them with concrete. The

parson wonders also at San Francisco matrons sitting down
on the cable-car tracks up Nob Hill, to prevent losing their
antiquated but beloved vehicles. He wonders, also, over those
famous "Daughters" who have joined themselves together to
guard their American heritage, who chained themselves to
Washington cherry trees, to keep them from being chopped down
when the Jefferson Memorial architects thought trees would spoil
the view. He wonders over Mrs. Iselin of Newport, who had
added no new names to her social list in twenty-five years. He
wonders as he wanders through Massachusetts and comes upon
a certain lake with an incredible Indian name, yet there it was
on a sign:

CHARGOGGAGOGGMAUCHANGOGOGGCHAUBUNAGUNGAMOG.

Fearing that this had been done during a printer's strike, he
finds that no! it is a totally serious name for a totally serious
warning—still used by all nationalist governments, including his
own, in every country on earth where the seats of the mighty
are; for the sign means: "You fish on your side, and I fish on my
side, and nobody fish in the middle."

Reaching for his Rousseau, the parson reads: "The first man
who, having fenced off a piece of ground, could think of saying:
'This is mine,' and found people simple enough to believe him,
was the real founder of civil society. How many crimes, wars,
murders, miseries, and horrors would have been spared the
human race by one who, plucking up the stakes, and filling in
the trench, should have called out to his fellows: 'Beware of
listening to this imposter! You are undone if you forget that the
earth belongs to no one and that its fruits are for all.' "

The parson longs to be the one to pull up these stakes, and to
fill in that trench, and to call out those thrilling words from his
pulpit down to his sitters. But they sit there so solid and satisfied
that he wavers. Next Sunday might be better anyhow, he thinks.
And contents himself with Ruskin: "It is probably much happier
to live in a small house and have Warwick Castle to be astonished
at, than to live in Warwick Castle and have nothing to be astonished at."

But even as he says the words, he realizes that the trustees know to a T what their pastor gets, per month, and so are now looking down their noses as they think: "Sour grapes!"

He longs to tack Epicurus on to Ruskin: "If thou wouldst make a man happy, add not to his riches, but take away from his desires." (But he sees the Chairman of the Board winking at his wife.)

Then God in His goodness gives such a poor parson St. Philip Neri—"Pippo Buono": the good Philip. Blithe, merry, rich enough and blunt enough to know how to deal with sitters in Rome, in 1544, and wise enough to make the ambitious tremble today.

For one day an onery young man told Philip Neri of his success in finishing philosophical studies.

"O happy you!" Pippo Buono cried affectionately. "*And then?*"

"Well, I aim to study even further, to become a doctor in civil and canon laws."

"O happy you! *And then?*"

"Well, then I shall inherit our family fortune; so I plan to marry, have children, and go right on rising in the legal profession."

"O happy you! *And then?*"

"Why, maybe I can earn even higher honors and get elected to the Rota."

"O happy, happy you! *And then?*"

"Well then I suppose I shall grow old and die like anybody else."

"*And then?*" Philip Neri asked in a whisper. But the young man was speechless.

"What must I do to inherit eternal life?" another rising young man asked the Master of Life. And it was this Master's own mother who foresaw, nine months before her Child was born, that after He came, the mighty would have to come down from their seats. The way Moses had refused to be called the son of Pharaoh's daughter. The way Peter Waldo gave up his wealth, in Lyons; and Francis of Assisi, in Italy; and Ignatius Loyola; and Leo Tolstoy; and William Wilberforce; and Lord Shaftesbury; and Wilfred Grenfell.

A reporter interviewed Sir Wilfred: "Give me the real low-down, Doctor! When you see your fellow surgeons earning big money in London, and making big names for themselves in Harley Street practices, don't you sometimes regret going off the deep end out there in Labrador, among rough fishermen?"

Dr. Grenfell looked with his sea-blue eyes straight through the reporter: "But maybe more fame has come my way than any Harley Street man gets from doctoring the idle rich! All any surgeon wants is plenty of tough cases to engage his skill— up in Labrador every disease is tough, and comes to me complete with fog and ice and danger and zero weather! Yet I live there with my beloved family working beside me, with thousands of friends all over the world supporting this work. So—you wanted the low-down? Well, this is the high-up!"

For as Bishop Brent once said: "You must melt your theology into poetry. But note that you must have a theology before you melt it!"

Whereupon all the well-to-do sitters with a theology began to melt it the moment the Tenor touches their pocketbooks by saying that he wonders as he wanders out under the sky, how Jesus our Saviour came for to die for poor onery sitters like you and like I.

After which the poor parson saw by the calendar that, moment by moment, Lent was approaching, and Good Friday with its three-hour agony, when it was written:

6. *And sitting down they watched Him there—*

They, so safe; and He, so stricken, smitten and afflicted, pulled halfway between heaven and earth.

"Spectatoritis," doctors call it today. Just watching somebody else struggling to win. Good Friday was crowded with such spectators. The Gospels give us these glimpses: "And all the people that came together to that sight, and beholding the things that were done, smote their breasts, and returned. And all His acquaintances, and the women that followed Him from Galilee, stood afar off, beholding these things. . . . And they that passed by railed on Him, wagging their heads, and saying: 'Ah, Thou that destroyeth the temple, and buildest it in three days!' But when the centurion which stood over against Him, saw that He gave up the ghost, he said: 'Truly this man was the Son of God!' "

To be so familiar with such a sequence that it comes with no new freshness on any Good Friday creates the preacher's dilemma. For it had not been that way with Clovis, Master of all Frankish men, on the day of his baptism at Rheims a thousand and more years ago; for when Clovis heard this crucifixion story for the first time he clenched his fists and cried in agony: "If only I could have been there with my strong Frankish soldiers, this need never have happened to Jesus Christ!"

But sitters in today's pews simply sit and watch their preacher: "seeing they crucify the Son of God afresh, and put Him to open shame." What to say? How to phrase it? If even the Tenor does not stir such poor onery sitters like you and like I? Then the minister studies the Gospels, and decides to help his flock,

7. To sit where Jesus sat—

As a Boy, *sitting among the doctors,* asking and answering questions, so that these grown men were astonished at His answers. The preacher wishes he knew what the Boy asked! Did He go back to Isaiah Nine, perhaps? Asking how a mere Child could ever get to be called: "Wonderful"? "Counsellor"? "The Mighty God"? "The Everlasting Father"? "The Prince of Peace"? Could they please tell Him, for instance, how a Boy of twelve could carry the government upon His shoulders? And establish justice from henceforth forever? No doubt they sat stroking their long patriarchal beards, speechless at such a light in such a young face.

As a young Man, returning to Nazareth, *sitting in the synagogue* after reading Isaiah Sixty-one and daring to say: "It is about me that this is written! It has my home address on it!"

Sitting on a hillside, teaching: "Blessed are ye, when . . . Woe unto you, when . . . When ye pray, say . . . Ye are the salt of . . . Ye are the light of . . . Forgive . . . Follow . . ." All equally impossible to cope with, even after nineteen centuries.

Sitting by a well, talking to a woman no better than she ought to be; yet sharing with her such spiritual insights that the Greek

Catholic Church has honored her with a name—Photina! To
remind other women that it is quite enough to run home and
fetch nine men to listen to the Master; even if the men are somewhat rude about it, saying: "Now we believe! But not because of
what the woman told us!"

Sitting at meat in Martha's house; and with Zacchaeus; Levi;
Simon the Leper; with His disciples at the last supper; in the
home of Cleopas, at Emmaus; by the shore of the beautiful lake
where He Himself broiled the fish and broke the bread.

Sitting in boats in times of storm saying "Peace" to the wind,
and "Be still" to the waves; so that His best friends were frightened, and asked: "Who is this, that even the winds and the
waves obey Him?"

Sitting in Peter's house, curing an old lady's fever; sitting by
the bedside of the daughter of Jairus saying: "Get up, little
darling!" Sitting in the house in Bethany when Lazarus had died,
able to say at the tomb: "Come forth!"

Sitting by the roadside, blessing little important children whom
the disciples had considered of no consequence.

Sitting behind closed doors after the resurrection, when the
disciples were frightened; breathing on them and saying softly:
"Receive ye the Holy Spirit!"

Sitting at the right hand of God, from henceforth, expecting!
"And round about the throne were four and twenty elders sitting,
clothed in white raiment; and they had on their heads crowns
of gold. . . . And when He had taken the Book, the four and
twenty elders fell down before the Lamb, having every one of
them harps, and golden vials full of odours, which are the
prayers of the saints, *and they sang a new song* . . . and I beheld,
and heard the voice of many angels round the throne; their
number was ten thousand times ten thousand and thousands
of thousands. . . . And every creature which is in heaven, and
on the earth, and in the sea, heard I saying: 'Blessing and honor
and glory and power be to Him that sitteth upon the throne,
and unto the Lamb forever and ever.' And the four beasts said:
'Amen!' And the four and twenty elders fell down and worshipped
Him that liveth forever and ever."

After which the Tenor on earth sang with those in heaven the

"Sevenfold Amen" (Stainer) for all the seven sitters in the seven pews in the seven churches.

[*Note:* This chapter may be given as a semi-dramatic meditation: seven chairs on the platform, turned sideview toward audience; the seven sitters, one at time, silently come to sit in these chairs, seen in silhouette, e.g. *first,* carries armful of big stuffed paper bags, each with huge black dollar signs; *second,* in rags, gropes blindfolded toward chair, sits hands outstretched, palms upward; *third,* sits bowed over slightly, handkerchief held motionless over eyes; *fourth,* sits with finger on lips; *fifth,* in purple, furs, with orchid; *sixth,* turns head to stare fixedly above audience; *seventh,* continually turns pages of Bible, reading. *Tenor solo* is old Appalachian Carol: "I Wonder As I Wander"; music by John Jacob Niles may be ordered from G. Schirmer, Inc., 3 East 43rd Street, New York City; 50 cents. To close the meditation, following poem used, while charwoman in apron sweeps slowly from *first* past *seventh* sitter.]

Methought that in a solemn church I stood.
Its marble acres, worn with knees and feet,
Lay spread from door to door, from street to street.
Midway the form hung high upon the rood
Of Him that gave His life to be our good;
Beyond, priests flitted, bowed, and murmurs meet
Among the candles shining still and sweet.
Men came and went, and worshipped as they could—
And still their dust a woman with her broom,
Bowed to her work, kept sweeping to the door.
Then saw I, slow through all the pillared gloom,
Across the church a silent Figure come:
"Daughter," He said, "thou sweepest well my floor!"
It is the Lord! I cried, and saw no more.

George MacDonald

6

THE CHURCH IS NO CANDLE. BLOW ON!

Upon this rock will I build my church, and the gates of hell shall
not prevail against it.   MATTHEW 16:18

The title is something Edna St. Vincent Millay once said. But
the truth of the title, the whole truth, and nothing but the
truth is now being written on the pages of Christian history, by
Negroes.

"Perhaps you would like to read this bunch of letters just
received from one of my men down in Africa," Canon Max
Warren said last August (1954), handing over twenty or more
typed pages, "for I would like your opinion. They are having a
spot of trouble down there in Kenya, you may know. But perhaps I should warn you—this is strong meat!"

And it certainly was. Exactly as if the whole of the eleventh
chapter of Hebrews were being rewritten by African Christians
less than fifty years in the Church. Yet their candle unblowable!
unquenchable!

Canon Warren heads up all the work of the Church Missionary
Society of Great Britain, with nine hundred missionaries in his
charge. But, at the moment, he seemed proudest of Number
901—Samuel Muhoro from Limuru, Kenya, living in a furnace of
persecution: "I thank God for the power to endure which He
gave us, to enable us to speak in friendship to the Mau Mau who
came to attack us. Surely He was overruling and guiding us to
speak His words; for Christ said: 'Don't be anxious as to what
you will say, for the Holy Spirit will tell you what to say to
those who accuse you.' First I was made ready for this trying
experience. I was working in the parish of Njumbi, about twenty-

41

five miles west of Fort Hall. I had eleven villages under my care, at various distances from my home, some six or eight miles away; others, four or five. Each church consisted of saved ones or just ordinary church members. When the reign of terror began I was gripped with great fear, but I prayed the Lord to give me victory over this sin, and He did, so that I became very bold in this work. Off I went to each church where the Mau Mau were forcing people to take their old tribal oath with great violence, and many Christians were badly knocked about for refusing. Goats and cats and moles were hung all around, as a warning. In Njumbi Parish Church a he-goat was slaughtered and all its limbs broken, then straddled across the prayer desk with a warning letter, all in type, saying what a curse would fall on anyone who removed the carcass—to terrorize us. Many so-called Christians took the oath under this pressure, others stood firm, saying death was preferable to this return to old bestial barbarisms. . . . Thank God for them. For instance, two sisters whose husbands had been Christians, but had then taken the oath, were warned by their husbands to join the Mau Mau; when they refused, they were denied food and clothes; in the end, when their refusal to serve any but Christ persisted, they were trussed up and left to die at the commands of their own husbands. This went on and on until the saved ones were being hunted like wild animals and had nowhere to rest. Yet they went on living quietly wherever possible, in the middle of their enemies, with no soldiers or weapons to defend themselves with, only Christ. Fathers were scheming against their own children, mothers too, children against their own parents, brothers against brothers, sisters against sisters, friends against friends, in-laws against in-laws.

"One woman was hanged five times on a tree. Each time as she lost consciousness, she was taken down and asked to drink the tribal oath. On answering that Christ sufficed, she was strung up again. When they saw she was not going to give way, they told a man nearby to dig her grave as they would have to bury her, and she stood by, and watched what was being done! Even here she stood firm. Her witness was a great encouragement.

"In Njumbi where I had been pastor 1950-52, there was a young Christian couple and little child; they had been married in 1950. One night the Mau Mau came and strangled them to death. We then invited all the brethren to a wedding. 'What wedding?' they all asked. Rebekah and Ganthon had gone to heaven, but we placed them inside the church at the very place where they had once stood to witness to their love and be married.

"A great number of our saved ones have been put to death. At their funerals this is the hymn we sing:

> We are on the way to heaven,
> The dwellings of joy and love;
> The things you others love
> Lead you only to destruction.
>
> You say you are not going to heaven?
> Not going to heaven? not going to heaven?
> You say you are not going to heaven?
> We are on our way there!

"In Kiruri Church three hundred are now living at Weithaga, sixteen miles west of Fort Hall. There are no troops to guard them, all their possessions lost; but they help each other with food and clothes and money from the Church Missionary Society of Great Britain. . . ."

The letter went on and on, in detail. Samuel Muhoro wrote how he himself had been struck and wounded and stripped one dark night; over a month in the hospital recovering, with probable lameness for the rest of his life. He wrote also of Andrew Kaguru, a catechist who had been such a brave witness that the infuriated Mau Mau had chopped up his body in the most savage way, to get even; they had tied a wire around his body, dragging him away like a sheep; leaving five small children and another to be born later still in the mother's womb. It was horrifying to find no blood left in Andrew's body, presumably the savages had drunk all of it . . .

At this point Canon Warren began to explain: that Kenya once had been a pleasant happy valley in the British Empire. There were huge estates where white men lived more lavishly than was possible even back in England. But the Kikuyo tribe contended that these lands had all belonged to their ancestors. It is significant to notice that Jomo Kenyatta, the chief agitator, studied for two years at Moscow University, that he was a good friend of Paul Robeson, and used to use countless Communist terms in speeches to stir up his tribe, after his return to this colony in 1940.

Now Kenyatta is serving a long prison term, charged with complicity in stirring up this revival of old primitive traditions. Every new Mau Mau recruit is indoctrinated in the belief (1) that their early way of life is better than the white man's way, and above all (2) that he must pledge himself to denounce his Christian faith, never attend a mission school, and murder any Christian when so ordered. There is even training in how to mutilate a corpse, and how to nail a cat's head on the doors of all who refuse to join.

The raiding Mau Mau gangs are being rounded up, with as many as seventy thousand held in prison camps; but, in the thick forests, there are countless hideouts which neither the British soldiers nor their loyal African assistants can locate—so that the tragedy still continues.

But, in the thick of all this trouble, think how God has been working; no matter how revolting and devilish the persecution, His Spirit is prevailing. For within the past year there has been a sequel! You may have read Bremer Hofmeyr's report of it in The American Weekly for November 28, 1954.

Mr. Hofmeyr, himself, is a member of one of the old Afrikaans South African families, and a cousin was once Deputy Prime Minister under General Smuts. In his article he told how David Waruhui used his father's assassin to prove something convincing about Christian courage—for after he and his father had been converted, his father called the first anti-Mau Mau assembly. Since J. K. Waruhui was one of the senior chiefs in Kenya, his high position drew more than 50,000 men of the Kikuyu tribe. It was at his urgency that a resistance movement was started that day. But this so inflamed the Mau Mau against him that one dark night, on a lonely Kenya road, J. K. Waruhui was shot to death. Old tribal customs would have required David Waruhui to track down his father's killers, and kill them, in retaliation. But as a Christian he knew that he could not fight hate with hate. So the thing he did was heroic! *He and his family moved into the barbed wire encampment* where the British had imprisoned 1,500 Mau Mau ringleaders, among whom was Kimu, one of his father's assassins.

David sent for Kimu that first day, and spoke to him gently and courteously, as friend to friend. Kimu glared back sullenly. But day by day, moment by moment, at every visit and at any chance meeting, there was a lessening of tension. Until the afternoon when the young eight-year-old Wanjiri Waruhui offered Kimu a cup of tea. He took it; and spoke his first words. The next morning, as David was walking alone in the prison yard, Kimu actually greeted him, of his own accord.

After which, with the inevitability of gradualness, first Kimu and then others of these rebellious ringleaders began to recognize a Spirit at work among them. For David talked constantly of what Kenya could be like with absolute honesty, purity, unselfishness and love. In himself they saw all four, impersonated.

Today, five hundred of the fifteen hundred interned in that Athi River prison are with David, heart and soul. He is training them to go out, a dozen men together, into other Mau Mau prison camps to relive this same slow redemptive process. There is a mass demand for Bibles and hymnbooks, and hundreds are openly leaving the Mau Mau. One of the most conspicuous of these converts is Peter Muigai, son of the chief Mau Mau leader, Jomo Kenyatta.

For the Church is no candle. Blow on!

"Sire," said Theodore Beza, the Huguenot, to the King of Navarre, in John Calvin's century, "it belongs in truth to the Church of God, in the name of which I speak, to

receive blows and not to give them; but it will please
your majesty to remember that it is an anvil that has
worn out many hammers."

We have not journeyed across the centuries, across the
oceans, across the mountains, across the prairies, because
we are made of sugar candy.

from a speech by Winston Churchill,
in Ottawa, December, 1941

For like a child sent with a fluttering light
To feel his way across a gusty night,
Man walks the earth; again, and yet again,
The lamp shall be by fits of passion slain,
But shall not He who sent him from the door
Relight the lamp once more, and yet once more?

Matthew Arnold

7

FORGIVE US OUR FILIBUSTER

. . . and prayed thus with himself. LUKE 18:11

In the Senate, of course, a filibuster seems childish. Outchatter
your opponent. Make a marathon with your mouth. Say any old
thing and every old thing that comes to mind. Just keep mumbling
along. Tiring the other fellow out. And stop that vote from taking
place. How deplorable of grown men to stoop so low! We hope
the Russian papers do not copy it. And certainly not the Chinese,

with Confucius in their memories of how men of dignity should speak. Yes indeed, deplorably childish in senators.

But on my knees, how tragic to tire Almighty God with my trifling private filibuster, whatever the stream of consciousness brings forth from moment to moment, while the preacher prays in public—

Did I shut the kitchen window, I wonder? There's old Mrs. Dogood in last summer's hat, except, of course, that new rose. Funny how some women never see that a fresh flower on faded straw makes a hat look frumpish. But I suppose good taste is born in you or it isn't. I wish I had worn my blue suit, for it looks now as if it wouldn't rain, after all. I'm glad he's praying for the soldiers, since there sits Sam beside Sally—I wonder if she really wants that baby? Not that she can help herself now. I must remember to return *From Here to Eternity* tomorrow at the library, on my way to the dentist's. I hope he won't hurt quite so much this time. Incredible how we never outgrow our dread of going. Bob is just like me—a frightful fuss, beforehand. I tell him that the dentist says if only people would drink water after eating candy it would wash away the bacteria that start decaying teeth right off. Bob thinks his particular teeth are eternal. Boys never learn from parents; think we are decrepit old creatures. I heard that the dentist's wife is divorcing him. Poor soul; so gentle and all. Perhaps she likes a livelier man. I'm glad myself that Jim is so up-and-coming, even if he never notices one single thing I ever do. *Men!*

Why do ministers cover the whole earth in their prayers, I wonder? "And now for all Thy homeless ones, O Lord God, wandering like a river of human woe." He really uses lovely language. Speaking of rivers, I hope the plumber fixes that leak in the bathtub, for suppose it starts staining the living-room ceiling, what a mess to have painters all over the place again. But dear me, how long have we been in the house, anyhow? Ten years? Eleven? No, *nine*—for Bob was only a baby. I do wish he wouldn't tramp in with all that mud on his boots. A dozen door mats would never remind that boy to wipe those boots. He simply doesn't give a hang about his home. Treats it like a public dormitory, to sleep in; and leave. And me, like the chef in a restaurant: "What's for dinner?" Children weren't like that in my day. Mamma did us all a good turn. She was a good cook, too. I do wish I could find her recipe for that pudding—only two eggs, imagine!

Well, the prayer must be nearly over, for he's praying for "the President of these United States, in these dangerous moments in history, O Lord." All I can say is, I wish Mamie would stop wearing bangs; it hardens her face or something. But it must be fun fixing up that old farmhouse from scratch; with plenty to do with. I'd surely like to buy that old Chippendale sofa, it's definitely a bargain; but suppose Bob flopped himself down on it as he does on our divan now, that heirloom would be splinters! Anyhow, if we buy the sofa we can't take the trip to Canada this summer, and that will be educational for Bob. They tell me the streets in Montreal are all named for saints! What a lot of reverent things to think about everywhere I walk. Isn't it strange that Protestants pretend the saints are only for Catholics? But the saints got to be saints before a single Protestant was born. I simply love them, myself. But then I have these inner longings, all the time. I still remember when somebody told me, on October 28, that this was the date for St. Jude, one of the twelve disciples, and that he was called the "Patron of Impossible Things." Nobody really knows how he got that reputation. But I was so curious I went home and read his Epistle straight through at one sitting. Only one chapter, after all. But he certainly got everything in! All very brief brisk little scenes, like something on TV. Now Egypt; then Sodom; then the angel Michael fighting the devil; then Cain; next Balaam. By and by, clouds without water, carried about by winds! I memorized that verse: *"These are murmurers, complainers, walking after their own lusts; their mouth speaketh swelling words, having men's persons in admiration, because of advantage . . ."* it made me think of my own ambitious days, trying to climb up a social ladder before Jim earned quite enough to get us there. Now how does the rest of it go? Oh yes! *"But ye, beloved, building up yourselves on your most holy faith, praying in the Holy Spirit, keep yourselves in the love of God, looking for the mercy of our Lord Jesus Christ unto eternal life. And of some, have compassion, making a difference . . . pulling them out of the fire, hating even the garment spotted by the flesh."*

Probably there isn't another Protestant in this room with a patron saint! One to remember every October 28. I don't wonder, myself, why he is the patron of impossible causes—for it is about me he writes! It has my home address on it! Just think how windy and empty this frightful filibuster has been—while the preacher prayed in public, look at my private parade of problems! O Lord, I may be proud of having a personal saint, but Thou knowest what is in man—Thou rememberest my frame, and how dusty I am! So I am no surprise to Thee; but who else in all this congregation could sink so low as to outchatter the most disgraceful filibuster in Washington?

I ought to be thanking Thee for all my bliss! Those dear things of home, reminding me at every turn of loved ones gone and of those so precious, now. For there is ecstasy in human love, O God, as Thou didst know when Thou didst frame our mortal bodies in the lowest parts of the earth, when as yet there was none of them. I thank thee for these words the Psalmist said, for it helps me know Thy plan for all the bliss which Jim and I have had, and for Bob—so like us both, and yet so modern. Lord, I do indeed thank Thee, too, for the special skills at my fingertips —Thou didst plan them for me alone; on all the earth, nobody's fingerprints have ever matched mine, nor ever can! Such knowledge is too wonderful for me—but I pray Thee to bless the work my hands do; for when I am busy creating I feel that this bliss of accomplishment must be a little like Thy resting on the seventh day and saying of each thing created: "It is good!"

I had meant to thank Thee, too, for sunshine and for shade. For the charm of color in gardens and sunsets, in rainbows and flowers and birds. Thy beauty restores my soul. I inherited this bliss from Thee! When I think of my earthly ancestors, I ought to go around touching everyday improvements with deeper wonder—for I need no wax to turn into candles, no lamps to trim to let there be light; just a small button to touch, and lo! there is light. If only I could use Thee as I use electricity! It keeps my clothes ironed, my hair waved, my food cooked, my machines moving. But instead of thanking Thee in prayer, I use my telephone only to call the fire department and the police when there is trouble.

Lord God, I am like that statue I saw in the Metropolitan Museum—two men who looked exactly alike, wrestling together; one flat on the earth (as I am now), the other slowly arising from the struggle, face to the sky! Even Henry Barnard's title for his sculpture suits my present state: *"I Feel Two Natures Struggling within Me."*

Forgive me this filibuster, I beseech Thee, O God, and may the benediction of Thy disciple Jude come upon me: *"Now unto Him who is able to keep you from falling, and to present you faultless before the presence of His glory with exceeding joy, to the only wise God, our Saviour, be glory and majesty, dominion and power, both now and forever. Amen.*

We dream alone, we suffer alone, we die alone, we inhabit the last resting-place alone. But there is nothing to prevent us from opening our solitude to God. And so what was an austere monologue becomes dialogue.
> Henri Frédéric Amiel

Over the great city
Where the wind rustles in the parks and the gardens,
In the air, in the high clouds brooding,
There I am.
Think not because I do not appear at first glance,
Because the centuries have gone by
And there are no assured tidings of me,
That therefore I am not there.
Think not because all goes its own way,
That therefore I do not go my own way through all.

The fixed bent of faces hurrying in the street,
Each turned toward the light and seeing no other,
Yet I am the light toward which they all look.
The toil of so many hands toward such multifarious
ends,
Yet my hand knows the touch and twining of them all.
Make no mistake, do not be deluded—
Over the great city,
There I am.

Edward Carpenter; used by permission

8

DIMINUENDO?

As the clear light is upon the holy candlestick, so is the beauty
of a face in ripe age. ECCLESIASTICUS 26:17

Thirty-seven words, and Luke tells all we really know about her.
But one day in college a certain English professor put "A" on
a certain daily theme. The assignment read: *Describe a Woman's
Conversation with Her Doctor.* And a certain sophomore knew
enough to find the proper patient in the Gospel, fever and all,
cure and all. Yet there must have been more than met the eye
in Luke's two brief verses. But what? What? That was when
this eighteen-year-old began reading between the lines, putting
two and two together (with certain recent additions).

For the moment Peter walked indoors his wife called out:
"Mother's sick!" And Peter called back: "But the Master is here!"
So of course they took Jesus to the old lady's bedside. And as soon
as He touched her hand He said: "You have a fever! How did

you get it?" Not that He needed to ask—"for He knew what was in man." But He knew, too, that half the cure lay in an invalid's own discovery of the big barrier blocking her getting better.

However, the poor old soul hugged her secret closer. Far too frank to share with this particular Visitor. So then He said it for her: "I can see that you are worrying over something—what is it?"

She blurted out the truth: "Of course I'm worrying! Why shouldn't I? Didn't I think my daughter was fixed for life? Hadn't she made a good marriage? What with Peter owning his own fishing boat, in partnership with Andrew. But just look at him now! Traipsing all over the countryside with You, not catching a single fish, nor earning a single penny! As I look ahead I can't think what's going to become of us all."

Still with His finger on her pulse, the Master took her into His confidence: "That's only because you don't see far enough, then, nor appreciate Peter. Suppose I told you that I foresee Peter's becoming one of the most important men on earth! He will get written up in the world's best-selling Book. In fact, he will even write some of the chapters, himself—do you suppose it will be about your own daughter that he will write: *'and some men, even without the Word, will be won by the conversation of their wives'*? How thrilling for you, good friend, if he could also add: *'and by the conversation of their mothers-in-law, too'*! And how will you feel when I tell you that after I leave, Peter will preach such a successful sermon on Pentecost that three thousand persons will feel so pricked in their hearts that they will surge up to Peter afterward to join my church?"

"Did you say *three thousand*, Lord?" the old lady gasped. "Good gracious, our Peter as important as all that?"

The Master smiled at the bliss on her face: "Your fever seems to have left you!"

"And why not?" she chuckled cheerfully. "I never dreamed the dear fellow had it in him!"

"But didn't I tell him he was going to be a *rock*? And on that rock I would build my church?"

"Yes, I know You did, Lord. But You don't know Peter as I do. For he's really only a pebble!"

"And whose fault is that but yours? A woman your age should know better! Can a candle shine until somebody lights it? And if it blows out, relights it? Can a plant bloom until it gets enough sunshine and rain? It's a tragic trait to keep doubting a person's possibilities. To live under the same roof with a man, expecting him to be tomorrow exactly what he was yesterday. Never believing in anything he attempts. Never bracing him up. But belittling him. Blaming him for having no backbone, when your own backbone should be bent over in perpetual prayer for Peter. Do you know how many times I have stayed under your roof? You do? Well then, how much have my visits changed your own viewpoints? You know how impressionable Peter is— so think what a personal part you might play if, instead of pestering him, you painted pictures of Peter preaching, Peter catching men instead of fish, Peter turning to you for inspiration whenever he reached your front door!"

The old woman's eyes began to twinkle: "Mercy on me! What a nice new notion, Lord; I must say I like it. Especially on top of those three thousand souls. None of the neighbors can equal *that!*"

The Master patted her hand gently: "Before you brag too loudly, perhaps I should warn you that I foresee his very popularity landing Peter in prison."

"*Prison?*" the ex-invalid repeated, her fever suddenly pounding back into her pulse. "But nobody in our family has ever been in enough disgrace to land in jail, Lord! What on earth will the reckless man do to deserve prison?"

The Master looked at her agitated face affectionately: "Come now, dear friend, must you always judge everything socially? What will the neighbors think? The fact is, it is going to become a high honor to be imprisoned for my sake. And it will come to Peter because he will do something spectacular. Do you recall the lame beggar lying by the Beautiful Gate of the Temple? You do? Well then, let me tell you that one day Peter and John will be on their way to worship there, when this cripple will start asking them for money. Peter will then say: 'Silver and gold have I none—'"

"That sounds like Peter!" his mother-in-law interrupted tartly.

The Master reproved her: "It puzzles me that a woman your age should still think of Peter only as a sorry wage earner. And judge of his story at the starting point instead of the finishing point. You dwelt on Peter's poverty. Well, let me dwell on his power! For he will be able to say to that beggar: 'Such as I have, I give; therefore, rise up and walk!' The cripple will leap to his feet, completely cured."

The old lady sat up speechless, every wrinkle wreathed into a question mark: "Simon Peter doing *that?*" she stammered, finally.

"The power of God—through Peter. Indeed, the time will come when his very shadow falling on the sick will cure them; and one day, in Joppa, he is actually going to raise from the dead a widow named Dorcas. Yet these very miracles will cause the priests to be jealous of his power; so they will imprison him. Couldn't you remember, however, that my Father and I will always be with Peter? And couldn't you comfort him on each home-coming by believing in the ability the Spirit will pour out on Peter? That is the real beauty of a stay-at-home life, you can create a climate where a man can become more than himself; he can be that plus which God intends him to be, and that you yourself expect him to be."

"That's quite a responsibility, Lord. Could you tell me how to begin?"

"Believe in him more! There is going to come a day in my life when I shall be on trial in Pilate's judgment hall, and Peter will be out in the courtyard warming his hands at a fire, when a maid servant will come along and twit Peter with being my friend; now why do you suppose he will deny violently that he ever knew me? Could it be because he had lived too long afraid of a woman's cutting tongue, and her unlovely spread of gossip about him up and down the street? Old age could be such a marvelous moment for you—all passion spent, but your serene belief in him creating character and courtesy."

The old lady looked crushed: "But he will never deny having

known You, Lord! He has been too proud of the way You have used his boat! He boasts about it, sometimes."

Our Lord looked at her tenderly: "Then let me share another secret—for you worry that Peter catches no fish, nowadays; but let me tell you that down across all the centuries of my church on this earth, Peter's fishing boat will have high honor paid to it in lands you never heard of, in languages you cannot speak! Over in Rome, for instance, the people speak Latin, and their word for ship is *navis*. So I can look ahead to the day—three hundred years from now—when people called by my name will build their churches in the shape of a ship—in memory of Peter's boat! All because we were all safe on board, together, even in storms. And a thousand years from now, in another language, the place where the congregation will sit will be called the *nave*—again in recollection of Peter's ship. How shortsighted it is for you to prefer a few fish for your cooking pot today when Peter will be remembered for so much more, everywhere on earth—tomorrow."

The old lady shook her white head regretfully: "It's more than I can take in. How had I better begin making myself over, at my age? You know, Lord, I don't get any younger as I get older! Where's all this energy to come from, when actually there's less and less of it every day I live."

"Less and less *talking*?"

"Well, no, Master! I do seem able to talk the same as ever."

"Good! Just talk better, and hint less—about lack of fish, that sort of thing. And how about *time*, less and less of that, nowadays?"

"No, Lord, I really have more and more time!"

"Good! Then spend it with Peter! Think him bigger. Talk him bigger. Plan him bigger. Pray him bigger. That is what more time is for—dreaming more and daring more. Forgiving more, too. For maybe it is here at home that our poor Peter practices his new seventy-times-seven arithmetic. On you! Match him by forgiving first!"

She was startled: "Maybe I was dwindling a little, Lord. But it is this bustling around that tires me out."

"But you won't need to bustle at all to do the beautiful thing

I have in mind. Just consider the lily! Perhaps you think a lily none too necessary. But have you never noticed the trouble my Father takes over beauty—just quiet unnecessary beauty? All His sun and rain and wind to help its loveliness and fragrance along. But is the fragrance in the bulb or in the bud or in the full bloom? Two of them all wrapped up in themselves, like little old ladies in shawls. A bit like yourself. Smaller and smaller each day. Determined to do less and less. When all you need to do is to unfold more and more, so that God can talk and think through you, so that Peter can be drawn home to the fragrance, and catch it! For Peter is too small himself, just now. For instance, a night will come when Peter will be up on the rooftop, praying; three times I shall have to send him a vision of a sheet let down from heaven, with fourfooted creatures in it. Three times I shall have to say: 'Rise, Peter, kill and eat!' But in the most virtuous voice he will answer: 'Not so, Lord, I have never eaten anything unclean.' "

The old lady sprang to his defense: "Now that's true! I will say that for Peter, he's as orthodox as they come!"

"Really too orthodox, then! For I came on earth to bear witness to the truth that nothing God ever made is unclean or second class. So right on the heels of the dream, there will come a knock at the street door, and as Peter goes down to answer I shall have to say: 'It's all right, Peter—*I have sent them!*' For he will find Romans there, inviting him to come to the house of Cornelius, to stay there and answer their questions about me. So Peter will go. How does that news strike you?"

She looked worried again: "I suppose that would depend on how long he had to stay. For I can't see where my poor son-in-law could *eat*, if he stays over a mealtime—for naturally he couldn't sit down at the same table with Gentiles, could he? Now, Lord, why do you look at me that way—you know our old custom!"

"But have you ever heard me say: 'I am the *Custom!*' Who is to eat at my table when I say: 'I am the *Bread*,' 'I am the *Vine*,' 'I am the *Water*'? In my sight, food is food; a table is a table; hunger is hunger; and God is God of the rich and the poor. If only our Peter could have someone at home spiritual enough to see why I came, instead of nagging at him the moment he gets indoors: '*What? no fish again today?*' "

The old lady blushed and braced herself briskly: "You make me awfully ashamed, Lord. So just tell me what you see me doing the moment my fever leaves me completely?"

"I see you arising immediately and ministering unto all in this household!"

"Then do touch me, Lord!"

So He stood over her, and rebuked the fever; and it left her; and immediately she arose and ministered unto them.

OR, CRESCENDO?

But I will hope continually, and will yet praise Thee more and more. My mouth shall show forth Thy righteousness all the day. I will go in the strength of Thy righteousness, even of Thine only, O God. Thou hast taught me from my youth; and hitherto have I declared Thy wondrous words. Now also when I am old and grayheaded, O God, forsake me not; until I have showed Thy strength unto this generation, and Thy power to every one that is to come. . . . Thou, who hast showed me great and sore troubles, shalt quicken me again . . . Thou shalt increase my greatness, and comfort me on every side.

Psalm 71:14-18, 20-21

Then Mr. Despondency's daughter entered the river and passed over to the other side singing, but so low that no one could hear what she sang.

John Bunyan, *Pilgrim's Progress*

He who ceases to grow, becomes smaller; he who leaves off, gives up; the stationary condition is the beginning of the end.

Anonymous

But the path of the just is as a shining light, that shineth more and more unto the perfect day.

Proverbs 4:18

9

THEME FOR SOPHOCLES

For our light affliction, which is but for a moment, worketh for us a far more exceeding and eternal weight of glory; while we look not at the things which are seen, but at the things which are not seen.   2 CORINTHIANS 4:17-18

Where are all those devoted women who used to work worsted mottoes in colored wools for preachers and doctors to hang on office walls? They may be out in the waiting room, themselves, of course—eye on the door, impatient to get in for their own appointments. But how cathartic to start embroidering mottoes again; short sentences, provocative enough to prick a patient into proper perspectives. The likelihood is that within four minutes, out may come a memorandum pad to copy down the titbit. Surreptitiously, perhaps.

"Just something suggestive for my neurotic neighbor," the lady may confide, if caught in the act of jotting it down. (For on some streets some people really do love their neighbors as themselves.)

Suppose, for instance, that you have been the one to embroider for your doctor this stray sentence from Percy Bysshe Shelley: "If I so much as stub my little toe, in three minutes it becomes a theme for Sophocles."

In case a patient begins copying within four minutes, but seems uncertain about Sophocles, you may pull out of your handbag—as nonchalantly as possible—a number of scraps of paper, each with something sensible which Sophocles wrote.

Simply say, as you hand these over to the unknown lady: "Incredible, isn't it, to think that Athenians exiled Sophocles for being frank? This top quote sounds like the Constitution of the United Nations, doesn't it? You know how it goes—'Since wars begin in the minds of men, it is in the minds of men that the defenses of peace must be constructed.' Now, match Sophocles!"

The stranger will read with surprise: "Grant, O God, that we may be of the number of those who are born not to join in hating, but to join in loving." "O ye deathward-going tribes of men, what do your lives mean except that they go for nothingness?" "It is money that sacks cities and drives men forth from house and home, warps and seduces native innocence, and breeds a habit of dishonesty." "Kindness is ever the begetter of kindness."

"Dear me!" the lady may say; "was Sophocles a Christian, then?"

"No! He lived before 500 B.C. But God gets into everybody, some time or other. I suppose that what Shelley meant about the stubbed toe was that dramatists notice all of us, every moment, to get ideas for their themes—you know how some people magnify their own woes and their own wants, as if nobody else existed?"

"My goodness, yes!" the other patient explodes. "Why, I have a neighbor, you simply wouldn't believe how that woman can pester the life out of me . . ."

But of course you do believe her. For you have a neighbor, yourself. In order to escape any post-mortems you show her another motto: "The least pain in our little finger gives us more concern than the destruction of millions of our fellow men." (William Hazlitt, 1778-1830.)

She may agree. Or she may be literal, as the sick so often are; for suppose she says that she has never had any trouble with toes or fingers, herself; but oh! this pain in her neck; all because her husband keeps the window . . .

This would be a good time to turn her poor stiff neck toward Bobby Burns's motto:

> Ah, gentle dames! It gars me greet
> To think how mony counsels sweet,
> How mony lengthened sage advices
> The husband frae the wife despises.

And of course, if she shows too sharp a satisfaction, lead her further down the wall where a single fresh rose stands underneath George Matteson's prayer, written in his diary the day before he composed the hymn, "O Love That Will Not Let me Go"—

Dear Heavenly Father: I have thanked Thee a thousand times for my roses but never once for my thorns.

I have looked forward to a world where I should receive compensation for my cross.

Teach me that my cross is itself a present glory.

Help me to see that I have climbed to Thee by the path of pain.

Help me to see that my tears have made my rainbow. Amen.

If the two of you are alone in the waiting room, how therapeutic to try humming the tune softly, recalling the words, especially the line "O Joy, that seekest me through pain, I do not ask to fly from Thee." For actually that is why both of you are keeping your present appointments!

Slightly embarrassed, it may seem wise to read these other mottoes:

> A sick tossed vessel
> Dashing on each thing—
> My God, I mean myself!
> GEORGE HERBERT, 1593-1633

Suffering is a short pain and a long joy. HENRY SUSO, 1300-1366

O God, from Thy great pain for me, remember my little pain.
MARGERY KEMPE, 1400

My health is very bad, but God does so much through me that I laugh heartily at myself.   ST. TERESA OF AVILA, 1515-1582

It is to be hoped that the doctor has some patient with enough leisure to cope with the well-known: "Give me a good digestion, Lord, and something to digest"; saving special scarlet yarn to add unmistakable emphasis to the line: "*This fussy thing called I.*" For no matter how this strikes the waiting-room crowd, at least the doctor may relax a little realizing that the human race has always been "fussy" ever since somebody wrote about "Digestion" on the walls of Chester Cathedral.

Much more recently some light versifier has said that when Shakespeare was Shakespeareing he know not he was Shakespeareing, and that when Meyerbeer was Meyerbeering he did not know he was Meyerbeering; ending up after a dozen other authors with the suggestion: Let each man go on himselfing and each man be himself. Paraphrasing poorly, you know that when a woman starts Sophoclesing she is *herselfing* into a theme for Sophocles, and when she is William Hazlitting and Bobby Burnsing she is herselfing so much that even chance acquaintances start psychoanalyzing her, long before the door into the doctor's inner sanctum opens.

For people babying themselves give away their secret at a glance. This draught. This hard pew. This unpleasant sermon. This poor light. This long wait. This unbalanced diet. This stingy helping. This wretched service. This lazy cleaning woman. This lonely house. This silent telephone. This ungrateful friend. This impossible life. Poor me.

Herselfing the days away!

She ought to be the one to embroider Emerson's suggestion: "If you do not quit the high chair, lie down and roll on the ground a great deal, you become nervous and heavyhearted. There is health in table talk and nursery play. You must wear old shoes and have aunts and cousins."

Even St. Jerome wrote all this in similar vein to Laeta centuries earlier, about how to bring up her little daughter: let her play with girls who are prettier than she is and with more toys, so that she can be jealous but learn to get over it.

All the quotations so far have been purely prophylactic and without affection. But Samuel Rutherford can always be trusted to say the true thing tenderly. A Scottish saint, long in prison for his faith, yet able to frame such gems as these three:

Would to God that I had not myself but Christ.

Yes! you seem to be in a bad way. My advice is "Take you a house next door to the Physician, for it will be very singular if you should be the first He ever turned away unhealed."

There be some would follow Christ, but with the reservation that Christ would cry: "Down crosses," and "Up umbrellas," and the summer sky and sun till we be all safely landed in Heaven. I know you have not so learned Christ, but that you intend to fetch Heaven, to take it with the wind on your face; for so both storm and wind was on the fair face of Christ, your lovely forerunner all His way.

When a woman asked the surgeon, just before her operation: "Doctor, how soon after the anaesthesia wears off can I expect the full use of my mind?" "Madam," he said, "I wouldn't count on it at all, if I were you!"

But restoring minds was something the Great Physician always did. In Luke's gospel we read of "Mary called Magdalene, out of whom went seven devils." You wish that Luke, who was explicit enough about other miracles which Jesus did, had enumerated those demons for you. But now the best that you can do is to name seven modern evil spirits which make men and women break down. Self-pity, self-love, overindulgence, indifference to others, idleness, aimlessness, godlessness.

"This is the sin of thy sister Sodom, pride and fulness of bread, and the idleness of all her daughters, and the fact that she did not care for the poor and needy"—this was Ezekiel's report.

Speaking of fingers, Dr. Hocking of Harvard offsets William Hazlitt perfectly when he says: "No religion is a true religion which does not make men tingle to their fingertips with a sense of infinite hazard."

Think of the infinite hazard ahead of Mandombe, one of the earliest Christians to be baptized at Banza Manteke, in the Belgian Congo. In those days there was no remedy for sleeping sickness, and Mandombe's wife was one of the victims. When it became known that a cure might be found if someone were willing to go to England to be experimented upon, Mandombe offered to go. He was told that only someone who had sleeping sickness would be of any use, so he went away in sorrow. But before many weeks he was back again, his face glowing as he cried: "Now you can send me! I have it! I am ready!"

It was pointed out to him that he would have to stay in England a long while, perhaps even die there, far from his loved ones. But he still insisted: "Yes! Yes! send me!" This was even braver than you may guess, for Congo people like to die in their own village and be buried in the "village of the departed," nearby.

Mandombe went to England with a medical missionary. When he was near death, the English doctors offered to send him back to Congo. But he simply asked: "Have you found the cure for sleeping sickness yet?"

"No, not yet," they said, "but the secret is nearly found!"

"Then you finish your work; I am not going home."

You may know that today sleeping sickness has been brought under control. But did you know that in a certain hospital in London there is a special plaque in memory of Mandombe, who "tingled to his fingertips with a sense of infinite hazard"?

Undoubtedly it was that way with Father Damien the day that he had to say to his patients: "*We lepers!*" One of the nurses at Molokai was asked what sort of a place this leper asylum was: "It's a Ticket Office to Heaven!" she answered.

Mary Reed had the same sort of Ticket Office, and she came and went through its gates. But her entrance was heroic. For she had been on furlough at home, and had gone to her doctor to diagnose a strange new set of symptoms. Every specialist said the same thing. But the gallant young woman sailed for India without telling her parents the dreadful disease she bore. Very courageously she entered a leper colony; and, after a few years of treatment, the disease left her.

Then she faced a strange decision. She had wanted to give her life to India, but it had turned on her with its most bitter sting. Almost any other young American girl would now have hurried home. But not Mary Reed! Samuel Rutherford would have understood why, with the winds of the high Himalayas blowing in her face, she opened a home for lepers on Changdag

Heights—and stayed there in that "Ticket Office to Heaven" until she was well over eighty years of age.

By contrast, there is a seminary professor's wife in this country. None too rich and none too poor, except that—to outsiders—life in that particular quadrangle looked highly exhilarating. But, she was none too well, either. So that she fell into conversing about her symptoms, until it seemed to everyone within earshot that she would never outgrow a single woe, but merely grow new ones, moment by moment. But that was before Mary Liu came from China for a year to study.

For Mary Liu is a major miracle.

Nobody knows how God could ever have made an editor out of someone who had neither hands nor feet, just one thumb on the stump of one arm, and the stump of a finger emerging from somewhere on the other. Not much, you must admit. But plenty for Mary Liu. And more than plenty for the professor's wife when this phenomenon came to her campus.

Mary Liu's story began when she was sold as a slave girl to a heartless and heedless young mistress, who used to mistreat the child so viciously that one day she simply tossed her out on a dump heap to die—having already burned both of her feet away. A missionary who was walking past heard smothered sobbing. Searched for the sound; and found this little mutilated mass of misery. In the mission hospital they could carve her a pair of wooden feet. But the mangled fingers and palms had to be amputated, with just the unrecognizable remnants of bones left to serve as hands. The frightened girl lay on her cot, gloomy and grumbling. But the nurses were gentle. There were dolls and candy and pictures. There were merry children all over the place. And one day, out of a clear blue sky, Mary Liu became the merriest of all. Learning to scamper on small new wooden feet. Never for a single moment letting any lack of fingers stop her from doing whatever the others were doing. And always sheer joy over each tiny triumph.

When she finished her schooling, she was made editor of two Christian magazines for Chinese women, *The Messenger* and *The Star*. When the Japanese took over her town, Mary Liu used her wits about preserving her precious stock of paper for the magazines. She had it stacked in dark corners, as if it were worthless stuff, or underneath other piles against the walls as if it were old forgotten back numbers, perhaps. While all the actual trash she stacked pretentiously in careful bundles and treated with such concern that when the inspectors came, this, of course, was what they carted straight out from under her nose, sure that they were hindering and not helping.

Meanwhile, over in America, the World Day of Prayer committee which sponsored her magazines through their annual offerings began marveling how Mary Liu seemed able to go on publishing month after month, year after year, when other Chinese enterprises had to stop printing from total lack of paper.

Perhaps it was natural, therefore, that when the war was over, Mary Liu should be brought to America to study; and, of course, *to be seen!* She was always so gay and festive that more sober people fell to wondering just what she found so funny! And especially the seminary professor's wife wondered.

"If I had no feet!" she said to herself, wondering how on earth she would ever get around the quadrangle—she who had two perfectly good feet which had never given her a moment of trouble! Yet here was Mary Liu flitting upstairs and downstairs as fleet as a dancer, and bubbling over with exuberance.

"If I had no hands!" the professor's wife thought; she who had all her fingers and thumbs.

"How on earth do you do it, my dear?" she was driven to ask.

Mary Liu looked her merrily in the eye: "But see, haven't I everything on earth to be thankful for?" she asked, in surprise.

And that was the day when the professor's wife started to drop the seven demons which had been possessing her: one by one self-pity and self-love began to be cast out . . .

"At least none of you will ever hear me complain again!" she confided to the seminary president, midway of this miracle of being made "every whit whole."

It makes you hope that her doctor can teach her the usual Afghanistan greeting—

He to her: "Staray mashy": "May you never be tired."
She to him: "Kwar mashy": "May you never be poor."

For it seems as if he would have one less bill to mail out for services rendered, on the first of each month.

[*Note:* This chapter has been presented frequently as a Meditation, by a reader; enacted in pantomime by a roomful of patients on the platform, who arose at intervals to study wall mottoes. Between various paragraphs, one of the patients sang appropriate stanzas of the George Matheson hymn.]

Magdalene at Michael's gate
   Tirlèd at the pin;
On Joseph's thorn sang the blackbird,
   "Let her in! Let her in!"

"Hast thou seen the wounds?" said Michael,
   "Knowest thou thy sin?"
"It is evening, evening," sang the blackbird,
   "Let her in! Let her in!"

"Yes, I have seen the wounds,
   And I know my sin."
"She knows it well, well, well!" sang the blackbird,
   "Let her in! Let her in!"

"Thou bringest no offerings," said Michael.
   "Nought save sin!"
And the blackbird sang: "She is sorry, sorry, sorry!
   Let her in! Let her in!"

When he had sung himself to sleep,
   And night did begin,
One came and opened Michael's gate,
   And Magdalene went in.
           Henry Kingsley, 1830-1876

This morne I used some words of persuasion to my
wife to forbeare to tell me what is past and promised

*here to become a good husband to her for ye tyme to
come and shee promised me likewise shee would doe
what I wished her in anything save in setting her hand
to papers; and I promised her never to wish her
thereunto.*   Adam Eyre, 1614

If it may be a lengthening thy tranquility.

Daniel 4:27

10

DOWN, FIDO!

The sin which dogs our feet.   HEBREWS 12:1 (Phillips)

No matter how breathlessly hot the weather seemed on that
August Sunday morning, suddenly it dropped to zero. For the
Ruling Elder announced that the visiting preacher's train was
delayed beyond church time, and so he was going to do something he had always wanted to do—he was going to give every
member of the congregation an opportunity to preach for five
minutes! Ushers would soon distribute paper and pencil to help
them collect their thoughts.

With cold feet, hands like icicles, and minds in deep freeze, the
congregation visibly shivered, and wished to be anywhere else
on earth than in this church hearing such paralyzing words. In
the end, however, it proved a rare experience; and has been
experimented with elsewhere ever since.

When everybody was equipped with writing materials, they
found that their five-minute sermons were to be written while
sitting quietly in their pews. No oratory. No weak knees. No

trembling hands. No butterflies in stomachs. Although what it did to consciences, nobody knows to this minute.

The Ruling Elder asked them to print in block letters at the head of the page a Bible verse from the book of Hebrews: THE SIN WHICH DOTH SO EASILY BESET US. In parentheses they were asked to put the translation given to that text in Phillips' *Letters to Young Churches*: "The sin which dogs our feet."

The Ruling Elder said he had a dog which loved him so devotedly that he had to keep saying: "Down, Fido!" This was all very well, with a pet; but with a pet sin which he let tag at his heels all day, it was disgraceful. No sensible man took his dog to his business; no preacher took his pet to his pulpit; no school teacher took Fido to her classroom. But the Christian took his besetting sin everywhere he went. Even to Church. And the Church was the only organization on earth made up solely of sinners! Deliberately and consciously, you joined because you knew you were one. But the Church, eventually, is supposed to become "without spot or wrinkle or any such thing," Paul wrote. "Then what about that sin which dogs your steps? To which you are so completely faithful that you never let it out of your sight? or chained at home? leading you, instead of your leading it? jumping all over you? making spots and wrinkles from the marks of muddy paws?"

"Before you start writing, friends, let us sing that ancient church hymn: 'Art thou weary, art thou languid, art thou sore distressed?' For the likelihood is, you *are*! Just as I am. And every man on earth, who faces his conscience and his God. Suppose we let the middle aisle divide us, those on the left-hand side singing the first two lines, those on the right side, the last two lines. For in any such antiphonal singing we repeat a custom of the medieval congregations, and can begin to feel ourselves part of that great cloud of witnesses, all of whom were also sinners . . ."

After the hymn, the five minutes were spent in thinking. Over and over and over the organ repeated the tune "Stephanos," so softly that it was almost like silence. The Ruling Elder explained that since these papers were all to be anonymous, it might be well to print in block letters the sin which hindered and hampered, making for unhappiness. Perhaps one word would do. But probably a few defining words would spell out the true transgressions which led into trouble. After five minutes, the papers were to be folded, collected by the ushers, brought to the platform where he would read them aloud and drop them into a large copper kettle (on a metal stand) where he would then burn them. Since they would be reduced to ashes anyhow, and no penmanship could be recognized, this act of quiet confession should be done in the sight of God, and with a searching of conscience (while the music of the "Stephanos" melody asked its own questions, and the saints, apostles, martyrs, answered).

Then the ushers collected the papers. And in his gentle gracious way, the Ruling Elder opened and read the sins of those in that room. There was nothing unusual about these lists; everybody kept thinking: "But, good gracious, that's my sin, too!" They were this sort of thing: Hold grudges too long, never can forget and forgive. Find fault at home, nothing suits me, family upset. Worry over poor health and age, over no way to earn money; but why forget all His benefits, O my soul? Brood over wrongs done me, never really make up. Worry about my sales, blue all the time, cannot win customers by gloom. Nag at my family, regular old crosspatch at home. Cheat at exams, want to pass, but can't, without cribbing. Jealous of friends with finer houses, clothes, cars. Can't stop mourning over recent sorrow, neglecting dear ones still with me. Tongue too disagreeable, hurts people all day. Refuse responsibility; indifferent to needs around me. Selfish over TV set, turn on only my own favorites. Forget God until I need help. Waste money over trifles, begrudge it for church. Vain; think only about my looks. Read wrong things. Like my own way. Can't pray.

While the papers were burning, the congregation sang as a prayer, the first verse of "Art thou weary," then were given this responsive reading from Psalm 73, which was used antiphonally also:

Left: But as for me, my feet were almost gone, my steps had well-nigh slipped; for I was envious of the foolish, when I saw the prosperity of the wicked . . . they are not in trouble like other men; neither are they plagued like other men.

Right: Lord Jesus, who would think that I am Thine?
    Ah! Who would think,
    Who sees me ready to turn back or sink
    That Thou art mine?
    I cannot hold Thee fast, though Thou art mine:
    Hold Thou me fast,
    So earth shall know at last and heaven at last
    That I am Thine.

CHRISTINA ROSSETTI

Left: Pride compasseth them about as a chain, their eyes stand
out with fatness; they have more than heart could wish.
They are corrupt and speak wickedly concerning oppression;
they speak loftily. They have set their mouth against the
heavens, and their tongue walketh through the earth . . . and
they say: *"How doth God know?"* Behold, these are the ungodly that prosper in the world, they increase in riches.

Right: Oh, this world! this cheating and screening
    Of cheats! this conscience for candlewicks
    Not beacon fires! this over-weening
    Of underhand diplomatic tricks
    Dared for the country while scorned for the counter!
    Oh, this envy of those who mount here,
    And oh, this malice to make them trip!

ELIZABETH BARRETT BROWNING

Left: All the day long have I been plagued, and chastened every
morning. If I say: "I will speak thus," behold, I should offend
against the generation of Thy children. When I thought to
know this, it was too painful for me; until I went into the
sanctuary of God, then understood I.

Right: Let us have a Church that dares
    Imitate the heroism of Jesus;
    Seek inspiration as He sought it;
    Judge the past as He judged it;
    Act on the present as He acted;
    Pray as He prayed;

Work as He wrought;
Live as He lived.
Let us have a Church for the whole man:
Truth for the mind,
Good works for the hands,
Love for the heart;
And for the soul, that aspiration after perfection,
That unfaltering faith in God,
Which, like lightning in the clouds,
Shines brightest when elsewhere it is most dark.

THEODORE PARKER

Left: Thus my heart was grieved, and I was pricked in my reins.
So foolish was I, and ignorant: I was as a beast before Thee—

Right: Remember the spider weaving a square,
And that you did it everywhere.
Remember the cat tormenting a bird,
And that you did it in deed and word.
Remember the fool mistreating the good,
And that you did it whenever you could.
Remember the devil and treachery,
And that you did it when you were he.
And then remember not to forget,
That you did it, and do it yet.   JAMES STEPHENS

Left: Nevertheless I am continually with Thee; Thou hast holden
me by my right hand, Thou shalt guide me with Thy counsel,
and afterward receive me in glory. Whom have I in heaven
but Thee? and there is none upon earth that I desire, beside
Thee. My flesh and my heart faileth; but God is the strength
of my heart, and my portion forever.

Right: Christ with me, Christ before me, Christ behind me,
Christ in me, Christ below me, Christ above me,
Christ at my right, Christ at my left,
Christ in the heart of everyone who thinks of me,
Christ in the ear of everyone who hears me.
I bind myself this tide
To the Christ who died.   ST. PATRICK, "The Deer's Cry"

Right: Wherefore, seeing we also are compassed about by so great a cloud of witnesses, let us lay aside every weight, and the sin which doth so easily beset us, and let us run with patience the race which is set before us, looking unto Jesus —the author and finisher of our faith.

Belong to God and become a wonder to yourself!
An ancient unknown saint

Religion's all or nothing; it's no mere smile
Of contentment, sigh of aspiration, sir—
No quality of the finelier tempered clay
Like its whiteness or its lightness, rather stuff
Of the very stuff; life of life, and self of self.
Robert Browning

11

ENLARGE THE PLACE OF THY TENT

Enlarge the place of thy tent, and let them stretch forth the curtains of thine habitations: spare not, lengthen thy cords, and strengthen thy stakes; for thou shalt break forth on the right hand and on the left; and thy seed shall inherit the Gentiles, and make the desolate cities to be inhabited.   ISAIAH 54:1-3

Christians hardly expect the *Arabian Nights* to equal the Hebrew prophets. But at least once Scheherazade almost outmatched Isaiah. Poor woman, she was in desperate need of outthinking, outplotting and outwitting the fearful fate hanging over her head.

So she wove a tent out of whole cloth—out of her own imagination, really—just to keep herself alive another night. For you must have heard how, for a thousand and one nights, she thought up tales to keep the Sultan amused, since he had the unhappy habit of marrying a new wife each evening and killing her off the next morning.

It took ingenuity, therefore, to fascinate him by endless entertainment, and that was why she made Prince Ahmed receive from the fair Paribanou a tent so tiny that he could hide it in the hollow of his hand, or fold it into his pocket. Yet whenever he wanted to open his tent, it could extend out and out and out wide enough to form a canopy of protection over his entire army or over his entire city. Any civil defense committee on earth would welcome such a safety device, today! Although locally—tucked in each citizen's hands—this tent exists already: tangibly and intangibly, visibly and invisibly. For anybody's hands folded in prayer can open in compassion, enlarging the room under his own private tent, stretching forth the curtains of his own home, lengthening his own tent pegs until he could stretch space on the right hand and on the left, keeping his city from desolation. So that no matter where he goes in town he walks on every street to the thrilling tune: "Immortal tidings in your mortal hands."

Isaiah mentioned more of God's plans for the homeless: "For a small moment I have forsaken thee, but with great mercies will I gather Thee, saith the Lord, thy Redeemer. . . . O thou afflicted, tossed by the tempest, and not comforted, behold, I will lay thy stones with fair colors, and lay thy foundations with sapphires. And I will make thy windows of agates, and thy gates of carbuncles, and all thy borders of pleasant stones. And all thy children shall be taught of the Lord; and great shall be the peace of thy children."

So then Isaiah's gorgeous refuge outglittered Scheherazade's inconspicuous little tent; and, far from being a mere fairy tale, this book could be filled with a thousand and one true tales of true tents hidden in actual hands to hide inhabitants and protect the children of the desolate.

In India, only yesterday, Pandita Ramabai did it. For she

knew from her childhood what desolation was like—in the great famine of 1877 she was nearly starving, and prostrated herself day and night before idols on the godshelf. When no answer came, her parents sold all their jewelry; then all their clothes; then all their cooking utensils; after which they went out in the forest to die. First her father perishing, then her mother, then her sister. With the Hindu dirge for the dead sounding on every side, over and over, as sorrow came to other families:

> O! thou apple of my eye, O! my darling,
>   my blissful paradise;
> O! thou apple of my eye, where
>   hast thou hidden thyself?
> O! my golden jewel, O! my eyes,
> O! my flower, where hast thou
>   hidden thyself?
> Is this anyone's curse upon me?
>   O! the apple of my eye!

Growing up alone, Ramabai studied Sanskrit and ancient manuscripts. Then, somehow, she was taken to England for a while where she could not help seeing how superior Christianity was. Then she was baptized. After which she began hearing about George Müller and the China Inland Mission. To herself she said: "If others can trust God this way, why not I?"

Back in India, with this tent of tenderness hidden in her hands, Pandita Ramabai lived through the tragic famine of 1896; she saw girls dying right and left, and so she vowed: "I must save them! I will depend upon God and not man . . . I began to take in these starving girls, keeping them first outdoors, under the trees, for shelter. I asked God for money for shelter, and He has sent me over $25,000. Already He has sent me over five hundred girls; and if God sends them I will take a thousand more!"

The thousand came. And she took them!

But think of one woman with no private resources in a land of timid women, drawing plans and superintending the construction of immense buildings; directing a hundred teachers, matrons, workers; providing more than a thousand girls with food, education, training them how to sew, weave, farm, nurse, cook, run dairies and oil mills. Yet with time left over to imitate Isaiah's brilliant tent of refuge—for she named her gates "Salvation" and her walls "Peace," and she even laid out the center of her gardens in dramatic designs, with the decorations of her flowerbeds spelling out Scripture texts in praise to God who kept providing such substantial tents for two thousand child widows.

And who was this George Müller who gave Pandita Ramabai her first idea of widening hospitality? A hundred years ago in Bristol, England, almost anybody could have pointed out his house, and told you what a reckless clergyman Mr. Müller had become. Refusing a regular salary for preaching. Quite sure that God was dependable and trustworthy. Even Mrs. Müller agreeing to sell everything they owned on earth—parting with all their household furnishings. That sort of reckless sweeping thing! Although every woman knows how sticks of furniture gather memories across the years, so that a chair is always more than a chair. It is also all the people who have sat in it. Admiring the workmanship. Even breaking it down bit by bit, until the cushions sag, the legs loosen, the needlepoint frays, and even the curious creakings call to mind words said on a certain day which changed everything. A lamp is more than a lamp. It is also the day it was bought, the faces it has lighted at nightfall. Yet Mrs. Müller let all these possessions go gladly; it was almost as if she could hear across the Atlantic Ocean about that same time the voice of Emily Dickinson telling the world that God's residence is next to mine, His furniture is love!

For the next thing Bristol knew the first orphanage in all England had been started under the Müller roof. If people wondered where these reckless foster parents found money to feed so many hungry young stomachs, certainly the Müllers never told them. Long before undertaking this new enterprise in faith they had made at least five risky decisions: to live on a day-to-day, meal-to-meal basis, never to tell anyone except God about the needs of their orphans, forbidding their helpers to tell outsiders, never to borrow, and never to use money given for one thing for something else.

Only at night, on the pages of his own "Journal," would George

Müller write down his prayers to God for tomorrow's lacks. And always the next morning that prayer was answered. Such heavenly hospitality shook England! It was like the widow's cruse of oil that failed not. It was like the curtains of Isaiah's tent stretching left and right. It was as unbelievable as Scheherazade making up a tale to keep herself alive another night, for the Müllers kept alive their immense family of orphans, night after night. Every room in their house seemed like another prophet's chamber, as if Mrs. Müller had said to George: "Let us, I pray thee, make a little room on the wall; and let us set there a bed, a table, a stool, and a candlestick; and it shall be, when the prophet cometh to us, that he shall turn in thither."

Grand Rapids has never yet made furniture so famous!

> A tent pitched in a world not right
> It seemed, whose inmates every one
> On tranquil faces bore the light
> Of duties beautifully done,
> And humbly, though they had few peers,
> Kept their own laws, which seemed to be
> The fair sum of six thousand years'
> Traditions of civility.

> ANONYMOUS

Christians reading of the Müllers and Pandita Ramabai have always felt conscience-stricken, especially if their domestic design for living has been: Me and my wife, my son John and his wife —us four and no more.

With them George Eliot once shared her own version of Scheherazade's secret tent: "The invasion of our private lives by the larger destinies of mankind." This is almost always quite a nuisance. Always rather risky. But at least it answers a major Christian question without unchristian apologies: *What do ye more than others?*

Fritz and Marta Legatis answered it moment by moment under their roof in Breslau, during the war. For no matter how often every day the Gestapo knocked at their door, ordering them to take down the sign on their wall reading SOCIETY OF FRIENDS; just that often did Herr and Frau Legatis nail it back in place. Their son Gert kept bringing fellow students home with him from the University of Breslau to attend Quaker meetings. The contagion of such courageous Christianity caused many of these uncertain young Germans to give up Nazi tendencies and join this Society of Friends. When the Jews in Breslau were rounded up and put into concentration camps, out from the hands and the home of the Legatis family came food parcels and friendly letters, and a constant concern for the families of prisoners. In cases of death, Legatis hands had the necessary comfort to share. Until, in themselves, this one family became a modern version of Paul's letter to the Church in Corinth: "I know that if this earthly tent of mine is taken down, I get a home from God, made by no human hands, eternal in the heavens. It makes me sigh, indeed, this yearning to be under cover of my heavenly habitation, since I am sure that once so covered I shall not be 'naked' at the hour of death. I do sigh within this tent of mine with heavy anxiety— not that I want to be stripped, no, but to be under cover of the other, to have my mortal element absorbed by life. I am prepared for this change by God, who has given me the Spirit of its pledge and instalment" (2 Corinthians 5:1-5 [Moffatt]).

This is Paul—tentmaker himself—weaving Isaiah's and Scheherazade's protectiveness over Jews, Greeks, Romans, bond, free, male, female, wise, foolish. Love seeking not its own.

Any more than André Philippe sought his own safety in his little home town in France, in the mountains of Douvaine, near the Alps. For the French police sent word one Saturday that by Monday morning—under strict directives from Vichy—all refugees being cared for in an old people's home by Mme. Philippe, were to be taken away, and sent back to concentration camps; all adults into slave labor.

But, on that fateful in-between Sunday morning, Pastor Philippe said to his Protestant parishioners the same quiet sentence which the Catholic priest said to his congregation: "We have heard that the friends in our midst are going to be taken away tomorrow morning. But—you are Christian! And—you are French! So of course you will know what your duty is!"

Then, from hands folded in prayer, a literal tent began extending to the right and to the left: visibly, invisibly. For by Monday morning not a refugee was left in town. Under cover of darkness all Christians had lent their hands to leading all Jews into escaping across dangerous Alpine passes into safety in Switzerland. All two hundred and fifty of them saved by hand!

Another pastor did this very same thing, alone, until our soldiers in Korea pitched in to help him. For one day Ye Yun Ho went out to sketch the city dump heap in Seoul. But he was startled to discover that in this jungle of old discarded packing cases and tin cans hundreds of homeless children were hiding. Ravenous! Ragged! Rough!

A ready-made parish, if ever there was one. Without waiting for ordination, the young Presbyterian seminary student moved right into the dumpheap, to become "moska," which is Korean for "pastor." He knew on how many gateposts in town there hung the sign: "HANG BONG PUL MYONG"—"Address unknown."

But these children had a known address. The G.I.'s chipped in to help Ye Yun Ho build his church for dead-end kids, and American readers of Time magazine sent even more, so that the brick church had a brick steeple, and there was enough to build a ten-bed hospital, next door. Pastor Ye had the good fortune to marry a medical school graduate, Dr. Chong Young-Duk; and all was going well when the Communists took over Seoul, and Americans began bombing them out again. Mr. Ye feels that religious bombers must have tried to avoid harming the church, since it and the houses nearby were all that escaped destruction. Even the church organ stood intact. Even the hospital medicines, instruments, mattresses.

When the Hi-Y Club in Appleton, Wisconsin, read all this, and found that Pastor Ye needed clothing and supplies for resettling his children, they sent him box after box. Then later, when they heard that Ye wanted to study in America, Appleton youth dug down in their pockets for five hundred dollars to bring him over to Lawrence College in their own town.

It troubled the Christians in Appleton to learn what Ye was discovering about them. He thought America was a big and beautiful land. Even Wisconsin barns were beautiful; and much, much bigger than Korean churches. Nowhere did he see slums like the poor little boxes back home. Even in Chicago, slums were three stories high! He went, of course, into book stores. The covers of magazines shocked him: in a country with plenty of clothes, so many pictures of people with nothing on! This need to be naughty without necessity stunned him. And another thing: the dining rooms! So much to eat; but so few saying grace in gratitude for all this plenty. So many churches, too. Yet so many people never going. All their great generosity he respected deeply; but how could he help recalling words which another tentmaker wrote: "And though I bestow all my goods to feed the poor, and have not love, it profiteth me nothing."

Another college town had trouble with such love, three years ago. Yet propped before me as I write is a newspaper picture of Rozella Switzer's parlor in McPherson, Kansas, where her own tent began extending over the whole community that Christmas. In the picture seven Nigerian students from West Africa are sitting around her tree, their interesting names appear underneath: Elijah Odokara, James Craig, Isaac Grillo, Emanuel Thompson, Daniel Onyema, Augustine Njoku-obi, Joseph Obi. All the dark faces, smiling; all the white teeth, flashing; all the dark eyes, sparkling. But John McCormally, who reported this party in *The Hutchinson News-Herald* on December 25, 1952, filled four columns on page one with a memorandum of much less merry moments when seven students started to shop early, wrap carefully.

With Augustine Njoku-obi it came with his first meal in a restaurant. He had been ordered to the kitchen to eat it. Joe Obi, in another cafe, had been seated out in another kitchen so near the sink that the dishwasher splashed soapy water on his food. He could not eat, and ran back to the college, afraid for his life. The other boys had trouble with barbers refusing to cut their hair, with department stores demurring over selling suits; although the weather was freezing cold the citizens seemed more frigid. Inside the college walls there was no discrimination whatever. But Rozella Switzer who had graduated there, herself, knew that this was not enough. The story of other walls and other roofs was treacherous stuff to get into letters from McPherson to

Nigeria. After all, as local postmistress, mail was all-important! So she called up the manager of a large department store.

"Luther," she began, "would you spend fifty bucks to stop a war that's going to cost billions?"

"Are you nuts?" Luther Palmer asked. Mrs. Switzer explained how McPherson had seven chances, moment by moment, day after day, to whip actual Communists already at work stirring up trouble in Nigeria. Augustine Njoku-obi had told her that his roommate at school in Nigeria always kept Stalin's picture over his bed, saluting it every morning. What absolute common sense, therefore, to give Augustine some decent democracy to describe in America.

When Mr. Palmer agreed, Rozella Switzer called up his three business competitors to tell what Luther would do. And of course they promised to do it, too. Then she took her seven Nigerians down town. Each boy got a winter suit, an overcoat, a pair of warm gloves. They also began getting a glowing glimpse of McPherson generosity. Especially in Rozella Switzer's white bungalow with its salmon-pink shutters. Especially when *The News-Herald's* candid camera snapshot was enlarged to 5½ x 7½ on the front page, showing seven boys on her parlor floor, in front of Rozella's mantlepiece where eight Christmas angels in a row held outstretched hands over Joseph Obi's head. Mr. McCormally did not need to report their message. For moment by moment since the Year One it has always been the same brief ten words—like a Western Union telegram to the world: "Glory to God . . . on earth peace among men of goodwill."

Wanted: another McPherson!

And I stood up to see till they folded up that old tent . . . and I saw till the Lord of the sheep brought a new tent, greater and loftier than the first; and set it up in the place of the first that was folded up. And all the sheep were within it.

The Book of Enoch 90:28-29

O Lord, the children of my people are Thy peculiar
    treasure,
Make them mine, O God, even while I have them
My lovely companions, like Eve in Eden!
So much my treasure that all other wealth is, without
    them, but dross and poverty.
Do they not adorn and beautify the World,
And gratify my Soul which hateth Solitude!
Thou, Lord, hast made Thy servant a sociable creature
    for which I praise Thy name,
A lover of company, a delighter in equals;
Replenish the inclination which Thyself hath implanted,
And give me eyes to see the beauty of that life and
    comfort
Wherewith those by their actions inspire the nations!
Their Markets, Tillage, Courts of Judicature, Marriages,
    Feasts and Assemblies,
Navies, Armies, Priests and Sabbaths, Trades and Busi-
    ness,
The voice of the Bridegroom, Musical Instruments, the
    light of Candles and the grinding of Mills
Are comfortable, O Lord, let them not cease.
The riches of the land are all the materials of my felicity
    in their Lands;
They are my Factors, Substitutes and Stewards,
Second Selves, who by Trade and Business animate my
    wealth,
Which else would be dead, and rust in my hands.
But when I consider, O Lord, how they come unto Thy
    Temples, fill Thy Courts, and sing Thy praises,
O, how wonderful they then appear!
What Stars,
Enflaming Suns,
Enlarging Seas of Divine Affection,
Confirming Patterns,
Infusing Influence do I feel in these!

Who are the shining light of all the land (to my very
    Soul:)
Wings and streams
Carrying me unto Thee,
The Sea of Goodness from whence they came.

                                        Thomas Traherne, 1634

1 2

THE VOICE OF ONE HUNDRED FAMILIES

But I say, Have they not heard? Yes, verily, their sound went into
all the earth, and their words unto the ends of the world.
                                        ROMANS 10:18

Part of the fun of growing somewhat older is the freedom to
stop any stranger on any street, and speak to him as if you had
known him all your life. For in the end, of course, you really do!

So my friend Anna from Chicago—by far the world's friend-
liest soul—went walking down a certain Kentucky street one day
when she saw a tall dark stranger coming toward her. She
planted herself in his path, and held out her hand in greeting:
"Forgive my stopping you! But I simply have to ask—you aren't
an American Negro, are you? You see, my brother is a missionary
over in Nigeria, and he keeps sending me pictures of his African
friends; and it fascinates me now to notice that the shape of your
face is exactly like the shape of their faces! So that *is* where you
come from, isn't it?"

"Yes, it is!" the young man grinned. "In fact, I have just come
over—last week! To study at the college here for the next two
years."

"Splendid!" Anna cried cordially, shaking his hand all over

again. "And that means you have had your first Sunday in town. How did it go? Church, I mean, and all that? For I suppose you are a Christian?"

"Oh yes, indeed I'm a Christian! And the man who converted me in Nigeria comes from this church in this town; indeed, they still support him. So of course that was the church where I went last Sunday."

Anna nodded: "Good! And how did it go?"

He hesitated; "Well, not so good maybe. I haven't quite decided yet. I suppose I had dreamed up a dream about this church. I suppose I thought it must be the most perfect church in America, all because it had been supporting my missionary at the very moment when he had been converting me! Anyhow, I could hardly wait for Sunday morning to come. All through the opening part of the service I kept waiting for the place we always have, over in Nigeria, where people stand up and tell the wonderful things God has done for them that past week. But when it seemed as if they weren't going to have that time here, and when I saw the deacons carrying the offering plates down the aisle, then I couldn't wait another minute! Up I got and praised God that this very collection could go right on supporting their same wonderful man in Nigeria who had converted me. It seemed too good to be true, I added, that here I was— standing in his own church, among his own people. So I thanked God all over again for being called to study where he studied, and to worship where he worshiped."

"Of course you did!" Anna agreed. "Weren't the people terribly touched?"

"Maybe yes! Maybe no! I couldn't tell."

"How do you mean, you couldn't tell? I should think it would have been as plain as day."

"Yes? Maybe it was as plain as day, then. For ours is the sort of plain church where committees are free to work quickly. So, after the morning service, some committee met. They voted then and there that it would be better if I attended the Negro church in town after this, instead of coming back to them."

"No-o-o?" Anna groaned, as if she could not believe her ears. "Oh, surely not? Not like that?"

"But yes," he sighed, "just like that!" Then because she looked heartbroken, he began patting her arm to comfort her: "There! There! It's really all right. I guess it's really all right. I keep saying to myself that maybe I sounded conceited—thinking I was Exhibit A of all their missionary money coming true at last! As if I were sort of a last chapter in the Acts of the Apostles getting written in their town. I haven't thought it through yet. But I keep praying that God will help me to see this thing straight."

"We had better pray that God will help *them* to see this tragic thing straight," Anna said indignantly.

But that was something God could not do in that town. Not then. And not yet.

For as the Chinese proverb says: "Public Opinion is the voice of one hundred families." And the first hundred families in town liked being the first families in town. Public opinion raised its voice against change—nothing was more risky than change. Nothing! *Nothing?* Not even the fact that nothing could sound choicer for Red Chinese orators to quote and requote till their sound went into all the good red earth! Or for Red Russian newspapers to publish and republish till their words went to the ends of the world; or for Brown Americans to see through and wait a little longer for all God's children to put on their shoes and walk all over God's heaven—everybody talking about heaven ain't going there; heaven? heaven? Yes, on earth; in Kentucky. And all the forty-eight states of mind, heart, soul, strength and public opinion where Christians love neighbors as themselves.

Once there was a traffic court where the officer in charge made all the worst offenders copy ten times over a startling article from *Reader's Digest* entitled: "And Sudden Death." Instead of a sermon some Sunday morning, how equally startling to set some congregations to copying ten times over (while kneeling) the prophet's protest against breaking God's bridge of brotherhood:

Have we not all one Father? Hath not one God created us? Why do we deal treacherously every man against his brother, by profaning the covenant of our fathers? . . . The Lord will cut off the man that doeth this, the master and the scholar, and him that offereth an offering unto the Lord of hosts. And this ye have done again, covering the altar of the Lord with tears, with weeping, and with crying, insomuch that He regardeth not the offering any more, or receiveth it with goodwill at your hand.   MALACHI 2:10, 12-13

For it might become—after ten copyings—as embarrassing as the native song of the Choco Christians in Columbia, 94 per cent of whom are descendants of Negro slaves brought to South America, centuries ago, yet still lifting up their voices to sing:

> Are not Negroes too baptized
> In the true baptismal font?
> Is there some other font
> More shining and more rare
> Somewhere behind, beyond,
> Where white men are baptized?
> I, who am ignorant,
> Would make this prayer:
> If to be white is virtue
> That I be whitened
> With Thy whiteness, Lord.

> *The One bethought Him to make man*
> *Of many-colored dust,*
> *And mixed the Holy Spirit in*
> *In portions right and just,*
> *Each had a part of mind and heart*
> *From One Himself, in trust;*
> *Thus came the brown and yellow man,*
> *And black and white and red,*
> *So different in their outer look,*
> *Alike in heart and head—*
> *The self-same dust before their birth,*
> *The self-same dust when dead.*
>   Pai Ta-Shun, Chinese poet

Not till the sun excludes you, do I exclude you,
Not till the waters refuse to glisten for you
Do my words refuse to glisten and rustle for you.
                                        Walt Whitman

13

PLIMSOLL MARK

"Master, Master! We perish!" LUKE 8:24

Nowadays nobody knows exactly who Mr. Plimsoll was. Although every ship still carries a "Plimsoll Mark" painted around its water line to show what load she dares to carry: beyond which—danger!

But landlubbers and even people called pewholders care nothing about such precautions. You cannot escape hearing them say, apropos of nothing visible at the moment, in a quite ordinary tone of voice: "If I had my way I would put all the blanketyblank so-and-sos on a ship, and sink them out in the middle of the Atlantic Ocean!"

Just to simplify something or other. A job? rent? security? social position? recognition?—*something*, anyhow. Just to purify local history. Just to start fresh, without any old blanketyblanks to mess things up. Suddenly you know what Nero was like. And what Hitler was like. And what Stalin was like. And even the politer Pilate. Standing there washing his hands in public, and saying: "I am innocent of the blood of this good man. But *you* see to it! Go along, get rid of Him if He's in your way."

You never get over meeting such frightful indifference face to face.

Just as Dr. George MacLeod had not forgotten, when he

startled a group of Presbyterian preachers at Buck Hill Falls by telling how he went from Iona to South Africa to speak to another group of preachers. The Christian worker sent to escort him to the meeting said, en route: "You're going to give it to them red hot, I hope?"

"Red hot!" Dr. MacLeod promised.

"Good! Fine! Perfect! They need it! For if I had my way I would put every one of these bloody Negroes on a ship and sink them all out in the middle of . . ."

But the man who is rebuilding the island of Iona in the pattern of early Christian brotherhood had had a totally different idea of "red hot"—and he sizzled against ship-sinkings and selfishness in high places, regardless of Plimsoll Mark.

Just as the writer of these lines cannot seem to erase the memory of a certain clergyman down on a Florida beach saying that if he had his way he would put every Jew in the world on a ship and sink them out in the middle of . . .

"Jesus Christ, too?" she managed to ask.

But no! Of course not the Lord of the Church. The clergyman's Church. One had to draw the line somewhere. But she began remembering the tragic new legend making the rounds of Germany that very year—how Herr Hitler required every schoolteacher in the Fatherland, on a certain day, to draw the line drastically, by saying: "Will those of you with Jewish fathers please stand. Now turn! And walk out of this room, and never return."

In every schoolroom the same sad shuffling exodus. After which each teacher was required to give this second order: "Will those of you with Jewish mothers please stand. Now turn! And walk out of this room, and never return."

In one such classroom this second group stood rooted to the floor, looking up spellbound at the wall above the teacher's head. Puzzled by the tragedy in their eyes, the teacher, too, looked up to see the Man on the Cross painfully loosening each hand from the nails through His palms. Painfully He loosened each foot from nails through the insteps. Then, slowly and painfully, this solitary Figure made His way down the aisle of that schoolroom, and out of that door. After which all the other children who had Jewish mothers also, turned to walk out the same door behind Him, not to return. Not as long as Herr Hitler ruled the Reich. Not as long as he wanted Plimsoll Mark to sink below its water line. Not as long as six million Jews could be liquidated in Nazi concentration camps, sunk out in the middle of . . .

So that when T. S. Eliot said that we had become a lot of godless decent folk, he forgot to reckon with Plimsoll Marks, or preachers on Florida sands facing out toward the middle of . . .

Equally unforgettable was the day in a New York apartment hallway when the tenant from 7B met the tenant from 7A, waiting for the elevator. Apropos of nothing whatever, instead of "Good morning," 7B greeted 7A with the words: "If I had my way I would put all those blankety-blank Japanese on a ship and sink them out in the middle of . . . "

As one lady to another—godless? Yes! Decent? No! Plainly her mood outexploded, outwrecked, outmatched Pearl Harbor. Moment by moment all day 7A debated: "Dare I warn her of the penalty hanging around her own neck? Dare I lay my Bible on her doorstep, open at Mark Nine, verse forty-two: "Whosoever shall offend one of these little ones that believe in me, it were better for him that a millstone were hanged about his neck, and he were cast into the sea"?

Until the middle of the Atlantic Ocean hardly bears thinking about! Such overcrowding, with all those ships slowly sinking below their Plimsoll Marks. Negroes from Africa, drowning. Perhaps even boatloads of Negroes from the U.S.A.—who knows but somebody somewhere may have packed their steamer, too, and sent it off to its doom, to keep white supremacy whiter. Six million Jews from Europe, dead. Millions more, drowning. Seventy million Japanese drowned to suit the tenant in 7B.

And now, at the suggestion of their own Lord and Maker, shiploads of church members in good and regular standing find themselves in this terrible tumult at sea. Frantic with fright they call: "Master, Master! We perish!"

The identical panic which Pearl Harbor produced. Lock up all aliens! while our own unchristian practices come back to hang around our own necks, to sink us. Such items as signs over doors cooking up indignation against us at the ends of the earth, when one door reads: "WHITE," the other: "COLORED." Such items as signs at hotel entrances: "GENTILE CLIENTELE ONLY." Such items as signs in Shanghai parks: "NO DOGS OR CHINESE ALLOWED." Such items as an article in a newspaper in India, anticommunist, yet saying: "The Chinese are Asians who were treated like coolies in their own land by arrogant western races. They [the Chinese] have now turned the tables. As Asians we cannot but feel some satisfaction."

Sign for sign, Christian nations equaling unchristian nations. Herr Hitler with his sign in Vienna, in December, 1939: "NO JEWISH GOODS UNDER THE CHRISTMAS TREE THIS YEAR," matched by General McNarney's signs in Berlin barracks to prevent the American army from giving food or candy to hungry German children: "THERE IS TO BE NO SENTIMENTAL NONSENSE ABOUT BROTHERHOOD AND GOODWILL THIS CHRISTMAS." No wonder the tide turns against the selfish. With Davy Jones's locker piling boat on boat, out in the middle of . . .

Moreover, there have been actual ships which actual clergymen wanted to sink, out in the middle of . . . In 1682 Reverend Cotton Mather warned Governor Higginson of grave and eminent danger:

There be now at sea a ship called *Welcome*, which has on board 100 or more of the heretics and malignants called Quakers, with William Penn, who is the chief scamp, at the head of them. The General Court (of Massachusetts) has accordingly given sacred orders to Master Malachi Auscott of the brig *Porpoise* to waylay the said *Welcome* slyly as near the Cape of Cod as may be, and make captive said Penn and his ungodly crew, so that the Lord may be glorified and not mocked on the soil of this new country with the heathen worship of these people. Much spoil can be made of selling the whole lot to Barbados, where slaves fetch good prices in rum and sugar, and shall not only do the Lord great good by punishing the wicked, but we shall make great good for His minister and people. Yours in the bowels of Christ, Cotton Mather.

Needless to say, this was the moment in our country when Quakers were put through horrifying ordeals—their tongues bored through, their ears cut off, public floggings, and death itself. Elizabeth Hooton and Mary Fisher, tied at the rear of wagons, were forced to walk into Boston, flogged ten times in each town through which they passed, stripped to the waist. By Christians who had come to Massachusetts to worship God according to the dictates of their consciences. But denying to Quakers the right to worship in quiet, waiting for more light yet to break through them.

In England George Fox received the same kind of treatment, as his Journal recounts:

> & When I began to speake they fell on mee, & ye clerke uppe with his bible as I was speakinge and hitt mee in ye face, yt I blaade exceedingly in ye steeple-house & so ye people cryd letts have him out of ye church (as they caled it); & when they had mee out they exceedingly beate mee & threw mee over a hedge; & after dragged mee through a house Into ye street stoninge and beatteinge mee: and they gott my hatt from mee which I never gott againe, & I was all over besmeared with bloode.

When Henrik Ibsen wrote *Peer Gynt,* critics said Peer Gynt was Norway and all its selfish self-sufficiency. But Peer Gynt's schemes and excuses make disturbing reading anywhere on earth: perpetually brooding over past grandeur and neglecting every present duty, until the Button Moulder could say to him that he had been designed to be a shining button on the vest of the world, but—his loop had given way.

Nowhere does his loop give way more graphically than in the scene where the stage directions state that Peer Gynt's steam yacht is in the offing; but he himself, on shore, is boasting to some crafty new acquaintances what good fortune has sailed on board that vessel—mostly earned from selling Negroes in Carolina and idols in China! He admits that his business hovered on the "outer verge of the allowable"; and so, as he grew older, conscience suggested that every spring he ship idols to China, but every fall, ship missionaries—supplying all they needed: stockings, Bibles, rum, rice; all at a bargain! He boasted how nicely neutralized things were, since for every idol sold the missionaries got another coolie well baptized.

The scene shifts to Peer Gynt's discovering that his crafty listeners have actually sailed off at a furious speed in his yacht. In staccato phrases he starts imploring God to help him: It is I, Peer Gynt—make them back up that boat—make them lower that gig —stop those robbers, Lord! make something go wrong with the rigging—hear me—let everybody else's business wait—the world can take care of itself for a while—but help me get on board that boat, Lord!

Then, even as Peer Gynt orders God around, his exasperated eyes see an unbelievable sight. His yacht blows up! And disappears from sight, right out in the middle of . . .

Ibsen might have had Psalm Seventeen in mind (where David prayed: "Lord make me the apple of Thy eye!") for Peer Gynt had wanted just that, and was breathless over this swift answer— he, rescued; the robbers, perished! What a marvelous feeling of safety and peace to find himself "specially shielded." The remainder of the play keeps upsetting his sense of special shielding, so little deserved.

Yet, moment by moment, vocal prayers all over the world have fallen into that category:

O Lord, we approach Thee this morning in an attitude of praise and also of complaint. When we came to Canada we expected to find a land flowing with milk and honey, but instead we find a land peopled with the ungodly Irish. O Lord, in Thy mercy drive them to the uttermost parts of Canada, make them hewers of wood and drawers of water; give them no places as magistrates, policemen, or rulers among Thy people. But if Ye have any favors to bestow, or any good land to give away, give it to Thine own peculiar people, the Scots. Make them members of Parliament; rulers among the people; but the ungodly Irish—take them by the heels and shake them over the mouth of hell; but Lord, don't let them fall in, and Thine shall be the glory forever. Amen.

No wonder that moment by moment an S.O.S. keeps sounding: "Master, Master! We perish!" And moment by moment lifeboats keep pushing off from shore, manned by all sorts of churchmen from all sorts of places—even if this rescue is the first ever attempted. For as Wendell Phillips used to say: "God never permitted any man to hold an ideal too beautiful for His power to make it practicable."

Bishop William Quayle explained us to ourselves when he said: "Christ was wistful for a world; He dwelt among races of provincials. The Jew, the Greek, the Roman were all provincials. Christ whispered, trumpeted, wept, sang, preached, lived, died —all framing a wide unprovincial word: the world."

It is always to be remembered, therefore, that whenever the storm grows so unbearably tempestuous that people on board cry out their double despair: "Master! Master!" then the Master repeats their name twice over, too: "Jerusalem! Jerusalem! which killest the prophets, and stonest them that are sent unto thee; how often would I have gathered thy children together in my arms, as a hen doth gather her brood under her wings; and ye would not!"

It was about this that Dr. MacLeod spoke—from Iona, in 1942:

The real danger in our land is that the Cross has largely got disjointed; the horizontal beam has got wrenched from the vertical beam; and the vertical from the horizontal. About a tenth of our nation —we churchmen—have concentrated on the vertical relationship without daring to relate it to the problems of the contemporary world, till actually the things of Sunday have come to be called the things of holiness! Having given up our privilege of pain, we have thereby lost our spiritual power. The remaining nine-tenths of our people—impatient of Church irrelevance—have tried to solve the problems of the horizontal—all the relationships between man and man—without any reference to whose world it is. If we of the so-called spiritual have lost our power, it is equally true that the so-called practical men of the world have lost their way.

No. We cannot apportion blame: don't waste time with that. It is a divorce that has grown for generations—if not for centuries. But the hope of the world is that we both know now that we can't go on much longer—in this regard—as we are. The Church knows it has lost its spiritual power: and folk know they have lost the way. The hope of the world is that our joint bankruptcy is going to make us look at the Cross again: and it is only in that sign that we will conquer.

There is going to be a revival. But it will be of a new kind. God will bring it through those who refuse to think of holiness except as it covers the whole of life. And through those who refuse to think of man's relationships to man except in the sight of God.

Only then will a Masterpiece emerge: because we will have been mastered.

Part of this Masterpiece emerged in the suggestions which came forth from the Amsterdam Assembly of the World Council of Churches, six years later, in 1948:

We have to ask God to teach us together to say NO and to say YES in truth. NO, to all that flouts the love of Christ, to every system, every programme and every person that treats any man as though he were an irresponsible thing or as a means of profit, to the defenders of injustice in the name of order, to those who sow the seeds of war or urge war as inevitable; YES, to all that conforms to the love of Christ, to all who speak for justice, to the peacemakers, to all who hope, fight and suffer for the cause of man, to all who—even without knowing it—look for a new earth wherein dwelleth righteousness.

At which time—the Book of Revelation assures us—there will be *no more sea*. And nothing can ever be sunk again out in the middle of . . .

When all is said and done, our resemblances to the savage are still more numerous than our differences from him.
Sir James George Frazer, *The Golden Bough*

For centuries Christianity treasured the great commandment of love and mercy as traditional truth without recognizing it as a reason for opposing slavery, witch-burning, torture, and all the other ancient and medieval forms of inhumanity.   Albert Schweitzer

I, a poor sinful man, who have been born in sin, and, since my birth all the days of my life in manifold wise have offended against Thee, confess from my whole heart

*before Thee, O holy and righteous God, most loving
Father, that I have not loved Thee above all Things,
nor my neighbor as myself.*

Prayer of Olaus Petri, from the Swedish Liturgy

*We break the new seas today—
Our eager keels quest unaccustomed waters,
And, from the vast uncharted waste in front,
The mystic circles leap
To greet our prows with mightiest possibilities;*

. . .

*And, maybe, Golden Days,
Full freighted with delight!
And wide free seas of unimagined bliss,
And Treasure Isles, and Kingdoms to be won,
And Undiscovered Countries, and New Kin.*

John Oxenham, *Bees in Amber;* American Tract
Society and Methuen & Co., Ltd.; used by
permission.

14

MY DARLING FROM THE DOGS

Deliver . . . my darling from the power of the dog.

PSALM 22:20

The entire class in Sociology fanned itself out through certain
sections of Baltimore. All eyes! All ears! Into the worst slums in
town. Down dingy streets. Up trembling tenement steps. Into
overcrowded rooms. Armed with filing cards, the class asked all
the hundred and one questions suggested by their professor at

Johns Hopkins. Listing all the hundred and one answers about the particular boy or girl whose name appeared at the top of their cards. With every scrap of extra observation carefully noted, also: as to *parents*—co-operative or unco-operative? concerned or unconcerned? clean or unclean? careful or careless? away all day? home all day? observant or unobservant? As to the *tenement room or rooms*—unsanitary? overcrowded? other families sharing these small quarters? were they neat or neglected? were there saloons nearby? houses of prostitution? what other types of vice? how does the corner cop regard this household? where do the children play? what do they play?

All so searching and scientific that when the class met to pool their investigations, two hundred of the cards could be clipped together at once into a card catalogue called: HEADED FOR JAIL. Everybody agreed there could be no other outcome but crime, or theft, or worse, for children so obviously going to the dogs.

After which, in due time, this class graduated; and separated widely. Undoubtedly taking social service jobs elsewhere. Undoubtedly fanning out into other slums in other cities. Asking important questions. Listing significant answers. Until all their new superiors said: "Thoroughly trained! Johns Hopkins, you know!" And meanwhile two hundred cards lay neglected in a filing cabinet, turning slightly yellow at the edges as the slow years passed. Five years—eight years—ten—twelve—fifteen—eighteen—twenty—twenty-two—twenty-three—twenty-four years passed. New students coming; learning; going. But the old cards still in the cabinet.

Then, in the twenty-fifth year, another new sociology class stood in need of another new project for investigation. Then somebody came across two hundred old cards clipped together and announcing coldly: HEADED FOR JAIL. Curiosity was quickened: "Here's our project! Let's track down these two hundred children to see what's happened to them by this time."

Therefore, another class fanned through the same sections of Baltimore. Up the same trembling tenement steps. Hunting old names. But always directed elsewhere. And elsewhere again. Until the old names were located. Until the old questions were asked again, and new answers added.

Then finally this class, too, met to lay all their cards on the table and pool their discoveries. Only to have the surprise of their lives! For card by card, case by case, one hundred and ninety-eight of these children had become excellent citizens. Capable, conscientious businessmen. Church members, too—Catholic, Protestant, Jew. And only two of the two hundred headed for jail ever got there.

Excitement boiled over! Everybody dug back into his statistics for the reason why. Only to come across one name on every single card: "Aunt Hannah!" A schoolteacher there in that slum section so devoted, day in and day out, that no child within her radius ever could go to the dogs! Every card retold the same story with slight variations . . . I was the worst kid in her class. You never knew such a bad egg! Cops always on my tail. Nine times out of ten they got the goods on me, too. But one day Aunt Hannah kept me after school. She looked at me, all sort of gentle-like. She asked how come a smart kid wasted himself away on such rotten stuff? She painted quite a tall picture of what she could see me doing some day. Boy! it was quite some picture. All so gentle, still. Then she said: "Come around to dinner, Sunday." Boy, was it good? I can remember yet—chicken! a *whole* chicken! And a great big piece for me. With more, when I got through the first. And she still talked gentle and long and quiet. After that, how could I ever let Aunt Hannah down? So you find me here—see my doctor's shingle? I'm the neighborhood M.D. now, keeping other kids straight.

One hundred and ninety-eight times this loving-kindness took hold and stuck and never let go. Grown women had the same story to tell: She seemed all wrapped up in me. I was indispensable. Living where I lived at home, it was warm and wonderful to feel wanted at school. To feel admired. To turn into somebody worthy of being admired. Aunt Hannah never made a job of it. It was all a grand game and we both loved playing it. If something bad happened, tell her. If something sad happened, tell her. She was ours. We all knew *that!*

One hundred and ninety-eight times patience had done its perfect work. Aunt Hannah herself was extremely matter-of-fact:

she said that all she did was just loving them as if they were her own boys and girls. Until, of course, they were! All it took was time and tirelessness. More a mother than mothers are. Nobody goes to the dogs if he has somewhere better to go.

This second batch of sociologists sat there stunned, and humbled also. They were probably too young and unbiblical to add what the greatest Investigator undoubtedly wrote invisibly over each card: "My mother and my brothers and my sisters are those who hear the word of God, *and do it.*"

There are no working plans for a Christly world, save by the expansion of the home in the world, so that no human being shall be motherless.

Frances Willard

Lord, Thou didst teach, forgive me for teaching, for bearing the name of teacher which Thou didst bear upon earth. Give me supreme love for my school. Make me more a mother than mothers are, that I may be able to love and defend as they do what is not flesh of my flesh. May I succeed in making of one of my girls my perfect stanza, and in her bequeath Thee my most enduring melody against the day when these my lips shall sing no more.

Gabriela Mistral, teacher and poet, Chile

The song is to the singer, and comes back most to him,
The teaching is to the teacher, and comes back most to him,
The love is to the lover, and comes back most to him.

Walt Whitman

15

JUST WHAT GOD HAD BEEN WAITING FOR

When the fulness of time was come, God sent forth His Son, made
of a woman.   GALATIANS 4:4

She was exactly what God needed just then. And there has never
been any other woman of whom something so superlatively
sacred could be said. Yet nobody has ever had such an incredibly
hard time getting accepted by Protestants! Or being recognized
properly. Or praised properly. Or imitated properly. It has been
as if, in order to prove that no! no! no! we are *not* Catholics, we
have let Mary severely alone. Actually more anti-Catholic in our
attitude than pro-Christian.

Of course, at Christmas we are a trifle more venturesome. There
is often a box on the top shelf of the hall closet marked "Crèche."
It is quite all right to lift it down when December comes, undo
the string, unfold the tissues. We fetch forth the crib, the Infant,
the cow, the sheep, three shepherds to stand on the right-hand
side, three wise men to kneel on the left; and then, oh yes! here
is Mary, draped in blue, to bend over the crib, pondering. We
dust her off gently; and with so much else to divide the attention in the familiar scene, even the most authentic Protestant
feels safe in her presence.

But, moment by moment, New Year's comes; the tree drips
needles all over the carpet; the children head back for school;
so out comes the box marked "Crèche." Back go all the Holy
Family, safely wrapped in tissue paper until another December
rolls round.

But midway of every year comes May. With Mother's Day
down on every Protestant calendar. And I dare to recall to your

98

Protestant minds that beloved and brooding little figure. So exactly what God had been waiting for! Forget any prejudices, pro tem; reject any misconceptions; simply recall that when Paul wrote "in the fulness of time God sent forth His Son, made of a woman," that particular woman was special in God's sight.

And what were His requirements for mothering this special Child? Few as the references to her are in the Bible, they are all delightfully direct and down-to-earth. God does not choose dreamers, but doers. And from that afternoon when Gabriel appeared before her to announce the Saviour's birth, through Good Friday when she stood sorrowing at the foot of the cross, until the Day of Pentecost when the disciples waited patiently with her in an upper room for the Holy Spirit to come, Mary offers too perfect a pattern for motherhood to be missed by worried modern mothers buying books on "How To" and "What To" and "When To."

Indeed, one could fill a book with famous quotations. St. Augustine, remembering Monica and noticing more reluctant parents in Rome, wrote: "Give us other mothers and I will give you another world." Mary was just such a special mother; and her Child was just such a world-making Saviour. Every Protestant remembers how Paul wrote to Timothy: "They will be saved through motherhood, if they continue to be loving and holy, and sensible as well" (I Timothy 2:14 [Goodspeed]). Yet all the time, long before Paul's letter, a wholesome country girl had been displaying just that necessary faith, that necessary loving-kindness and holiness, that necessary common sense. Moreover, she put into words her unforgettable formula for motherhood. All any Protestant parent has to do is to read between the lines to see a new world coming.

For here was a village virgin identifying herself with the entire human race! For those who accept prenatal influences, the fascinating fact of history is how her famous Song sang itself deep into her Child's consciousness through His entire life. Not only, of course, because Mary sang it. But because she *knew enough to sing it*—knew enough to gain this glorious glimpse into God's divine intention for everybody everywhere, tomorrow and tomorrow and tomorrow, through all generations, till time should be no more. Indeed, her Song offers a simply stupendous study in "How To," "What To," "When To." And for modern mothers it should be a *must!*

For here you are today—scared to death about tomorrow: bombs, Russia, China, multiplying clashes between classes and masses East and West. Yet there was Mary, in a similar setting, living all her life in occupied territory, foreseeing how common-sense courtesy could come true through her Boy. Line by line, therefore, look at her Magnificat as God making known to a mother what He aims to do on earth; and a completely poor, completely ignorant small-town stay-at-home mother sensible enough to think it would work!

My soul doth magnify the Lord, and my spirit doth rejoice in God my Saviour—

This, of course, is Mary's special message to expectant mothers. With conception she began identifying herself with the One Supreme Creative Force of the universe, letting every thought about God's greatness become larger and larger, richer and richer, dearer and dearer; finding daily delight in His divine design for her life. Magnifying and rejoicing are momentous words for a country girl to choose: a divine-human encounter.

For He who is mighty hath done great things unto me, and holy is His name—

This is Mary still identifying herself with Majesty, and probably recalling ancient sentences from Scripture:

For unto us a child is born, and the government shall be upon His shoulders, and His name shall be called Wonderful, Counselor, the Mighty God, the Everlasting Father, the Prince of Peace; and of the increase of His government and of peace there shall be no end.

Thrilling things to think about this unborn Baby. But tantalizing, too! "How To"? "What To"? "When To"? But then, somehow, from somewhere, old authentic answers dawned on her:

He will gather the lambs in His arms and carry them in His bosom, and shall gently lead those that are with young. . . . Surely He hath borne our griefs and carried our sorrows. . . . Even to old age, even

when the hair is hoary. . . . The chastisement of our peace is upon
Him and by His stripes we are healed.

"How To" bring up any Child to be and do and carry through
all this? Can any good thing come out of narrow little Nazareth?
Mary planned that it would and could and should! It is her hint
to other mothers to start such sensible concern early.

He hath scattered the proud in the imagination of their hearts,
He hath put down the mighty from their seats—
O Mary! Mary! We shudder at your nerve! Imagine airing such
riotous revolutionary stuff in the hearing of certain congressional
committee members from Wisconsin. Enough to ride a modern
woman straight out of church: "Easy, sister, easy! None of that,
now," earnest deacons would whisper uneasily. But Mary seemed
to dip into the future, far as human eye could see, and identified
herself with that great day of the Lord when Caesar Augustus
would go, and Herod would go, and Pilate would go; but not
her Son, who, from generation to generation, would increase. Big
thoughts for a small-town girl? But that is what a woman's intui-
tion is for: to leap lightly and slightly ahead of little inconsequential matters!

We, knowing our statistics, can count Christianity's growth
from 12 followers to 872,000,000 church members. We, knowing
our history books, can see that yes, eventually the mighty were
put down from their seats: Alexander, Tamerlane, Attila, Napoleon, Hitler, Mussolini, Stalin. Only the other day a little girl
asked in a puzzled way: "Mummy, who was Hitler?" *Hitler!* with
six million Jews liquidated in his reign of terror, and ten million
Christians displaced! Yet, through all the storm, Mary's Son still
saying: "Peace, it is I!" And brave spirits proving it to be true.

He hath exalted them of low degree—
Here Mary identified herself in faith with everyday, ordinary
people on small side streets in tiny, undistinguished towns; Mary
somehow sensing that even unlearned fishermen and tax collectors
could write best sellers sold the whole world over. For she is
recorded to have said at a wedding, to simple servants when the
wine gave out: "Whatsoever He saith unto you, do it!" Any woman

like that teaches a dramatic lesson in democracy any day: everybody everywhere matters equally; although many a mother in many a town trains up her child to "move in the best circles, darling"; and eventually, alas! in the best triangles, too.

He hath filled the hungry with good things—

By identifying herself with those who starve Mary lived on later in her Son's pictures of the Last Judgment and of Dives who never dreamed of filling even one hungry stomach with good things; so that Mary should stab other mothers into attempting immediate aid for famine sufferers, recalling that other mother whose boy's picnic lunch once fed five thousand on a green hillside. To teach each child the miraculous multiplication of mercy sealed into every church envelope every Sunday! To help him visualize his own feet soon walking to strange doors; his own hands giving food; his own eyes shocked by so much misery on earth; his own heart troubled by human despair. This is the very least any mother can do in describing each week what utter excitement it is to fill an offering envelope. Kindling a divine imagination; awakening a divine response.

And the rich He hath sent empty away—

What imagination here? Never deliberately to pamper children with an overabundance of expensive gadgets? Never to consider luxuries and legacies more desirable than duties? To read and re-read about the Rich Young Ruler, brought up to prefer *plenty* rather than *sharing*, and so turning sorrowfully away? (And perhaps to recall 1931, when rich men jumped out of high windows as the Depression proved what they had been living for.)

As He spake to our fathers, and to Abraham, and to his seed forever—

How fitting that Mary could close this spaceless, raceless, timeless tribute by identifying herself with the ageless echoes of those haunting words: *"Forever . . . "* on and on and on and on, moment by moment, all generations, all nations, kindreds, tribes. All countries. All centuries. *"Forever"*? Just as, at this moment, you too are involved in the seed of all mankind. For right where you live, a redeemer is needed. Right in your own neighborhood. Right on your own doorsill. Emily Dickinson once said about Amherst,

Massachusetts, that the madonnas she saw were those that passed the house every day on the way to their work, carrying little saviours in their arms. For this is what God is still waiting for. Other mothers. Other arms. Other saviours.

And if you have ever been merely sentimental over Mother's Day, accepting tokens of appreciation as your right, then here is sterner testing from someone for whom God waited many years, till the fullness of time had come. Till a woman in a small town could identify herself with the entire human race. Till her Son could be sent forth repeating her Magnificat in practically all His parables, all His beatitudes, all His attitudes; even saying: "My mother and my brothers and my sisters are those who hear the word of God, *and do it!*"

[Inviting his imaginary audience into the Madonna's Porch in the Cathedral at Amiens, Ruskin wrote:] Only, if you come at all, good Protestant feminine reader— come civilly; and be pleased to recollect that Madonna worship never did any human creature any harm—but Money worship, Wig worship, Cocked-Hat-and-Feather worship, Plate worship, Pot worship and Pipe worship have done, and are doing a great deal; and that any of these, and all, are quite million-fold more offensive to the God of Heaven and Earth and the Stars than all the absurdest and lovingest mistakes made by any generations of His simple children.
John Ruskin, *The Bible of Amiens*

The Storke shee rose on Christmasse Eve
And sayd unto her broode,
"I now must fly to Bethlehem
To viewe the Sonne of God."
Shee gave to each his dole of meat,
Shee stowed them fairlye in,

And far shee flewe, and fast shee flewe,
And came to Bethlehem.
"Now where is Hee of David's line?"
Shee asked in house and Halle.
"Hee is not here," they spake hardlye,
"But in the Maungier Stalle."
Shee found Hym in the Maungier Stalle
With that most Holy Mayd,
The gentyl Storke shee wept to see
The Lord so rudlye layd.
Then from her pauntyng breast shee plucked
The feathers soft and warme,
Shee strawed them in the Maungier bed
To keep the Lord from harme.
"Nowe blessed be the gentyl Storke
Forevermore," quothe Hee,
"In that shee sawe my sadde estate
And showed such pitie.
Full welcome shall shee be
Full welcome shall shee be
In hamlet and in Halle
And hight henceforth the blessed byrd,
And friend of babies alle."

from the flyleaf of a sixteenth-century prayerbook,
in Yorkshire.

16

ALL MY HEART THIS NIGHT REJOICES

Fear not: for behold I bring you tidings of great joy.   LUKE 2:10

Hardly anybody in polite society needs to talk about a certain ugly word. Yet if you had been in Germany that year, and young, or even not so young, it would have been the constant dread of your days and nights. The reason for never going outdoors alone. Nor staying indoors alone. Nor wanting to hear footsteps on the stairs. For every German woman lived under the sinister spell of it, by way of some snatching soldier. And nobody altogether escaped the revolting experience, Fraulein Elsa included.

But when the Teacher Training School opened in the East German Zone at the end of the war, she tried her best to forget these unmentionable memories as she applied for entrance, and was accepted by Dr. Maria. Dr. Maria, with the haunting face of a madonna grown wise in this sisterhood of suffering.

"I am among the fortunate ones in having escaped bearing an unwanted baby," Fraulein Elsa confided.

"Then you are indeed fortunate!" Dr. Maria nodded—she who had shielded so many through their tense times.

But all too soon Fraulein Elsa returned in a tragic mood: "It seems I was mistaken, Dr. Maria! There is to be a child, after all —but I cannot tell you the utter impossibility of having this baby, fathered by that brute! No, I will not, will not, will not bear it! So now you must help me get rid of it. You will know the name of some safe doctor?"

Dr. Maria sat back in her chair: "Just a moment, my dear Elsa; I have two things to say. God always knows about a woman when she is totally innocent, as you are innocent. And God always knows about any baby, that it is totally innocent, too. Therefore, He will think that your child, as every child, has the absolute right to be wanted, and to be properly loved!"

"But that is too much for God to expect! I will not bear the baby of an unknown soldier—indeed, Dr. Maria, indeed you must tell me how to get rid of it!"

"But you are not unknown to God, and the baby is not unknown to Him, either. So I say it again, my poor Elsa, God never intends any child to be unloved, uncared for!"

"No, no! You ask too much; you and God ask entirely too much of a decent woman. I will not have this indecent baby!"

Dr. Maria grew stern: "Then you will please leave this room at once, Fraulein Elsa. What will God think of a decent woman calling any innocent child indecent? That is indeed too much! With all my heart I sympathize with you over this bitter unwelcome event. But it need not be sordid. For you owe this particular baby God's own particular protection, from this good moment on!"

"Never! Never!" cried Fraulein Elsa, slamming the door behind her. And in all the months when the baby kept on coming, she kept on plodding through her training course in alternate moods so morose or tempestuous that she was never out of Dr. Maria's mind. For a woman that bitter might do almost anything.

Then came Christmas. That first Christmas after the war when everybody seemed brokenhearted—missing members of their families, homesick for homes now rubble or friends unheard from. With everyone on her heart at once, Dr. Maria did two things for Fraulein Elsa. Although flour was exceedingly scarce, she had been saving out enough to bake a small cake, and hoarding enough sugar to make a gay icing in old traditional Christmas patterns around a tiny candle. Also, she went through the big box of Presbyterian relief materials from America until she found the very article she needed—a baby sweater, knitted in blue angora wool, unbelievably little; unbelievably lovely. With an urgent prayer, Dr. Maria wrapped her package, and hurried to Fraulein Elsa's door.

"I know why you have come!" the young woman said sharply.

"You want to take me with you to our Christmas Eve chapel service. Well, I have no least intention of hearing any carols, this year, Dr. Maria; or seeing any cradle with any little Christ child lying in it, and Mary looking down, all so calm, all so contented! It's quite, quite different with me, I assure you. And nothing you say can possibly change my mind!"

Dr. Maria raised her eyebrows: "What conclusions you do leap to, my dear Elsa! See, I came merely to leave you this littlest of presents—I had saved up a thimbleful of flour for a wee cake, and tried my hand with the old-fashioned icing my grandmother used to make. But I seem hopelessly out of practice. Yet how rich a blessing I do pray for you, this Holy Night!" She kissed Fraulein Elsa's forehead and hurried off on other errands.

And then it happened. The miracle no woman could resist.

Caught off guard, Fraulein Elsa opened the box and lifted out the elaborate little cake. Waves of memory swept over her. For in her own family kitchen, in the good old days, just such cakes had been iced with the same patterns—pink scrolls, green loops, and even this white lettering around the red candle: "HEILIGE NACHT." Homesick for old childhood days of this Christmas "holiness," Fraulein Elsa was about to taste Dr. Maria's treat when her eyes noticed the tiny sweater . . .

"Of such a smallness!" she smiled, lifting up each laughable little sleeve.

"Of such a softness!" she sighed, stroking the smooth wool gently.

"Of such a blueness!" she whispered. And no sooner had she breathed these words than she buried her face in the little sweater, remembering a day in the high Alps. Someone down in the valley had been yodeling, when suddenly she had come upon a small plateau carpeted with forget-me-nots. Of a heavenly blue, like this! She had fallen on her knees, to clasp a handful of the innocent blue flowers between her palms, burying her face in that mass of tender color, and praying: "Ah God! Ah God! I thank Thee for hiding so much pure beauty up here where nobody else may ever see it, all season long! As if Thou didst grow it just for me."

Deep down in the valley the yodeler seemed to call back, in three liquid notes: "Just for you! Just for you!" And she had vowed that the rest of her life forget-me-not blue would remind her of this high and healing moment. Yet *now? Now?* Was there no balm in this blue, also?

With the little sweater still in her hands, Fraulein Elsa rose from her knees and hurried straight to the school chapel, where the only light glowed deep inside the manger. She heard someone reading Matthew Two: Where the wise men had gone home another way . . . Where the Holy Family had been warned to flee into Egypt . . . Where Herod had slain all the Jewish babies left in Bethlehem. Fraulein Elsa shuddered: "It sounds like Germany!"

Then a solo voice seemed to sing straight to her sorrow that best-loved of all German carols:

> All my heart this night rejoices,
>   As I hear,
>   Far and near,
> Sweetest angel voices;
> "Christ is born," their choirs are singing,
>   Till the air,
>   Everywhere,
> Now with joy is ringing.

Someone with a violin then repeated the exquisite "Ebeling" melody, as if in memory of the yodel: "Just for you! Just for you!" For here, too, there came the same three liquid notes: *"Till the air, Everywhere."* She buried her face in the soft blue sweater, while strange sentences streamed through her consciousness: *With her own little Innocent safe in her arms, how stricken Mary must have felt about the slaughter of all those other small innocents. And yet, no wonder that she should also rejoice; for could she not see to it—she and her Son—that no such outrage should ever happen again? He that is mighty hath done to me great things, and holy is His name . . . He shall bring down the mighty from their seats . . . He shall exalt them of low degree . . . He shall feed the hungry with good things . . . O Lord God, in Ger-*

many, too, let this miracle come true! Not only Dr. Maria's beloved little cake, for me alone; but show my baby and me what we can do for all these wartime waifs wandering up and down every street—vicious as little wolves; jostling! stealing! sleeping in dark doorways! hiding in rubble! Lord God, are not all these little lost innocents Thy children? And to think that I could have let my own child be like one of them! Make me a mother of the motherless. Teach me Thy ways; it is what I am here for; surely it is what Christmas is for. O Father in heaven, forget-me-not! Forget-me-not!

The solo voice continued singing:

> Hither come, ye heavyhearted,
> > Who for sin
> > Deep within
> Long and sore have smarted;
> For the poisoned wounds you're feeling
> > Help is near,
> > One is here
> Mighty for their healing.

As the violin once again repeated the haunting notes of "Ebeling," Fraulein Elsa's petition went even deeper: *Forgive me for thinking there is no sorrow like my sorrow which has been done unto me. For, see, I have this roof over my head, and these friendly students around me, and this precious unseen child within me, just waiting to be born. But out in those beastly boxcars, other human beings crowded like cattle, shunted for days on some isolated siding. Starving there. Foraging for dry roots, as food. Homeless, hopeless, helpless! So I am the only miserable mortal in all Germany, am I, Lord? So I have no family left, have I? Until suddenly come all these refugees who could be mine! Is only my baby to be wrapped in this heavenly blue warmth? While other babies freeze as I pass by? Didst Thou hear, Lord: as . . . I . . . pass . . . by . . . on my two good feet? Able to use my two good hands? With every German street now so full of the legless, the armless, the crippled. Do make me wise enough to share some treasure with them, before I go home—another way. For how*

can it be really Christmas if I bake no little cake and knit no little sweater to show somebody else how they matter to me?
The soloist sang another of the Gerhardt stanzas:

> Hark! a voice from yonder manger
>   Soft and sweet
>   Doth repeat:
> "Flee from woe and danger,
> Brethren, come, from all that grieves you
>   You are freed;
>   All you need
> I will surely give you."

Fraulein Elsa heard the violin again: *How that music sounds like my promise that day up in the high Alps! But now I must go down, down where people live, Lord. Forget-me-not! When my baby puts little arms through these blue sleeves, teach them to reach out, embracing everybody everywhere. Give each of us enough tender mercy and loving-kindness to spare. What else is Christmas for? What else am I for? What other glad tidings could there be?*

When the students began filing silently out of the chapel, Fraulein Elsa rose from her knees, still holding the blue jacket with such obvious delight that Dr. Maria thought of a verse in Isaiah: "The redeemed of the Lord shall return with everlasting joy upon their foreheads!" Although the actual words which she found herself praying echoed Jesus Christ: "I thank Thee, O Father, Lord of heaven and earth, because Thou hast hid these things from the wise and prudent, and hast revealed them unto babes. Even so, Father; for so it seemed good in Thy sight."

After which it was rather a letdown to have the baby arrive wrinkled and weazened and anxious-looking, like some disgruntled old lady whom nothing could please. But to Fraulein Elsa she seemed perfection.

"Did you really ever see such a baby in all your life?" she asked Dr. Maria.

"No, I really never did!" the professor answered truthfully, equally appalled by the ugliness of this tiny girl and the high approval of her mother. Indeed, this absorption seemed so complete that Dr. Maria felt she should test it: "They tell me you are to be House Mother in our orphanage when you graduate, Elsa. But you aren't too wrapped up in your own child to forget all the others, are you?"

Fraulein Elsa stared at her in surprise: "Forget? But who's forgetting now, Dr. Maria? Hasn't every child in this world the right to be equally wanted and equally loved? Already they all seem like my very own! Ever since I first touched that forget-me-not blue angora I began wanting every single cold miserable little creature on earth to be warmed by its beauty and tenderness. It keeps making Christmas out of every day in my year—to love that hard! to have enough goodwill to go around! To see if ugly babies can't become the happiest of all!"

"I see!" said Dr. Maria. "Yes, I knew you would."

For once more, wrapped in the clothes of the Babe Jesus, there had been enough to build a bridge for all men.

[*Note:* If using this story in public, it will be more effective to stop at intervals to let a soloist sing each of the three stanzas; then to tell Fraulein Elsa's thoughts while an actual violin plays "Ebeling" as background music.]

> *He cam al so stille*
> *To His modir's bour*
> *As dew in Aprille*
>   *That falleth on flour.*
> *Hee cam al so stille*
> *Ther His modir lay,*
> *As dew in Aprille*
>   *Yt falleth on spray.*
> *Modir and maiden*
>   *Was never none but shee,*
> *Well may suche a ladye*
>   *Goddes modir bee.*
>   Fifteenth-century carol

*Try to become little with the Little One, that you may
increase in stature with Him.*

St. Bonaventura

17

BECAUSE MARK'S MOTHER LOANED
HER UPPER ROOM

The Lord shall count, when He writeth up the nations, that this
man was born here.   PSALM 87:6

Archbishop William Temple used to say that the most important influence in any child's life is the conversation overheard
in his home. And because Mark's mother had a big house in
Jerusalem, with a large "guest chamber, furnished" (Mark 14:12)
the likelihood is that Mark grew up overhearing Mary his mother
and Barnabas his cousin and Peter, the family friend, talking
about the new faith which was sweeping through Galilee like
wildfire. All sorts of great painters have painted that room—
Leonardo da Vinci in "The Last Supper," for instance. But it is
even better to paint it in your own mind's eye, with all the occasions when it was probably used—the Last Supper . . . that tre-
mendous day of Pentecost when so many were quietly waiting
together with Mary, the mother of Jesus, and suddenly it happened! That startling Spirit of the Living God, completely changing everybody present. Later still, in that same room, the meeting
for prayer because Peter was in prison—and all the time there
he stood outside, knocking at the door; with the little maidservant
Rhoda running upstairs to say so, but too flustered to have
opened the door to let him in.

Think, also, of the amazing row of plaques which could be placed beside that door, although who would know how best to decide their order?

> THE LAST SUPPER WAS HELD HERE
> JESUS CHRIST VISITED HERE
> PENTECOST HAPPENED HERE
> MARY THE MOTHER OF JESUS STAYED HERE
> ST. PETER SLEPT HERE
> ST. MARK WAS BORN HERE

This may be leaping to conclusions. But writers and readers love to leap; and Mark could have agreed with a wide variety of authors—with *Melville* in *Moby Dick*, asking for a condor's quill and Vesuvius for an inkstand, to produce a mighty book you must choose a mighty theme; with *Ruskin*: "This is the best of me; for the rest I ate and drank, and slept and loved and hated like another . . . but this I saw and knew . . . this, if anything of mine is worth your memory"; with *Dante* who warned the readers of his *Divine Comedy* that everything had a fourfold meaning, and would never be understood by those satisfied with surface sense only. And surely Mark would be at one with the anonymous old *Mandarin:*

> All around the margin
> Of any consignment of print
> Is a continuous flock of readers
> Leaping to conclusions—
> Excellent conclusions for them, no doubt,
> But not necessarily the author's.

So that although John Mark himself participated in none of the scenes about which he wrote, he "saw" them through Peter's eyes and "knew" them through Peter's heart; for all of the early church fathers were agreed that this Gospel was actually Peter's Memoir, told to Mark in Rome, in those flaming days when Rome burned and Nero fiddled, blaming it all on the Christians; later killing both Peter and Paul. Thought of from this angle, Mark's thirteenth chapter takes on an even more fiery tinge—

for he had lived through such horrors, and lost his two best friends on earth.

At this point a curious matter needs to be mentioned. For Peter's whole life can be traced on page after page of this little book—vivid and blunt and blundering. But who could ever guess that Mark had known Paul exactly as well? Traveled with him on all sorts of hard missionary journeys, seen Paul sweeping whole cities in Greece, through the power of the Holy Spirit? Yet Mark still chooses Peter's viewpoint—and fills all thirty feet of his parchment roll with pictures of Peter: leaving his nets, sailing his fishing boat, climbing a mountain, warming his hands at a palace fire, denying, hearing a cock crow twice, weeping; and all too often not quite knowing what on earth was happening to him.

While the only hint of Paul's enormous influence may be in the last line of Mark's book, where he adds that the disciples went forth preaching, *"the Lord working with them"*! Their Lord, absent. Yet ever-present, also. For as someone has said: God kept on working after His Book had gone to press.

And who could know this better than Mark, who had seen the Spirit working with Peter and Paul, with Silas and Barnabas; and of course with himself so vigorously that all later Gospel writers copied whole sections of his book. The vigor comes out in violent verbs, which the other writers toned down politely! Mark alone told how the Spirit *drove* Jesus into the wilderness; the Pharisees trying to *catch* Jesus in his words; the *toiling* in the rowing; the mob *railing* at him, *wagging* their heads. All his descriptions of illness, like the Gadarene demoniac and the boy at the foot of the Mount of Transfiguration, could be directions for a TV drama. It is a splendid literary experience to go through the book with a red pencil, underlining each of these vivid scenes. If Mark was not there, Peter was! And Mark is short on the sermons Jesus preached, but long on the compassion He showed in His miracles; so that was what Peter remembered best in his last days in Rome, was it?

Artists who study symbols wonder why St. Mark is always pictured in Christian art with a lion. Mark, so little brave that he is supposed to have been that young man who ran away from the mob in Gethsemane so fast that he lost his linen cloak, and fled naked to his home. Mark, who did an even worse running away when he left Paul at Perga, in Pamphilia, when the preaching grew much too dangerous. Leaping to our own conclusions, might the lion mean that Mark grew strong enough to face one? or was the lion there because Mark alone, in his first chapter, writes that Jesus was in the wilderness "with the beasts"? And how about the phrase from Peter's Epistle, that the devil is like a roaring lion going about seeking whom he may devour? For in a biography of Peter, Peter's Epistles crop up in certain other places, very interestingly. Whereas Paul wrote letters also, but traces of them are very hard to find in Mark.

Another portrait emerges from this book with lovely clarity. The Master who was always in a hurry: "straightway" doing this, or "immediately," or "forthwith." St. Francis de Sales once said that the only tense which matters in the Christian life is the present tense! And Mark's quick pen was all present tense. Do run through his book in a hurry yourself, and underline with a blue pencil those 48 "straightways"!

But even before you open the covers you can probably restore Mark's whole book from three dozen key words: who and what do you connect with "wilderness," "locust," "prepare," "latchet," "beheaded"? What pictures come to mind from the words: "nets"? "fever"? "roof"? "bed"? "cornfield"? "Sower"? "candlestick"? "swine"? "loaves"? "fishes"? "rowing"? "crumbs"? "dogs"? "transfigured"? "disputing"? "children"? "millstone"? "colt"? "hosanna"? "mite"? "spikenard"? "pitcher"? "bread"? "cup"? "kiss"? "cock"? "purple"? "early"? "spices"? "risen"? "go"?

For the way to value something is to realize how you would feel if you lost it. The way China has twice lost the sayings of Confucius! Twenty-two hundred years ago it was the emperor Chin Shih Huang who wanted all history to start with himself, and therefore collected every Confucian book in the kingdom to be burned—"the Slope of the Burning Books" the Chinese still call it. Chin also dug a deep ditch and buried alive three hundred scholars who refused to give up their books. But all this time there was Fu Sheng; ninety years old, too trembling in his hands to paint any of the characters, too husky in his poor old voice to be understood by anybody but his little thirteen-year-old grand-daughter, yet knowing all the Five Classics by heart. So, moment by moment, word by word, the girl wrote down that old man's words; and Confucius came back to China.

But all over again history is now repeating itself in China. Moment by moment Confucius is being burned, on orders of Mao Tse-tung! Scholars must turn out their libraries. Book stores must empty their shelves. For what has communism to do with the things Confucius taught—filial piety, brotherly love, loyalty to friends, "all within the four seas are brothers"?

Perhaps a Christian ought to recall that Jan Huss was burned at the stake, and William Tyndall also, for daring to let the Bible speak Bohemian and English. Perhaps all women should remember that Henry VIII had signs at the street corners of London, reading: "No Woman, no Artificer, no Artisan, shall be allowed to read the Bible in the English language either to himself or to another, on penalty of imprisonment and death." Like any prohibition, the ultracurious were aroused and simply had to find out for themselves what this forbidden Book said. So copies were secretly bought. Secretly read. Secretly loved. And England was secretly changed.

Just as anyone can be secretly changed by reading for himself the swift sentences and lively lines in Mark's Gospel. Not as a study, complete with Concordance, Commentary, and Professor So-and-So's latest research in the Greek texts, with footnotes to trip you up every inch of the way. Study should come later, of course. But read the book first because Mark's mother loaned her Upper Room, because Pentecost happened in that house, be-cause Peter slept there, because Rhoda was too delighted to be sensible, because Barnabas was Mark's cousin and straightened him out so splendidly; because Rome was burning and Mark thought: suppose this picture of Jesus was lost? Suppose Peter's memoirs never got written?

In a way, this sounds like the morning newspaper. In fact, why not make it into today's *Daily Times?* A surprise is in store for you if you do! Try sending to The American Bible Society (490 Park Avenue, New York 21, N. Y.) for three copies of their separate edition of St. Mark, at two cents apiece. You will notice at once that a page of this tiny Gospel is about the width of a newspaper column. Eight columns make up a page. Spend an hour cutting up two of your Gospels, pasting them in continuity along the length of each column. The likelihood is that the two will come out even: Mark, and your home-town paper.

The moral of this being, that if you never flinch from reading one page of your newspaper at a sitting, why quail from catching all of Mark's message in sixty minutes? His speed is sensational. If you should choose headlines for his reporting, you would need lively verbs and few nouns; and this would be a wise practice, because it would force you into a keener awareness of the author's Christ.

Then, having cut up two of the small copies of Mark, use the third copy for discovering certain basic ideas Mark was presenting. The margins are not very wide, but bold black block letters can be placed there as you go through the book again and again, finding the following facts. (It might simplify your search if you listed all these letters on the inside of the front cover, first.)

Let a large capital P stand for Peter; then go through the Gospel writing this large initial wherever Peter is mentioned: his memoir emerges perfectly. Note that the big fisherman is to be made a fisher of men (1:17). See how often Mark mentions *Ships*; put an S in the margin, while finding Peter.

Obviously Mark is as crowd-conscious as modern reporters! Go through the Gospel again, putting M in the margin for *Multitudes*. In an amazing fashion they throng on Jesus, pressing Him on every side, so much that the disciples could not even eat properly. From being friendly, eager, curious, in the opening chapters, notice that later the Multitudes come at Jesus with swords, mob Him, smite Him, rail, wag their heads, shouting "Crucify Him!" The portrait of Jesus will come clearer if you also write J in the margin; for wherever He was, the crowd gathered.

Two other dramatic words in Mark's life of Jesus are *"looking"* and "*going*," with L and G in the margin. Notice in chapter 3:5 the slow penetrating quality of that gaze: "And when He had looked round about Him with anger, being grieved at their hardness of heart, He saith unto the man: 'Stretch forth thy hand.'" And when Peter rebuked Jesus for foretelling the Cross, notice in 8:33: "But when He had turned about and looked on His disciples, He rebuked Peter." For could Peter in Rome ever forget Peter in Galilee being called "Satan"? Or could Peter forget that special look which Jesus turned on the rich young ruler, "loving" him (10:21)? This will be a rich and tender search.

The *comings* and *goings* make more disturbing reading, as the letter G is put in the margin. Bishop Brent loved to speak of "Christ's agile feet"—well, here they are! For the major words in all His ministry were certainly "Come!" "Follow!" "Go!" You will note, therefore, how "Jesus came preaching" (1:14); "and they were in the way going up to Jerusalem, and Jesus went before them; and they were amazed; and as they followed they were afraid" (10:32); see also 14:28 and 16:7: "I am risen and *go before you.*" Then that indestructible inescapable "Go ye!" in 16:15 which will always disturb Christian consciences.

You will recall how it sent William Carey from a cobbler's bench to India; and how old Dr. Erskine shouted to the Moderator of the Scotch Presbyterian Church in 1796: "*Rax me that Bible!*" For the Assembly delegates had just found it "improper and absurd to propagate the Gospel abroad" when all of Scotland was not yet saved. Opening at Mark 16, Dr. Erskine thundered out the two unforgettable words: "Go ye!" By all means, therefore, underscore every "go," "went," "came," "followed," "brought." For as an old Arabian proverb says: "There are only three kinds of people in the world—the Movable, the Immovable, and those that Move!" For the rich young ruler whom Jesus looked at and loved, came running; but was actually "Immovable" about his great possessions. (All the characters in this book can be gauged by these three standards; as Peter had told Mark!)

At every turn you will come across "amazement" and "astonishment"; an A in the margin can show this reaction which Jesus aroused wherever He went.

There are wonderful *"Women"* in this book; a W in the margin will identify them. Every one of the stories has color and charm, whether in the witty reply of the Syrophoenician woman which pleased Jesus so much; or the fragrance of Mary's spikenard which filled all the house. Our Lord said that this story of her gift would be told wherever His own story was told! But this has proved equally true of every person in the book. How about that wretched maidservant in Pilate's palace? What would she have thought about her mean taunting tone going down in history for nineteen centuries? Or Peter's even more dreadful denial? And how could a poor widow dream of her eternal fame, with every Mite Box in every women's missionary society named for her small gift?

Remembering this widow, there are certain uncomfortable juxtapositions of texts in Mark's Gospel wherever money is mentioned. With a dollar sign, $, in the margin, the meaning in 12:1-9 retells Christ's own life story; 12:13-17 was aimed by the Pharisees to catch Him on the money question; 12:40 denounces scribes who devour widows' houses; 12:41-44 brings the little widow herself to the treasury: "Disciples, see these mites!" Jesus said. But in the very next verses the heedless disciples shout: "Master, see these stones!" The temple so costly! The mites so paltry! In 14:3-9 the money contrast between the costly spikenard and the miserly man is very marked; especially with Judas leaving that very room to go out and sell Jesus for money to His enemies. This is vivid contrast in writing. Just as in 10:17-31 where the rich young ruler appears; 10:35-45 where two of the disciples irritate the others by seeking prime importance; and 10:46-52 an actual blind man begging as the blind disciples had just begged!

No wonder Mark could write that "the common people heard Him gladly." This self-initiated search can explain why, especially if the letter C in the margin marks the countless "cures," and a question mark, ?, lists the queries and answers. Mark's opening sentence shines clearer after such a study: *"The begin-*

ning of the good news of Jesus Christ," and Mark's closing thought: "God *working with them*," ought to lead new Erskines into shouting: "Rax me that Bible!" whenever the Movable prove Immovable.

One last way of making Mark more memorable centers in chapter 12:10-11: "The stone which the builders rejected is become the head of the corner; this was the Lord's doing and it was marvelous in our eyes"—Christ quoting Psalm 118, referring to His own life. You can see it afresh, yourself, by thinking of Cinderella; for hers is no fairy story—it is the underlying motif in every person's life who is rejected, then accepted; low, then lifted; a very poor widow, but noticed by the Son of God Himself with admiration; a beggar, seeing; Jairus' daughter dead, but waking. The whole redemptive thread of the divine-human encounter traced. Peter, a Cinderella, himself. And of course, Mark: with his lion; now unafraid.

Now for the art of catching fish, that is to say, how to make a man—that was none—to be an angler by a book; he that undertakes it shall undertake a harder task than Mr. Hales (a most valiant and excellent fencer) who in a printed book called A Private School of Defence, *undertook to teach the art or science, and was laughed at for his labour. Not but that many useful things might be learned by that book, but he was laughed at because that art was not to be taught by words, but practice; and so must angling!*

Izaak Walton, *The Compleat Angler*, 1654

Every man's life is a fairy story written by God Himself.

Hans Christian Andersen

18

DON'T CROSS YOUR BRIDGES UNTIL . . .

Between us and you there is a great gulf fixed; so that they which
would pass from hence to you cannot.   LUKE 16:26

The rest of their lives the beggars used to stand on the shore,
staring and staring at the bridge. Their bridge! Built as they
never dreamed it could be built. Without any least intention on
their part. So that their feelings about it were always mixed.
Some pride. More perplexity. Much petulance. Oh, that prince!

For by this time everybody in the city of Florence realized
what the Medici prince had done. He had been told and retold
for many years that a new bridge was needed over the River
Arno. But even in Renaissance Italy there were city fathers who
hated hints aimed at their pocketbooks. This prince, however,
was one of the more ingenious Medicis, for he agreed publicly
that yes, indeed—a bridge! But privately he had large placards
printed and posted at the street corners:

NOTICE:
IF THE BEGGARS OF FLORENCE WILL COME
TO THE MEDICI PALACE
THEY WILL BE GIVEN
A NEW SUIT OF CLOTHES
ON
FRIDAY MORNING, AT 9 O'CLOCK

Needless to say the poor ragged creatures flocked there in
droves. At the appointed hour the gates were flung open, and
everybody surged into the cobblestone courtyard. Standing on
the palace steps, the prince shouted four sharp orders—one to

the servants: "Shut the gates!" Two to the beggars: "Take off your old clothes!" (which they did; and immediately their next instructions were:) "Put on your new clothes!" (which they did. Then, to the servants:) "Open the gates! Drive them out quickly!"

When this, too, had been done, lo and behold! plenty of money was found tied up in the old clothes of the beggars to build the bridge. And to this day men still call it The Beggars' Bridge.

So then when a beggar stood on one side of the Arno, to watch his bridge being built, he felt a dozen different ways about it: *annoyance*—at the trick which had brought in plenty to build this spectacular span; *disgust*—at his own stupidity in letting the thrill of mere clothes blind him into leaving behind his real valuables; *pride*—that this beautiful structure bore his name, no matter how reluctant he may have been to build it.

Fortunately for us, the Prince of Peace does not build His bridge through any trick. But, stone by stone, span by span, moment by moment, He turns us into architects and donors, forever letting us build it freely—hilariously—reluctantly—as the case may be.

Did we think there were only three jubilant things to leap over the landscape: a plow, to furrow the fields? a car, to lick up the miles? a ship, to skim over the waves? But a bridge leaps, also! Moment by moment tying Florence to Fiesole, Brooklyn to New York, Oakland to San Francisco; citizen to citizen; ourselves to everybody everywhere.

This, then, is much more than mere history. Much, much more than just the Ponte Contadini over the Arno. It is all of life built over every dividing line. Wherever two or three are met together, there He is in our midst to become our Bridge of Peace, uniting both sides—provided we give Him what we have wrapped up in our clothes. And what do we have?

Our Master's own story of Dives tells all. For although Dives wore purple and fine linen, and fared sumptuously every day, eventually he took the part of the despised beggar he had taken pains never to see. The drama in it is disturbing:

Butler (behind Dives' chair at this sumptuous table; hems and haws to get attention. Then, discreetly): "Pardon me, milord."

Dives: "Yes, James, what is it?"

Butler: "That beggar, milord! He is at the gate again."

Dives (annoyed): "What on earth does the fellow want?"

Butler: "Bread, milord. He has none."

Dives: "Then let him eat cake!"

Or is this Marie Antoinette? (Any Marie Antoinette, bored over beggars.) Until that tragic time—later—when roles get reversed, and Lazarus is given the nicer spot while Dives draws the nasty one. Disgruntled and desperate, hear him begging for one drop of water, please! or at least, please oh please, let a prophet go to my five brothers to warn them to pay a lot more attention to others around them.

"Alas, no!" a voice explains. "Between you and us a great gulf is fixed. And you never cared a rap before, about building a bridge. So now it is pretty late to want one!"

This is, of course, our Master's other story of The Last Judgment, where not even the saints fully understood Who it was they had been feeding and dressing and loving at their gates—moment by moment. The sinners were naturally puzzled also: "But Lord, when saw we Thee starving, naked, in prison?"

"When saw we Thee?" that is our clue. Even our proverb tells us: "Don't cross your bridges until you come to them!" But when you do come to them, recognize them. And give gladly to the Prince of Peace all that is wrapped up in beggars' old clothes. What is wrapped up?

Even beggars can look at the person nearby:

In one of his best-known poems the famous Negro poet, Countee Cullen, tells us that when he was only six he went to Baltimore and rode in a streetcar where a little white Baltimorean stared at him in such an unfriendly fashion that, although he stayed a long time in Baltimore, that's *all* that he remembers! That haughty look.

No wonder the ancient *Sarum Primer* prays: "God bee in myn eyes and in myn lookynge"—for now that even advertisements show us cool supercilious ladies looking down their noses in disdain at unstylish sisters, it is high time to develop within ourselves An Apostolate of Affectionate Regard, dedicated to looking at anyone as if he or she really mattered. St. Augustine gives us this bridge: "O Thou who lovest each of us as if there were only one of us."

Even beggars can smile:

Ninety-eight muscles needed for a frown; only sixteen to smile with! And not any empty simper. Nor Mona Lisa's cryptic "Come hither" expression. Art critics tell us that the painter had mysterious music playing whenever she sat for his picture, just to keep this smile up to par. (But how would Leonardo have felt last year if he could have overheard a child from the Boston slums say in a museum, after one quick glance at a copy: "Her's fixing to steal something!") No, there is some kindlier bridge for smiling, a larger tenderness and deepening interest. Even wordlessly, it speaks.

Even beggars can shake hands:

After reading Vincent Van Gogh's letters to his brother Theodore it becomes noticeable that he ends each of them: "I shake your hand." The hand of this painter so unappreciated in his lifetime that he could not even earn fifty dollars a year, and so had to be supported by Theodore. The hand of this beggar whose glorious bright colors brought a million visitors to the Metropolitan Museum, one hundred years after his death. The hand of this beggar who went to live with coal miners, to gain "the feel of the trade." The hand which copied twice over *The Imitation of Christ* to feel the wonder Thomas à Kempis felt, and build the same bridge. "I shake your hand." It is a very simple thing to do. But at the moment we join the church it is called "The Right Hand of Christian Fellowship." And moment by moment, it always is this. Anywhere. Everywhere.

Even a beggar can talk:

Henri Roser's sister Elizabeth told me in New York about the "speechless" bridge her famous Pacifist brother once built in

Poland, in a train, traveling with strangers. It had been a long tedious day—customs inspection on leaving Cracow, passport inspection, and so forth. But at the hour of the Angelus he opened his New Testament. As the darkness deepened outdoors the motion of the train made him drop asleep, temporarily, and his New Testament fell to the floor. It woke him. But, much quicker than he, a Russian peasant across from him stooped to pick up the small Book. He was surprised, however, that she did not hand it back, but began turning the pages curiously.

Then suddenly she stood up, reaching toward the rack above her for her peasant bundle. She untied it, and took from between a loaf and some cheese a thick Book, bound in red, old with use. The other travelers watched her thumbing through her own Bible. Then Henri Roser took back his copy and found his French text: "For He is our peace, who hath made both one," from Ephesians Two, verse fourteen. Pointing to it, and gesticulating, he asked her if she could not find this, also. When she managed to reach the verse, what pointing and nodding and smiling and handshaking built their bridge of Christian fellowship! Then their further conversation from the benediction in the Bible: "Grace to you and peace from God our Father and the Lord Jesus Christ."

Yes! Yes! she nodded, her broad face radiant with smiles. She drew from her coat two pieces of paper: one, a Certificate of Baptism bearing the seal of a Ukrainian Church. The other, a work contract issued by the French Ministry, authorizing her to come to the north of France as a servant—in the house of a pastor friend of Henri Roser.

Everybody in the compartment started talking at once: a German lady, a Polish couple, a Czechoslovakian, another Ukrainian. Not that another word was necessary! The whole place was full of the invisible Presence. For the beggars all had what it takes. They had come from the east and the west, from the north and the south, and had sat down together, exactly as St. Luke reported our Lord's words: "And they shall sit down together in the kingdom of God." On earth! As in heaven.

Even a beggar can share his last crust:

Eating together has always been a sacrament of safety. Even among primitive people. The guest under the roof, safe, pro tem! Probably this accounts in some unconscious fashion for the success of men's luncheon clubs—Rotary, Lions, Kiwanis, and so forth: in an insecure world how good and how pleasant it is for brothers to dwell together in unity. But how tender that tie when it can cross generations and oceans and prisons, as in the case of Dr. Anna K. Scott and her son-in-law Dr. Henry Waters, in their relationship with Sister Pomegranate in China and her granddaughter. It began with a bite by a mad dog when Dr. Scott was able to save Sister Pomegranate's life and turn her into a Bible woman, thus saving a whole family. Eventually their granddaughter became a nurse, escaping in the war years to the same hospital in the Philippines where Dr. Waters was surgeon. But when the enemy took over the Philippines also, the tables were turned: and it was the doctor now who was in trouble, and Sister Pomegranate's grandchild who was safe outside prison walls. Safe. But poor! Yet deeply worried over food for the imprisoned doctor. Every crumb she could possibly collect was secretly passed inside the prison doors, through a trusted Filipino. So that Dr. Waters managed to live through the terrible siege. "Lord, when saw we Thee hungry and fed Thee, or sick and in prison and came unto Thee?" The Last Judgment, Dives, is enacted daily: moment by moment somebody somewhere is your concern!

Even a beggar can give some gift:

Fred Igler—student pastor at the University of Pennsylvania —tells of one student badly injured in a battle somewhere in the Pacific, and captured by the Japanese. With both arms broken, and both legs fractured, the poor fellow lay in utter discomfort on his hospital cot, suddenly conscious of a Japanese face staring at him so steadily that he grew uneasy. For how could he defend himself, with arms in splints? or escape, with legs in casts? Yet this terrible face of a man with too many teeth haunted him like a bad dream, for he was always there, staring.

Then one day the Japanese threw something at him; in considerable embarrassment turning away. It was a gift—a bath towel wrapped around a bar of soap. A bonanza in wartime! And it led to their delight in one another. For the real story grew out of a preesnt from America which this Japanese had cherished all his life. For, years earlier, a project of "World Friendship among Children" had sent a shipload of many thousand dolls, dressed in the United States, for distribution among Japanese children. And this boy had drawn a perfect beauty! Nothing could part him from it. So that now, with belated gratitude, he shared this treasure of his own at a time when soap was impossible to find and any woven goods a godsend.

Stone by stone, span by span, moment by moment, beggars build this bridge. For there is a great gulf fixed. And we are always approaching this abyss. But wrapped in our clothes is God's plenty!

O God, whose tunic, woven from the top throughout,
betokens the unity of the faith and the sacrament of
peace, grant to Thy Church peace in Thee, peace to all
peoples and nations; and to this congregation here pres-
ent that peace which Thou Thyself hast founded and
commanded Thy disciples to keep; and without which,
as Thou has taught us, none can be well-pleasing to
Thee. Grant this, O everlasting Father, through Jesus
Christ, Thy Son, our Lord, who is our true Peace, and
unbroken Charity, living with Thee and the Holy Ghost,
one God in Trinity, forever and ever. Amen.
                                Mozarabic Missal, A.D. 687

Interlinked, food-yielding lands!
Land of coal and iron! land of gold! land of cotton,
    sugar, rice!
Land of wheat, beef, pork! land of wool and hemp!
    land of the apple and the grape!

Land of the pastoral plains, the grassfields of the world!
Inextricable lands! the clutched together!
Walt Whitman

There goes but a pair of shears betwixt an emperor and
the son of a bag-piper: only the dyeing, dressing, press-
ing, glossing makes the difference.
John Marston, *The Malcontent*, 1604

And when I think that Michel Angelo
Hath leaned on me, I glory in myself.
Henry Wadsworth Longfellow,
"Old Bridge in Florence"

19

IN THE NAME OF THE BEE AND THE BUTTERFLY AND THE BREEZE, AMEN

The bee is little among such as fly, but her fruit is the chief of sweet things. Boast not of thy clothing and raiment, and exalt not thyself in the day of honor; for the works of the Lord are wonderful, and His works among men are hidden.
ECCLESIASTICUS 11:3-4

When Emily Dickinson thought of the line in our title, she was not linking unrelated things. For people have noticed for centuries that before the first man dreamed up his first bridge over impassable precipices to a further shore, bees and butterflies had been doing it daily in their line of duty. And spiders, even more tangibly, of course.

Distances meant nothing. A breeze could carry them across, if only they could get caught up in an air current going their way. And, curiously enough, for fertilization of fruits and flowers and grains, God has depended upon such inconsequential creatures —seemingly so frivolous, dancing their days away haphazardly. Yet actually like clockwork in keeping all their dates on time, with over 100,000 species of plants which could never form seeds without bee, butterfly or breeze.

Consider this bee: *five eyes*—three simple ones on top of the head, two compound ones with thousands of lenses; *five thousand nostrils*—enough to smell an apple tree half a mile away; *two sets of wings*—which can be hooked together in flight, so that they flap as one: 16,000 times each moment; 20 miles an hour; 7 miles, nonstop. No matter how zigzag the dizzy dance, always that beeline straight home to the all-important hive and the next big job to be done there. Acting as street cleaners, water carriers, nurses, sentries, masons, engineers, air conditioners, electric fans —often fanning twelve hours at a stretch, indoors; on top of twelve hours of gathering honey, outdoors. All that dipping into dandelions and blossoms in obedience to God's holy ordinance that "while the earth remaineth, seedtime and harvest shall not cease." This is beautiful business, expertly done. A mere mortal feels almost a heartbreak, however, over the discovery that to make one pound of honey one bee would need to travel 50,000 miles, more than twice the distance round the globe. And, actually, a single teaspoonful of honey in six weeks is a bee's entire life quota. But his buzz is not a grumble, merely his motor working overtime.

And all this labor without being spoken to twice—no reminders, no reproaches from a foreman. For mystical reasons the liturgical Church has always prescribed that candles used at Holy Communion be made from beeswax; and without any hesitation even the most nonliturgical is touched by this lovely tribute paid to such a pure and faithful "worker in the vineyard."

This chapter, then, hopes to fill out Emerson's statement that "the air is full of sounds, the sky is full of tokens; the ground is all memoranda and signatures, and every object covered over with hints that speak to the intelligent."

Tin Pan Alley made up a ditty not long ago about climbing aboard a butterfly and taking off on a breeze. Almost like Emily Dickinson. But not quite. And certainly not intelligent! For escapism is never enough. It is power to pollinate all the flowers of tomorrow and to bridge the unbridgeable that is the real life.

Hans Christian Andersen tells of a butterfly which had a thrilling time flying freely from flower to flower, learning all the deep, wild, wonderful outdoor secrets. But, in the end, the butterfly was stuck on a pin and hung on a curtain indoors. After listening to houseplants talking, the butterfly observed wisely: "One can hardly believe a plant in a flowerpot; they are too much among human beings."

It is at this point that the word "continent" paints a picture: *con,* together; *teneo,* to tie; therefore: *"lands-tied-together."* Not only by bees, butterflies and breezes. But other small creatures with wings.

Bird lovers with Protestant backgrounds must frequently wonder whether North America would be Catholic now if Columbus had reached our hemisphere in March—when birds might be migrating north—instead of in October, when he followed flocks of land birds flying south, feeling that they must mean business. As indeed they did. For Cristobal Colon lived up to his "Christ-bearing" forename, both planting the Cross and propagating the Faith wherever he set foot. And those birds which tied lands together, that October, determined something momentous in 1492: that this nation under God should be left open for Pilgrims, Reformers, Lutherans, Quakers, Huguenots, to flee to.

Of eight hundred American varieties of birds, one hundred and twenty-five varieties migrate. Their inborn urge to make this long uncomfortable trip, their awaiting some almost mystical signal to start, is one of Emerson's "hints" that all life proceeds on God's spiritual basis. Why should all the shy birds fly by night? Warblers, sparrows, vireos, juncos, finches, thrushes, wrens, hummingbirds. To be safer from capture, of course. But (in Don Quixote's happy phrase: "The little birds of the field have God for their

Caterer") their uncomfortable night flight ends on a branch—for they are berry eaters, and can nibble at their leisure. The bold and strong-winged birds are insect eaters and fly by day. Orioles, bluebirds, robins, grackles, swallows, swifts, larks, crows, bobolinks. *"Your heavenly Father knows."* Just as Jesus knew, the day He told the parable of the sower, where some seed fell by the wayside; but the birds were fed! The Father who knows when a sparrow falls, knows when a seed falls and a bird spots it. (Another of Emerson's "memoranda and signatures.")

All garden club members will be richer for remembering that back in the days when the Conquistadores returned to Spain from Peru and Mexico they brought home gifts, as all good husbands do. And what was more portable than seeds? Especially with such surprising stories to share. For instance, sunflower seeds! Over in Peru, the men would say, in all religious processionals the sun-worshipping Inca priestesses would carry tall yellow sunflowers as ceremoniously as Catholic priests carry crucifixes. All because this particular flower kept its face turned toward the sun when he rose, and turned toward the sun when he set. Therefore the Inca priestesses ate the sunflower seeds. Curious? Well yes, of course; but it may have seemed as much of a Eucharist rite for an Inca as the Loaf and the Cup seemed to a Christian. The husbands also brought back to Spain all sorts of other seeds from flowers which were sun-turning: morning glories, four o'clocks, heliotrope, marigolds, cosmos, zinnias, nasturtiums.

There must have been considerable suspense in many an old Spanish garden, waiting for these strange seeds to bloom in a new climate and in unknown soil. Would the flowers ever come? When they did, spectacular and vivid, all was well. Spanish bees enjoyed their flavor, and helped to spread the species. But many Spanish fathers also helped, by going over the Pyrenees to France, carrying gifts in their pockets for French hosts and hostesses. And again, what more portable or unusual than seeds from the New World? When the flowers bloomed in France, and the French bees improved each shining hour, then once more there were lands tied together so delightfully, that when Frenchmen crossed the English Channel into Britain it seemed like a pleasant piece of courtesy to take along some seeds. So that by the time the Pilgrims began crossing the Atlantic toward their bleak and rockbound coast, practically every trunk had seeds from some old English garden, to keep the colonists from feeling homesick. Which meant that, moment by moment, ever since leaving Peru, flowers had been tying lands together, the long way round.

Although hardly a garden club member on her knees planting four o'clocks notices that even the seed envelope says in parentheses: "Marvel of Peru," under the impossible Latin name. But about that impossible Latin name there is a story, also.

For Carl Linnaeus was the famous Swedish naturalist who found it unfortunate that, in every foreign soil, each flower was given a different name. Therefore, he gave them Latin names, which need not be changed from place to place, no matter what other names people called them. All very universal and scientific, of course. But just as a "forget-me-not" sounds more unforgettably blue and familiar in English than the formidable Latin *"myosotis"* ever could, so a similar thing was happening to the Bible in Latin —it fell on deaf unloving ears, until John Wyclif gave men "God in English." Then devotion quickened—until that seed, too, tied lands together into one common cause called Christendom.

"Speak to the earth and it shall teach thee," the garden club member reads in the book of Job at breakfast. Then, outdoors, kneeling, the flowers turn into geography teachers, telling how they bridged these seas and those rivers to bring from Mexico dahlias, gaillardias, verbenas, petunias, lupines, poinsettias, and the heavenly blue morning-glories which the Mexicans call "The Virgin's Mantle."

Around the year 1600, it is probable that enough of these flowers bloomed in the Cathedral Close for the Bishop of Exeter and Norwich to put them into a sermon. We still have some of his words: "These Flowers are true Clients of the Sunne; how observant they are of his motion and influence. At even they shut up, as mourning over his Departure; without whom they neither can nor would flourish in the morning; they welcome his rising with cheerfull opennesse, and at Noone are fully displayed in a free Acknowledgement of his Bounty. Thus doth the good Harte unto God; when Thou turnest away Thy Face I was troubled, saith the man after God's own Harte; but in Thy Presence is life; thus doth the carnall Harte to the World, when that withdraws his favour, hee is dejected; and revives with a smile. All is in our Choyse; whatsoever is our Sunne will thus carry us; O God bee Thou to mee such as Thou art in Thyselfe; Thou shalt bee mercifull in drawing mee; I shall be happy in following Thee."

Actually, and far more briefly, the famous Carl Linnaeus said almost the same thing when he carved over the lintel of his plant laboratory: "LIVE BLAMELESS—GOD IS NEAR." For he wrote this in his notebook, too, after examining so many exquisite plants: "I saw God in His glory passing near me, and bowed my head in worship."

With insects, stormy winds, birds and flowers fulfilling God's will, bridging the globe, it is no surprise to discover that corn and wheat, fruit and vegetables, follow the same plan.

The early Aztecs called maize "the holy grain"; and the ancient Mayans said: "In the Time-before-Time corn was made by the gods before they made man." Planting, and then harvesting, were their chief religious festivals. In Santo Domingo today, before cutting the ripe grain the people will say: "The wheat is getting excited"; while after cutting it, they pray: "We thank Thee, and thank Thee again; we thank Thee all the time, God!" An old Gaelic saying matches this: "I too will turn my face to the wind, and cast my handful of seed on high"; while a Scandinavian saying is less jubilant but more brotherly: "I sowed my enemy's field with corn that God might continue to endure."

The first wheat planted in the New World was grown in the plaza before the Church of San Francisco in Quito, Ecuador. Near the ancient Cathedral of Panama City there is a bronze plaque to mark the grave of Friar Tomas de Berlanga, the Spaniard who brought the first planting of bananas to this hemisphere from Spain in the year 1519; the scientific name was "*Musa Sapientum*": "fruit of the wise men." It is astonishing to learn that all oranges, lemons, melons, grapes and sugar cane were also brought first from Spain to our hemisphere. And of six coffee plants presented by the King of France, only one lived through a violent storm at sea when drinking water gave out; but a faithful officer gave all his quota to this royal gift. Out of this single plant came the immense coffee plantations in Brazil, filling half the coffee cups in the world.

What a sermon there, for the Bishop of Exeter and Norwich! Or perhaps he would prefer a gentle dig at Scotch Presbyterians for refusing to eat the first potatoes ever introduced into Europe, brought over from Peru by Sir Francis Drake. The old Presbyterian prohibition coming from the fact that "it wad no be seemly, since potatoes no were mentionit in Holy Writ."

In case the Bishop felt too ecumenical (even in 1600) to enjoy jousting over a brother's scruples, at least he might be able to incorporate the cattle on a thousand hills, or some verse about keeping up with the horsemen. For all the cowboys in the United States and all the meat-packing companies in Chicago, Kansas City and Omaha, owe a debt to Pizarro who left 34 horses in South America, and to Cortez who left 15 in Mexico, and to De Soto who brought 116 horses to Florida in 1539, and to Ponce de Leon who brought 50—together with long-horned cattle. For until then, not a horse nor a cow had ever been seen in our country, nor in South America. Yet Argentina is now a vast meat-raising country, due to Pizarro's cattle, and the gaucho is indebted daily to those horses left behind. In our land the wild horses wandered off into the uninhabited pasture lands in Texas and New Mexico. Without such crossing and recrossing of things visible and invisible, tangible and intangible, the greatest pastoral movement the world has ever known could never have taken place: a drama crowded with valor and villainy, with cattle kings and cattle wars; and with the demands for more and more immigrant labor; on and on and on, the interlinked indebtednesses pile up; for this is a story which can have no ending.

AND NOW JUST A WORD FROM OUR SPONSOR:

I thought, "How I would rank
you among the sons, and give
you a pleasant land, the

goodliest heritage of all
nations!" And I thought,
"Surely you will call me
'Father' and will not turn
back from following me."

IN THE NAME OF THE BEE . . . THE BUTTERFLY AND THE BREEZE, AMEN

"O dreary life," we cry, "O dreary life!"
And still the generations of the birds
Sing through our sighing, and the flocks and herds
Serenely live while we are keeping strife
With Heaven's true purpose in us, as a knife
Against which we may struggle! ocean girds
Unslackened the dry land, savannah-swards
Unweary sweep—hills watch, unworn; and ripe
Meek leaves drop yearly from the forest trees,
To show above the unwasted stars that pass
In their old glory. O Thou God of old,
Grant me some smaller grace than comes to these!—
But so much patience as a blade of grass
Grows by, contented through the heat and cold.
                              Elizabeth Barrett Browning

The trouble with most of us is that we do not have suf-
ficent bees in our bonnets to pollinate the flowers of our
minds.   Chinese proverb

Let every seed that falls
In silent eloquence unfold its store
Of argument: infinity within,
Infinity without.
                    Percy Bysshe Shelley

2 0

PILLARS OF THE CHURCH

... our daughters like corner pillars. PSALM 144:12, R.S.V.

If only this chapter could be read with *Finlandia* playing low background music. If only some unseen member of the choir could sing softly: "We would be building: temples still undone o'er trembling walls their crosses scarcely lift." If only there could be aroused in the gentle reader the same atmosphere which tourists always feel in Athens when they look up at the Caryatids, realizing how that romantic row of women, carved from stone, have stood for over twenty centuries holding up the roof on their side of the temple. If only the spectator could stop thinking how tiresome and awkward that position must be—forever reaching up above their heads, supporting something. Then the reader might be enticed into putting two and two together: temples building+pillars supporting=the long long history of the Church, with a curiosity about who-did-what-when-where?

Søren Kierkegaard used to say that history can only be understood *backward*, but that it can only be lived *forward*. So if, with his nineteen-hundred-year memory, the reader looks backward, what countless Caryatids can be encountered, perpetually supporting the Church. Even the Apostle Paul could approve of this approach, since in a dozen places he reminded his own readers that they were the temple of God, which temple was holy; that Peter and James and John, who seemed to be pillars, upheld the Jewish side of the temple roof, while he—Paul—chose to support the Gentile side.

And although Paul announced that he did not permit a woman to speak in church, think how eternally indebted he was to four

Caryatids upholding the early churches he founded. There was Chloe, that Corinthian column of a Christian, who spoke up in no uncertain terms about the sermon-tasters dividing her church; obviously far too preacher-conscious, voting: "I am for Paul!" "No, no! give me Apollos!" "Peter for me!"

Twice over Paul repeats Chloe's identical words in his letter to the church at Corinth, adding: "The very idea! Was Christ divided? Were any of you baptized into Paul?"

There was Priscilla, also, with her three upholdings of churches—pillar in Rome, until she and Aquila were forced to leave, as Christian Jews; pillar in Corinth; pillar in Ephesus: where Priscilla not only straightened out the theology of the brilliant young Apollos, but Paul says that she and Aquila also "laid down their own necks for my sake." Apparently Paul considered Phoebe as dependable in carrying a letter from Corinth to Rome as the United States feels about its postmen, quoting the Persians: Whom neither rain nor snow nor sleet could hinder in the swift completion of their errands.

Few men have had three such courageous Caryatids supporting their work (or even lesser pillars in a panic, protesting: "Haven't I held up this corner long enough, Paul? My arms are nearly out of their sockets!") Yet Paul had Lydia also, that highly successful businesswoman and hostess who became pillar of his church in Philippi, and may even have gone back to start a church in Thyatira, her home town—since there is no record of any apostle visiting there. Incidentally, a study of Paul's sixteenth chapter in his letter to the Romans is rewarding, in that he mentions almost as many women as men, and sends a greeting to "the beloved Persis," which gives her a Caryatid character at once—Paul being Paul, and cautious as clergymen have to be about noticing women unnecessarily. Or even necessarily! For the reader must have noticed how church fathers—looking backward as they wrote church history—omitted Caryatids almost completely. Century by century commenting in detail about countless heroes of the faith who became pillars in "temples still undone" (*Finlandia* music playing softly); but hardly ever naming a heroine. This chapter, then, is just to keep the record somewhat straighter through a partial Who's Who of Caryatids, who also overcame difficulties about which the Spirit wrote: "Him that overcometh will I make a pillar in the temple of my God, and I will write on him the name of my God, and the name of the city of my God . . . and I will write on him my new name."

There would be many remarkable mothers of whom Anthusa was typical. Widowed at twenty, before her son was born, she refused to marry again in order to make this brilliant boy into her Christian dream come true. Later, when his famous teacher wanted Chrysostom to study for the law, the young man spoke of his mother's sole concentration on his career in the Church. Licinius, therefore, went home to see for himself what a pillar she was, and the words he uttered on leaving that house are a challenge to Caryatids in any century: "Good heavens! what women these Christians have!"

When Chrysostom longed to become a hermit, she led him to her bedroom and flinging a dramatic arm toward her couch she said that she had not borne him in pain on this very bed in order for him to isolate himself in the desert, but among the Lord Christ's needy people *in cities!* Therefore, with dedication as disciplined as Anthusa's, St. Chrysostom lived the rest of his life in great cities, serving as bishop, writing magnificent and moving liturgies still used verbatim in Eastern Orthodox churches and carried over into our own prayerbooks, and preaching sermons so eloquent that listeners called him "the golden-mouthed." Even across the long centuries between, the reader can catch some idea of the bishop's unforgettable technique, from this excerpt: "Recall that money is like water. It goes bad if it does not run. Don't think that you have done enough because you beat down your body with fasting. I don't object to your fasting, but helping others is more important. And don't ask for lovely things if they are made by blood. Recall: a ship has to be fitted and rowers enlisted, a man for the prow and helmsman. A sail is spread and an ocean covered. Wife and children are left behind. The merchant entrusts himself to the waves and goes to the lands of the barbarians and undergoes innumerable dangers. And for what?

In order that you may have colored threads to weave into your slippers!

"Better use your money for the poor. How many are there in Antioch? I should say fifty thousand. And how many Christians? I should say one hundred thousand, and the rest Jews and pagans. Now if the Christians were to bring in goods, and share them like Apostles, couldn't we take care of the poor?"

Shades of that Caryatid, Anthusa! Her son preaching (in cities!) to such wildly enthusiastic congregations that they had to be warned against applauding. But when the Empress Eudoxia erected a pillar of porphyry and silver to herself, with heathen rites held in her honor during church services, then Chrysostom thundered from his pulpit: "Herodias is dancing again! This Jezebel! This Salome!" The Empress banished the Bishop for three years to an Armenian village; and she burned down Santa Sophia. But the saint wrote flaming letters . . . and glorious liturgies still able to stir a listless listener.

Monica was another such mother as Anthusa, pillar in the Roman Church (whose similar story is told in a later chapter, about St. Augustine). And what would Ireland be without the motherly St. Bridget, always sharing God's plenty by baking thirteen loaves in every batch: twelve ordinary ones for the family, the extra large loaf for the passing Stranger, in the name of Christ. Gathering Irish princesses and peasants into cells at Kildare to educate them in the Gospels: outstanding Caryatid of the faith, overcoming colossal obstacles with wit and Christian charm.

English history would be unthinkable without Hilda, abbess of the men's theological seminary at Whitby—the Northumbrian princess who dedicated herself to the Christian life in the lovely old halls at Lindisfarne, and in 657 was considered enough of a pillar to hold up a monastery alone! Yet even with all the wisdom being instilled in her monks, today's readers love her best for saying to a simple cowherd in the stable: "Sing, Caedmon, sing!"

"But what shall I sing?" the poor untaught fellow cried—he without a word of Latin in his head.

"Sing of the beginning of created things!" she suggested. And for the first time in all England, the cowherd turned Genesis and Exodus into the mother tongue; singing the stories of Christ, accompanied by his harp. For encouragement is a Caryatid characteristic in any country on earth.

And compassion is a cosmopolitan pillar, also, in any Christian country. Even concern expressed as Lady Godiva dared to express it early one morning in Coventry, after vowing to Earl Leofric her husband that unless he lowered the outrageous taxes with which he was beating down the poor in Mercia, she would ride naked through the streets. Quite sure that even the citizens awake at dawn would honor her decent compassion by not looking out of their windows. The first of thousands of Christian women to protest dramatically the misuse of power, identifying themselves with the underprivileged in town! England has been full of them, all the way from Godiva to Hannah More, to Elizabeth Fry, to Florence Nightingale, to Margaret Bondfield, to Muriel Lester; and up in Scotland, Queen Margaret, of whom the Venerable Bede wrote that she fed eight orphans with her own spoon every morning; and that she and King Malcolm themselves served two hundred beggars daily in the palace dining hall at Holyrood.

What would Paris be without its little pale patron saint, the gentle Genevieve, who not only prayed the Huns away from the city gates one time; but, when they finally entered, so impressed the cruel Attila that he trembled at her judgments. The day he planned to slaughter five hundred captives, he led them secretly outside the gates to escape St. Genevieve's eye! But she heard about it in time, and arrived like a pillar of cloud by day to lead the entire five hundred prisoners safely back into the city. Tourists in the Pantheon today stare reverently at the pictures painted around the walls, by Puvis de Chavannes, in soft pastel colors depicting the brave Caryatid scenes in her life.

Later, in medieval Paris, there was that other pillar burned at the stake for daring to be Joan of Arc, listening to "Voices." No wonder that when Bernard Shaw wrote a play about St. Joan, he made one of his leading characters ask whether a Christ must perish in every generation for those who have no imagination.

By skipping other centuries in Paris, there would be a prison

where a pillar of the Huguenot Church had been imprisoned for
over thirty years for refusing to recant her Protestant faith. Every
day, in this firm upholding of her beliefs, Marie Durand used
to scratch on the wall of her cell the single word: "RESIST." No
Frenchman can forget that thirty years is 10,950 days! that a day
has 1,440 moments! so that her total of 15,768,000 moments is a
dramatic column, indeed! *"God lives in moments,"* a French
proverb says—and, moment by moment, He surely lived in Elizabeth Skobtzoff in Paris during the last war. For this Russian
refugee became the kind of Caryatid around whom other refugees
flocked for safety. She became famous for turning an old garage
into a Russian Orthodox Church; she painted the icons, herself;
she traveled to every suburb in Paris to restore their lost Christian
faith to Russian *émigrés* working in factories or to Russian students studying at the Sorbonne. She started and cared for a hostel
for young Russian girls; she opened a home for older people.
Every unemployed and underfed and underloved Russian in
Paris knew that under her roof would be love personified. She
became familiar to every salesman in every market as she tramped
around town buying cheap food to serve in her free canteen for
the jobless and the homeless. When the Nazi occupation swept
down on Paris, she hid in her house every possible Jewish refugee.
So perhaps it is not surprising that such a conspicuous Caryatid
could not be hidden! The Gestapo sent her to Ravensbruck,
where she was burned to death in the gas chambers there. But
news of her martyrdom touched everybody who had ever seen her
tramping Paris streets in her big men's boots, on her constant
errands of mercy; and her work was continued by other volunteers.

In Russia itself, it would be the name of Catherine Breskovsky
written in everybody's heart: *"Babushka,"* they called her—"the
little grandmother of the Russian revolution," who had forty
million peasants in her heart! Nobody asked her to put them
there. But her own father managed a rich man's estates, and she
saw what she saw. All those forty million serfs chained to the
land, tortured, abused, beaten, crushed. Forbidden to learn to
read. But, even as a girl, she decided to teach those on her own
estate to learn the thirty-five letters of the Russian alphabet.

She followed the teaching of Jesus literally all her life. And gave up her comfortable home, to go out wearing wooden shoes and a peasant scarf and apron, in order to visit villages and stir up the indifferent. Russian leaven! With the police always at her heels. So that out of her eighty-four years of life, fully fifty were spent in prisons. All for the sake of Christ and His little "lost" people. Once she was sent on the long five-thousand-mile trek to Siberia—by cart, by boat, on foot. All along the way, hundreds of peasants would run out to offer her a cup of tea or some candy: "See, how happy I am!" she cried. "Persecuted, banished, and yet beloved!"

In solitary confinement in that isolated hut in Siberia, she used to stand in the snow singing Grand Opera at the top of her voice. From gaiety? No! from the firm determination not to lose the power of speech in this endless surrounding silence—she who would have so much to say whenever she was released. This is such stuff as the pillars of the church are made of!

And although when her prayer for Revolution came true, it was a total disappointment (the cruelty of the Czar merely multiplied by the new men in power in the Kremlin), deep in the hearts of all Russians Babushka's name is written, and the name of her God. For she was one who "overcame," for their sakes; and people still so unhappy remember her fifty years of misery for their sake.

Pillars of the church of God in China? Their name is still legion, of course. But the really famous Chinese Caryatid would be Dr. Wu, president of Ginling College. During the early years of the war with Japan, this slender little woman undertook a herculean task in moving her college from East China to West China, fourteen hundred miles away. Yet her entire staff and almost her entire student body made it! On foot. By cart. Occasionally stopping to teach the illiterates, en route. Moreover, in thousands of separate bundles flung over their shoulders or balanced on poles, the college library was carried west, and much of the delicate laboratory equipment, also.

Honors were showered upon this heroic woman when the war was over; among others she was chosen to represent China at San Francisco, when the United Nations was formed. She sat among the delegates so brilliant and witty and intelligent that the Associated Press reporters called her "the darling of the Conference." No one can know how her life is lived in China now, of course; but such a spiritual column of courage must have deep inner stability; and we remember her with loving concern.

For as Dr. Carl Jung said in Zurich: "The modern woman stands before a great cultural task, which means perhaps the beginning of a new era." But actually, on *their* side of the temple, all Caryatids see that it is the same era as yesterday in the Church —a determination to be dependable supports: come wind, come weather!

Exactly as Emerson said about any era: "There is one mind common to all individuals . . . of the works of this mind history is the record. There is a relation between the hours of our life and the Centuries of Time.

"We as we read, must become Greeks, Romans, Turks, Priest and King, Martyr and Executioner, must fasten these images to some Reality in our secret experience, or we shall see nothing, learn nothing, keep nothing.

"We must attain and maintain that lofty sight where facts yield their secret sense, and Poetry and Annals are alike. Time dissipates to shining ether the solid angularity of facts . . .

"Every history should be written with a wisdom which divined the range of our affinities, and looked at facts as symbols."

[*Note:* This chapter has been presented outdoors by college students following a course in Church History; but could also be given indoors. Twenty-three tall slender girls in identical Grecian draperies became Caryatids as they took their places facing the audience one at a time, arms uplifted, while their life stories were read by the Reader. After each brief biography, however, the Caryatid turned, lowering her arms; for strapped on her back was a tall white (or gray) semicircular corrugated cardboard pillar, with a wider corrugated capital firmly attached at the top. This curved column was 36 inches wide; the capital 72 inches wide, 12 inches high. Long white tapes had been sewed across the inside of each column, serving to fasten the curved pillar both around the waist and also crisscross over the chest. At the end, while Emerson on "History" was being read, a small congregation came from off stage to kneel in four rows behind the Caryatids, dressed as Greeks, Romans, Turks, Queens in crowns, et cetera, remaining in prayer throughout the Studdert-Kennedy meditation. A harpist played *Finlandia* softly during all the reading.]

O gain that lurkest ungained in all gain!
O Love we just fall short of in all love!
O Height that in all heights art still above!
O Beauty that dost leave all beauty pain!
Thou unpossessed that makest possession vain,
See these strained arms which fright the simple air,
And say what ultimate fairness holds thee, Fair!
They girdle Heaven, and girdle Heaven in vain;
They shut, and lo! but shut in their unrest.
Thereat a voice in me that voiceless was:
"Whom seekest Thou through the unmarged arcane,
And not discernest to thine own bosom prest?"
I looked. My clasped arms athwart my breast
Framed the august embraces of the Cross.

                            Francis Thompson

When you enter it you hear a sound. Listen long enough and you will learn that it is made up of the beating of human hearts, of the nameless music of men's souls— that is, if you have ears. If you have eyes, you will presently see the church itself—

The pillars of it go up like the brawny trunks of heroes; the sweet human flesh of men and women is moulded about its bulwarks, strong, impregnable; the faces of little children laugh out from every cornerstone; the terrible spans and arches of it are the joined hands of comrades; and up in the heights and spaces there are inscribed the numberless musings of all the dreamers of the world. It is yet building—building and built upon. Sometimes the work goes forward in deep darkness; sometimes in blinding light: now beneath the burden of unutterable anguish: now to the tune of great

laughter and heroic shoutings like the cry of thunder.
Sometimes, in the silence of night-time, one may hear the
tiny hammering of the comrades at work up in the dome
—the comrades that have climbed ahead."

Charles Rann Kennedy, *The Servant in the*
House; used by permission

21

O YONGE, FRESSHE FOLKES, HE OR SHE

Rejoice, O young man, in thy youth; and let thy heart cheer thee
in the days of thy youth, and walk in the ways of thine heart, and
in the sight of thine eyes; but know thou, that for all these things
God will bring thee into judgment.   ECCLESIASTES 11:9

Somehow Chaucer's early English spelling makes his "yonge,
fresshe folkes, he or she" sound younger and fresher than lovers
we meet today. But think how much more happily they could
have lived forever after, if only Chaucer had let his Troilus and
Cressida spend their summer in a Student Christian Work Camp,
repairing a torn world instead of tearing it to pieces socially
in "worldlye vanyte." His warning words bear rethinking:

O yonge, fresshe folkes, he or she,
In which that love up groweth with youre age,
Repeyreth hom fro worldlye vanyte,
And of youre herte up casteth the visage
To thilke God that after his ymage
Yow made, and thynketh al nys but a faire
This worlde, that passeth soone as floures faire.
And loveth hym, the which that right for love

Upon a crois, oure soules for to beye,
First starf, and roos, and sit in hevene above;
For he nyl falsen no wight, dar seye,
That wol his herte al holly on hym leye.
And syn he best to love is, and most meke,
What nedeth feynede loves for to seke?

For it has always been wise Christian counsel to fix the heart on the unfailing love of God. Chaucer's Troilus and Cressida were young and brave and beautiful. But—as he told his fourteenth-century boys and girls—their tragedy was being too much wrapped up in themselves and their temporal happiness. Whereas today's yonge fresshe folkes, he or she, find in their outstretched hands a tent of protectiveness and a bridge to another world.

Take Madeleine Barot. Brilliant young brunette who had studied at the Sorbonne, won the *Prix de Rome,* and was completing four years in archaeology in Italy when all hell seemed to break loose across Europe. Instantly interned as an alien in Rome, she managed to be evacuated back into France by diplomatic train, reaching Paris the very day the Nazis marched in.

What to do? Madeleine Barot noticed Nazis ruthlessly clapping into prison camps all Jews, and any Christians who objected publicly to such injustice. It was then that CIMADE was born, impressive initials which stood for her equally impressive *"Comité Inter-Mouvements auprès des Evacués."* (Begun with a combined capital of only thirty dollars.)

"We can't just sit back and watch!" said she and three other yonge, fresshe folkes who walked straight into prison camps, asked the astonished guards to arrest them so that they could live and eat and sleep exactly like those interned—without proper food or proper shelter or proper care.

A rugged experience! Yet soon twenty-two other yonge, fresshe folkes joined CIMADE, all willing to be physically miserable if only they could conduct nursery classes, outdoor games, concerts, discussion groups, Bible classes for these wretched war victims.

When the Gestapo began rounding up more Jews into extermination camps, CIMADE took secret steps against such wholesale cremations: "This is no time to be legal!" they cried, and dared to go underground in their rescue efforts. Madeleine Barot herself managed to visit every concentration camp in France to set up the secret schemes; she personally enlisted hundreds of young Christians—many in their early teens—to help smuggle small groups of Jews under cover of darkness through hazardous barbed wire, across meadows and forests, up perilous mountain passes into Switzerland. Where the World Council of Churches took over.

Even when the war ended, a million miserable refugees from Poland, Yugoslavia, Rumania, Hungary and France itself were stranded—homeless, hopeless, helpless. Among these displaced persons CIMADE built barracks and opened Christian Centers, usually with two French and two non-French yonge, fresshe folkes in charge. Other church youth movements in Switzerland, Sweden, England and America sent volunteers. And even now, ten years later, they are still at it.

Or, take Agape. A village started in the heart of a young Florentine pastor, Tullio Vinay. He dreamed up a community of love where there would be no more Italians or Americans or Germans, no more Lutherans or Calvinists or Episcopalians. Just Christians. A place of great loveliness where people could come from the ends of the earth, shake hands, sit down, and talk about how to bring the Kingdom of God on earth. He chose a spot in the foothills of the Piedmontese Alps, wild and romantic, where his Waldensian ancestors had held out for centuries against papal persecutions.

Tullio and a thousand yonge, fresshe folkes from all over Europe and America felled trees, cracked rocks, poured cement foundations until three buildings of that dream village came true: a place devoted to labor and prayer. As Carlo Lupo said when they dedicated those great stone houses in that picturesque setting: "With all the respect we have for ecumenical councils and doctors of theology, we must recognize that theological discussion belongs to a past state in church development. Today's religious revolution is a social transformation, not the social transformation of the Marxists, who continue to see work as a hated necessity, but a recognition that work is an act of love."

The word "Agape" itself means brotherly love: the dream of a young Waldensian pastor built by yonge, fresshe folkes.

But think, too, about Thailand where twice over this same dream has materialized. The first scene is set in Chiengrai, in 1951. Of the forty-one campers two came from Burma, six from Japan, two from Malaya, two from the Philippines and twenty-eight from Thailand itself, met together with a missionary leader to build a rice granary and lay the foundation for a new church at the Christian Co-operative Farm, where sixty Christian families had been living a year.

But as Ikuyo Abe said later: "We gathered in our work camp not only to build the granary and the church, but to build bridges between nations, races, and cultures." For how she and George Ruiz from the Philippines had dreaded meeting each other! He hated all Japanese—had they not slain his father and brothers, and burned down his family home? He made up a tough talk to put Ikuyo in her proper place when they met. She had thought up a superior speech to use on him, too. But after one crew had been going full tilt all day, pouring concrete, and another crew kept carrying twelve bags of cement an hour to feed the mixing boxes, and a third crew kept rushing their tractor down to the river bed for fresh supplies of clean sand and gravel, and a fourth crew kept a bucket brigade going to supply water, with carpenters trying hard to keep ahead of pourers, and lumbermen keeping ahead of carpenters by supplying new boards for new forms, and Benjie, the camp elephant, shoving huge logs in place for the sawyers—then all that busy Ikuyo Abe said to George Ruiz was "Hello!" And all that any decent Filipino could say to such a decent Japanese was "Hello!"

Over and over this old sharp prejudice simply evaporated, with sixty Siamese families looking on with delight when Chantrakom stood up to speak. For everyone had watched with surprise this grandson of King Rama IV (the king in *Anna and the King of Siam*) enter a work camp. But nobody watched with more surprise than this young man himself: he who had never lifted a finger found himself lifting and lugging logs, and liking it. He was surprised at finding no barriers of class or race or nationality. He liked that too. And although he knew exactly what an upheaval he would need to go through with his Buddhist family, later, he said he had had a vision of Jesus Christ in action, and would like to dedicate the rest of his life to this Master, then and there.

That very evening this grandson of a King of Siam was baptized in the village chapel with two of the farmers' babies: himself a bridge from old aristocracy to new democracy.

In 1953 a similar miracle happened in the Philippines, even more dramatically. For at long last the work camp directors had cleared all papers for four young Japanese students to be permitted to enter the Philippines, with other Chinese, Korean, Siamese, Australian and American work campers, and forty Filipino students. Their project was rebuilding College Laguna in Los Banos, badly destroyed by bombs in the war. The clearances came through, finally. And all this time a certain Filipino ex-army officer had gone around fuming: "I will kill the first Japanese I meet!"

But who would want to kill four yonge, fresshe folkes down on their kness, clearing stumps from the bombed earth in a college backyard, leveling lawns, planting flowers? Even hauling bricks, pouring concrete. The two Japanese girls in particular made such a vivid impression that nobody could bear to think of their going back to Japan: "Why can't they stay and go to college here with us?" the Filipino students kept asking. And two scholarships were contributed so that Kazuko Nagatani and Kiyoe Nazata could study that year at Silliman University—to continue building their bridge of reconciliation. And to prove that they were building it, who should offer them free room and board in his own house but the Filipino army officer who had vowed to kill the first Japanese he met! Yet now he wanted his own family to see for themselves, moment by moment, what astonishing creatures these Japanese girls were?

And last, there is Anna-Brites Engne's story from Scandinavia. For Sweden seemed almost too secure to need a work camp:

no unemployment, no social problems, no poverty, no refugees. And for the past twenty years the small town of Hallstahammar had definitely voted that no, they did *not* want a church! So why on earth had all these yonge, fresshe folkes come to town to build a bell tower?

"We do not want you here! And nobody goes to church anyhow!"

Miss Engne was director of the group. And there they were: up at seven, praying out on their worksite by seven-thirty, determined to build away for dear life, not matter who said "No." Curious citizens strolled by to criticize, but lingered to admire such energy. Invitations arrived for supper parties down in the town. Certain younger Hallstahammarians started working, themselves. So that the bell tower was going to be ready long before their five weeks were over. They cleared away rocks and laid a perfect path up from the town to the tower. And still they were ahead of schedule. So of course the only sensible thing to do with leftover leisure was to start digging the foundation for the church itself. Never mind that nobody wanted the church! Never mind that the state had not granted permission! Never mind that not a blueprint had been drawn up to show what kind of a building this church would be. The yonge, fresshe folkes dug on and on. Deeper and deeper, wider and wider.

On the day when the bell tower was dedicated, twelve hundred people lined the newly-laid path up the hill. The bishop and pastors from nearby places formed a processional, followed by the jubilant campers themselves. Four of these yonge, fresshe folkes pulled the ropes, and let the bells ring out over Hallstahammar for the first time.

But departure from town was by no means the end of this chapter. For one hundred men and women volunteered four hours a night for six weeks, in order to finish the foundation. Every Saturday night when the bells were rung, windows and doors down in the town were flung open, and fully fifty persons climbed to the tower for prayers. Then there was a continued-in-our-next chapter, the following summer. For in 1954, campers came from England, Germany, Holland, Finland, Italy, Switzerland, America, as well as one from South Africa, one from Malaya, and two from behind the Iron Curtain. They did every imaginable job—masonry in the crypt and sacristy, cement on the floors, carpentry, and so on. It was thrilling to find that Hallstahammar wanted a *brick* church, with a *crypt*. The year before they had wanted nothing. But now this sudden gladness. Also they saw East confronting West, Hindu confronting Christian, and Hallstahammar itself confronting all these yonge, fresshe folkes. So that once again, as Peter warned: "Judgment must begin at the house of God." With a thousand work campers a summer changing viewpoints everywhere they go.

Mankind is now in one of its rare moods of shifting its outlook.
Alfred N. Whitehead

*What whispers are these, O lands, running ahead of you, passing
    under the seas?*
*Are all the nations communing? Is there going to be one heart
    to the globe?*
*Is humanity forming en masse? for lo! tyrants tremble, crowns
    grow dim,*
The earth, restive, confronts a new era . . .
Your dreams, O years, how they penetrate through me!
(I know not whether I sleep or wake.)
*The performed America and Europe grow dim, retiring in shadow
    behind me,*
*The unperformed, more gigantic than ever, advance, advance
    upon me.*

Walt Whitman

22

THE BASKET THAT OPENED A DOOR

Behold I have set before thee an open door, and no man can shut it.
                                                    REVELATION 3:8

Once before there had been a Tea Party in Boston, famous in American history because it started a war. But this one over in Brookline seemed simply suburban; side street, and all that. Just a few ladies in Mrs. Ropes' parlor for tea. Hardly enough to set off a revolution! Or win friends and influence people half a world away. Or open the tightest-closed door in Christendom.

But the first lady to see that straw basket on Mrs. Ropes' table cried: "Oh!" Then the rest of them cried: "Ah!" For who had ever seen anything so beautifully woven before? "But where on earth did it come from?" they asked in a chorus.

"Japan!" their hostess replied.

But nobody had ever heard of Japan: "Where is it?" they gasped. "Did Mr. Ropes find it on this last trip in his clipper ship?"

"Exactly! Not that he could get into Japan itself, of course. Nobody gets in! It's a hermit nation, they told him in China, where he bought this basket. It seems that in every port city of Japan there are huge placards warning outsiders away: 'No FOREIGNER MAY ENTER THIS COUNTRY ON PENALTY OF DEATH, NOT EVEN THE KING OF SPAIN, AND THE CHRISTIAN'S GOD HIM-SELF IF HE SHOULD ATTEMPT IT WOULD LOSE HIS HEAD.'"

The members of the Congregational Church in Brookline, Massachusetts, clucked their tongues and wagged their heads over such shocking statements. One of them said in dismay: "Really, we ought to pray that such wicked irreverence should stop!"

Everybody agreed. And the tea party turned into a prayer meeting then and there, that God might find ways of opening this hermit nation.

The moment they rose from their knees, however, one sensible soul said that surely just praying was almost too simple. Shouldn't they start something practical? Like giving money? So that when God opened the door they could send a missionary straight in? Why not begin by dropping some silver right now into Mrs. Ropes' basket, then go on meeting and praying and giving until something happened?

In 1827 this second Boston Tea Party became as demonstrative as that! Less noise than the first, maybe, but fully as much revolution. Since, moment by moment, mounting concern fired them. Month by month they met, prayed, gave. Year by year they deposited these gifts in a Boston Bank; and with that amazing arithmetic called Compound Interest, their original $600 grew into several thousands. But that door was still closed. Japan stayed as hermit as ever, with the same placards in the same port cities. The ladies in Brookline grew old and gray. Presumably they felt slightly disappointed.

"All this money, and no result!"

"All this money, and no use for it!"

For who in Brookline could see that moment by moment God had been moving in His own mysterious way somewhere else? stirring up all sorts of other people His wonders to perform? For while certain governments can hinder God temporarily, in the end nobody really stops Him. It simply takes a little longer than Brookline ladies liked. They had foreseen their money, *working*.

Whereas one dark night, in Nagasaki harbor, when a Dutch trading ship was sailing past, a Dutch New Testament fell overboard. Was a Dutch sailor leaning on the rail to admire the spectacular phosphorescence below? Perhaps. But no New Testament merely falls. For it had been caught in the net of a Nagasaki fisherman, who found it in his catch the next morning. The faithful fellow felt it was his duty to turn it over to Count Murata, captain of the port. And although this wealthy nobleman could not read Dutch, of course his curiosity about this small square Book was such that he dared do a clandestine and dangerous thing—secretly sending to China to see if the volume had ever been printed in Chinese: for then he might puzzle it out for himself.

Eventually this Chinese copy did reach him secretly. Sentence by sentence he tried translating it—secretly. And he shared the surprising story with his cousin, another nobleman. Moment by moment both their hearts were strangely warmed by the good news which seemed to sing out from the difficult Chinese script.

But . . . the placards still stood in every port city.

And Brookline dollars still drew interest in the Boston bank.

"Not yet!" God was saying.

But in His mysterious way He planted His foot upon the storm, exactly as the hymnbook tells us. Rather a terrific typhoon swept across the Pacific Ocean and blew a fishing trawler so far out to sea that the three fishermen lost their bearings, drifting for weeks until another storm cast their boat upon the coast of California, practically wrecked. As a page in Christian history, who can escape asking why three such strangers within our gates could not have been welcomed, brought to church, and introduced to Christianity then and there? So that a story started on the eastern shores of Massachusets could be continued on the California coast. But the west was sparsely settled in those early days. And foreigners were foreigners; slanting eyes were slanting eyes; an unknown tongue was an unknown tongue. So all that really happened was that somehow or other the three fishermen fastened their old trawler together again, and started back across the wide Pacific. And if the Brookline ladies had known about it, it would have seemed as if a heaven-sent opportunity had been lost forever. What with plenty of money in the bank! And all their praying! Fancy closing a door.

But God had other doors, and other wiser men also waiting and praying for the impossible to become possible. This time a German named Gutzlaff, living in China, but obsessed by the desire to carry the gospel into Japan. But, of course, those placards still stood in the port cities. So Gutzlaff stayed with his Chinese flock.

But a man could go on praying. So he prayed. Blindly, of course. Little dreaming that out in the middle of the Pacific Ocean three men in a tub were being buffeted hither and yon, in a panic lest they be cast up on Japanese shores, since it meant instant death for any long-absent Japanese subject to come sailing back to Japanese ports.

Early one morning some of Gutzlaff's parishioners knocked at his door and handed over three dazed and half-drowned fishermen whose ship had been wrecked the night before on their treacherous rocks. Nobody could understand a word they said. But everybody knew Gutzlaff's heart: wide and welcoming. Maybe he would not mind these weird new specimens? Gutzlaff gave one glance. Grasped God's glorious plan. Gripped three Japanese hands, grinning his welcome. For now he could learn Japanese from his three guests. It was as simple as that! Get some of the Bible ready to enter Japan as soon as the placards came down. So, moment by moment, they helped him retell in their own language the lovely life of The One who made the lame leap and the blind see—until there was the New Testament —ready! There was Gutzlaff—ready! There were three new Christian converts—ready! And over in Boston, plenty of money —ready!

But the placards still stood. And in the end, Gutzlaff died. In China! But that was by no means the end of his story. For the Chinese built a lighthouse on their treacherous rocks, in his memory. Rather an unusual lighthouse. For whenever the great light inside revolved in each new direction, the Chinese had built in a speaking device to call out over the waves his beloved name: "Gutzlaff!" "Gutzlaff!" "Gutzlaff!" So that—east, west, north, south—the name of the man who cared so much might remind them constantly that the knowledge of God shall cover the earth as the waters cover the sea.

But—not yet!

Not with those placards still up. Therefore, the money went on drawing interest in the Boston bank. Gutzlaff's Bibles stayed stacked in a Chinese church. Count Murata went on trying his best to translate the impossible Chinese into possible Japanese, to see what on earth this disturbing Book was about. Everywhere the revolution was working! Like yeast—nudging and dislodging and pushing. Like a bridge—linking and joining and connecting unrelated events.

Then came Jonathan Goble, able-bodied seaman, also obsessed with the dream of getting into Japan. It seemed sensible to enlist on a merchant vessel sailing to China. Then, one evening, near the Japanese coastline, Jonathan Goble broke his bold plan to the other sailors, explaining that as soon as it was dark enough he would jump overboard, swim secretly to shore, hoping to land on some unguarded beach where he could walk inland; learn the language; and live the rest of his life as a missionary.

The sailors said he was crazy! Hadn't he heard of the death-dealing placards? Well then, did he want to lose his head? Apparently he was willing to risk it. For they went down to their bunks, blue as indigo, after hearing the splash of his dive and seeing the strokes of his arms as he swam toward shore. All night they pictured him, drawn and quartered, tortured, beheaded. But in the morning there he was on deck again—rather shy, and totally disgruntled. He said he had landed on the beach at the very feet of a guard with a lantern! Apparently the Japanese felt this poor foreigner had fallen overboard from that ship discernible out on the horizon line. Somehow it seemed polite to put the stranger into his sampan and row him back to safety.

The sailors laughed until they cried: "Such luck! That will teach you your lesson!"

But no, Jonathan Goble was convinced that on some even darker night, farther north, his plan was worth trying again. No threat of a placard could stop him. So once more, the splash! Once more, that white body, swimming off into the black night. Once more, their ghastly visions of a beheaded Goble.

Actually an almost identical outcome brought him back to his ship, safe, but scowling. Another Japanese guard had found him on shore, and returned him courteously.

The sailors grew hilarious in their relief in seeing their shipmate unharmed: "Now you will learn!" they hinted.

But no, Jonathan Goble thought up a brighter scheme. How about being nailed up inside a barrel, he and a hatchet? For what guard would suspect an innocent keg bobbing up on some sandy beach?

Every sailor felt this was still more highly hazardous. Yet he forced them to nail him up and launch his barrel the moment the tide turned to run shoreward. They pictured him dazed and dizzy in his new doom. The next morning, however, he had again been brought back by a gallant guard who had spotted the barrel rolling over and over by the incoming waves, and then had watched with surprise as a man hatcheted open an exit, like a chicken out of an egg. Apparently it had looked suspiciously like foul play by shipmates . . . the least one could do was to give the poor fellow another chance, therefore.

Jonathan Goble acknowledged, then, that undoubtedly God had no intention of converting Japan by any clandestine conquest. So when his ship returned to America, he turned heaven and earth to enlist on Admiral Perry's flagship which the President of the United States was sending to the Emperor of Japan, with trade treaties designed to open the port cities. Legitimate, at last!

On a Sunday morning in 1853 Jonathan Goble stood on deck as they steamed into Nagasaki harbor. The sailors sang "All people that on earth do dwell." But the next morning when Admiral Perry went on shore to present the trade treaties, neither he nor the Emperor nor Jonathan Goble knew that a Dutch Bible had been fished from that very harbor, that Count Murata was fascinated by it; that Gutzlaff had slaved over translating it; that Brookline money waited in a Boston bank; that God does things by decades, sometimes.

Whereas Jonathan Goble was a man in a hurry. Dumbfounded that this time he was not even to set foot in Japan! For the President of the United States felt the Emperor should be given a year to think through the trade treaties. Therefore, the flagship steamed slowly away, and Jonathan Goble was the most disappointed man on board. Until a few days later when news spread over the ship that a Japanese stowaway had been hiding below decks, and had now emerged, starving. Nobody knew what to do with him. Nobody but Jonathan Goble! who sponsored him instantly; took him to his home; converted him; learned Japanese from him; translating the Gospel of Matthew in readiness for the day when trade treaties would be signed, placards would come down, and a Christian could enter with the first convert and the first gospel. For what did he know of Gutzlaff, and three earlier converts, and that roomful of waiting Testaments? Or, of a nearby Boston bank with enough deposits now to send several missionaries through the door.

For at long last that door did open. Mr. Goble and his Gospel and his convert entered. For many years he went around saying all the sentences he had always wanted to say, meeting all the Japanese people he had always wanted to meet. Purely as a by-product, it is perfect to know that Jonathan Goble is still in action on all Japanese streets. For his wife became an invalid, and it was for her personal comfort that this creative man invented the jinrikisha—now so familiar a Japanese sight that surely we should remember it in connection with a Christian intent on spreading the Good news swiftly.

This means that a Baptist missionary was at work. A Congregational collection was being spent. Lutheran Testaments were being distributed. And Bible societies everywhere were printing Holy Scriptures, Old and New.

One of them fell into the hands Neesima. As a youth he was puzzled by the idols on his family godshelf, so helpless to help themselves. He planted one outdoors, to see what would happen. The thing that happened was the growth of a grain of rice, part of an offering laid on the idol's palm—plainly more alive than the idol. It was then that he opened a Bible and read: "In the beginning God created the heaven and the earth." It was exactly what he wanted to know. So there was a big, able, alive God, was there? Since this astonishing Book had on its front page the words "Printed in New York City, U.S.A.," his next logical step was to get there quickly. So he stowed himself away on a ship headed for New York. When hunger drove him out of hiding, Captain Hardy adopted him as a son; put him through college;

and before James Hardy Neesima sailed home for Japan, he stood with outstretched hands in a large St. Louis auditorium, saying to the people: "How can I stir from this platform until you put into my hands money enough to build a Christian University in my country, in order that other boys as puzzled as I once was may learn about God?" Christians gave him that money; and Doshisha University still stands as his monument.

Everybody knows about Kagawa's life. How he moved one Christmas Day, many years ago, from a home of comfort down into a one-room hut in the slums. How not even tuberculosis nor trachoma are able to stop his incessant labors; his fellow workers say of his tireless energy: "He is so busy he forgets to die!" Even locked up in prison by his own people during the war, he said of his cell: "I could meditate with that wall."

So that the second Boston Tea Party led to revolution, also. But, decade after decade, a one-man revolution: which is the way God usually works. Looking back, the delicate spans linking land with land loom large and mystical, like some rare old Japanese print done in monotones—bridges bind distant banks! travelers toil across, faces bent over a Book! And it seems no surprise, therefore, that the Emperor took off his crown, or consented to read the Bible regularly with Mr. Kosaki of the Kyodan, or sent for Elizabeth Vining to open windows for the Crown Prince, as only a Quaker could open them. Almost as if the word of the Lord had come to the Emperor the way it once came to Ezekiel: *"Remove the diadem, and take off the crown; this shall not be the same: exalt him that is low, and abase him that is high. I will overturn, overturn, overturn it: and it shall be no more, until He come whose right it is; and I will give it Him"* (Ezekiel 21:26-27).

THESE JAPANESE PROVERBS ALL CAME TRUE!

No rock so hard but that a little wave could beat admission in a thousand years.

*Everything must wait its turn—peach blossoms for the
second month, and chrysanthemums for the ninth.*

Who travels for love finds a thousand miles only one mile.

The journey of a thousand miles begins with one step.

He who is in haste fishes in an empty pool.

*The trouble is that I am in a hurry, but God Almighty
is not!*

Theodore Parker

23

THIS WATCH CHAIN IS NEVER TO BE SOLD

There is that scattereth and yet increaseth.   PROVERBS 11:24

When your father is a preacher and marries a Quaker who is
only eighteen, anything can happen. And the thing that happened was his watch chain. The one that was draped in two loops
across his vest through the middle buttonhole. The whole thing
began with a Deficit (capital D) in the denomination. He broke
the news about it at Sunday breakfast.

"Darling," he said, "I hate to admit it, but our denomination
has come down with a dreadful Deficit! And the people at headquarters expect my sermon this morning to help wipe it out."

"Deficit?" she repeated, laughing. "But what on earth is that,
Henry? Thee makes it sound like a contagious disease."

Incredible how financially firm and spiritually sound these

Quakers are, he thought fondly. Then proceeded to picture the doom closing denominational doors all over the map.

"Good gracious!" she gasped. "So this is what I have married into?"

"I'm afraid so! But the point is that when I get through preaching, the ushers will come around with pledge cards. Just in case you never saw one before in a Friend's meeting, see—this is the way it looks. So grab one, sweetheart; and down here on this dotted line write our two names. Then up above, opposite the dollar sign, write in this amount of money—like this. Think you can manage?"

"Probably," she smiled sensibly.

But neither of them realized how totally different it would all sound when he let out his big voice eloquently, and began booming down at the congregation from his high pepperbox pulpit: "Do you realize what you have been doing, good friends? It is really nothing to you that all over India and Burma the sick are again being borne-of-four, as in the days when our Lord was here among men? But this time there will be no door for that stretcher to enter, for every one of our denominational hospitals will be closed. No doctor will be there—they will have had to sail home. No nurse. No clinic. No dispensary. So that the sick must suffer in pain until they die, with none to help them. Is it really nothing to you that all over China and Japan schools have had to be closed, causing thousands upon thousands of boys and girls to grow up unable to read and write, totally ignorant that there is a Book called the Bible or news of a Saviour who especially said: 'Let the little ones come unto me'? Is it really nothing to you that all over Asia and Africa churches must now be locked, and their matchless messages about Jesus Christ silenced, because missionaries must sail home?" On and on boomed his voice, painting pictures. Clearer and clearer grew the shocking situation.

But there was still another thing he could do with his voice. For after letting it out, he could gather it in! So, with almost unbearable softness, he gentled his tone, and whispered down as his eyes swept over his congregation: "And who started this sorry situation? Who but you? And you? And you? and you?" It was then that his eyes lighted on his little Quaker bride, sitting in her pew, shocked and stricken by this new concern. For how much worse than Henry had hinted at breakfast! If only she dared walk down that long aisle to the platform, and, standing on tiptoe, whisper up to the high pepperbox pulpit: "Henry, we weren't nearly generous enough at breakfast, were we? Would it be all right to double it?"

But how unthinkable to do anything as dramatic. So she took matters into her own hands; for when the pledge cards were passed out, with considerable exhilaration she wrote only her own name, down on the lower dotted line; then, up above, opposite the dollar sign, she dared to double the amount agreed upon at breakfast.

Probably this is the moment to tell a secret you may not know. But the truth is that many a minister who lets his voice out vigorously and gathers it in gently is often more moved than anybody else in the congregation. So much so that Henry felt conscience-stricken over the trifling sum which had seemed adequate at breakfast. But how on earth could a man signal to a Quaker across all those pews: "Double it, darling! Double it!" Since this was obviously impossible, he jeopardized his balance by leaning far down from his high pulpit to reach for a pledge card. Firmly he signed his own name. Firmly he doubled the amount mentioned at breakfast.

Whereupon both bride and groom walked on air until they met at luncheon.

"Let me tell thee what I did at church," she bragged boldly.

"But just let me tell you what I did," he interrupted.

"Ladies first!"

"Very well, my love, and what did you do?" as if a Quaker could do little. But she had done plenty! For between them they had pledged away their entire salary for the next six months.

There may be denominations where a preacher can go to the treasurer on a Monday and admit that when he had let his voice out on a Sunday he had rather run away with himself: "And so, my dear fellow, if it's all the same to you, suppose I cut that pledge in half?"

But not in that particular denomination. And not with that particular Deficit—so drastic, so desperate. Apparently the only possible thing was to ask the trustees for six months' salary in advance, embarrassing as that would be.

"They will guess at once that I ran away with myself," he sighed ruefully.

"But wasn't it God leading me and thee, Henry? And He never runs away with anybody! So we must not spoil His beautiful secret plan for us. The only thing for thee to tell thy trustees is that thee married a Quaker wife who is only eighteen years old, and that somehow the poor thing simply can't make both ends meet—so, thee needs thy salary in advance! Then our secret will belong to us, and we won't get laughed at."

On Monday, therefore, he said all this to the trustees. They stroked their chins thoughtfully, as trustees must, when handling sacred funds. But actually these guileless gentlemen considered this Quaker girl the most charming creature ever in their parsonage, and their vote to advance the amount was unanimous.

That meant that the pledge was paid promptly. But . . . the cupboard was bare; and two healthy young stomachs craved three meals a day.

It was then that he took to calling on his flock at mealtimes. Often the hostess issued no invitation, so Henry would sniff appreciatively: "Mrs. Van Rensaeller, what a marvelous smell!" Half the time she would rise and shut the kitchen door, apologetically: "My new maid! She never shuts it!"

The preacher and his bride landed on the sidewalk limp with laughter: "Henry, thee was hinting!"

"Of course I was! I'm starving!"

"I'm hungry, too," she admitted.

Because he simply adored her, he bent over solicitously: "Darling, are you sorry we did it?"

"No indeed!" and she wagged her head from left to right in no uncertain fashion.

"But would you do it again, if you had the chance?"

"Oh yes! Yes indeed!" And she nodded her lovely head up and down vigorously.

After that, it often happened that when they were in some

room with luscious smells, but no least hope of sharing the meal, Henry fell into the habit of catching Mary's eye and forming his lips into the question: "Sorry?" Always her head moved swiftly left to right, twice over. After which he shaped the next silent question: "Do it again?" And always her head moved affirmatively up and down as if saying: "Yes! Oh yes!"

Finally he said, with reverence: "Do you know what your little ritual means to me? I know that Quakers have small use for symbols, but do you realize that your precious head is actually making the sign of the cross? See—like this!" And he imitated her.

She was completely radiant about it: "Oh, how I thank thee, Henry, for putting something mystical into this discipline; for now I guess I can take it better! In His name! For His sake!"

It was then that he sold his gold watch chain for sixty dollars. To buy food. And although you have often heard that money went further in those days, it still could not go nearly far enough. And where the congregation used to see a gold chain in two loops draped across the preacher's vest, sparkling in the sunlight when he let his voice out or gathered it in, now there was simply a shoestring in two loops, threaded through the middle buttonhole, which pleased nobody.

So certain bolder members mentioned it to Mary: "Why does your husband wear a shoestring these days?"

"He likes it; doesn't thee like it?"

So that their secret was still their secret. Just as their hunger was still their hunger, and knew no holiday.

Then, when the six months' ordeal ended, with the prospect of a salary again, the preacher was called to a big city church. And the preacher's wife was just enough wiser in the ways of congregations to choose one woman in the new church to be trusted with the secret—*trusted to tell it,* that is!

"I don't want thee to think that my husband is a country bumpkin because he wears that shoestring. You see, it really represents six of the most memorable months of our lives, when we carried the whole world on our shoulders. Can thee count up? That makes twenty-six endless weeks and 182 endless days of never having nearly enough to eat. But out of it we made this ritual—see, the sign of the cross, to say: 'No, I'm not sorry we did it!' And: 'Yes, I'd do it again!' I knew thee would love knowing what a beautiful blessing came to us both. My husband sold his gold watch chain, to buy food."

"Oh!" cried the woman who had been trusted with the secret. "Oh, you poor young things!" So of course she could not keep it! After which the shoestring seemed like a silent sermon to every pocketbook.

Then came Christmas. With a tall tree loaded with presents for everybody, given out by a giant Santa Claus. At last only one tiny box was left, up near the topmost star. Taking it down, Santa Claus called: "Will the minister please come forward."

When Henry lifted the lid of the jewelry box a card read: "THIS WATCH CHAIN IS NEVER TO BE SOLD FOR FOREIGN MISSIONS." He wore it all the rest of his life, draped in two loops across his vest, threaded through the middle buttonhole, sparkling in the sunshine whenever he let his voice out or gathered it in. But it was more than a watch chain, really! The two loops were like the spans of the bridge the beggars built—because, wrapped in their clothes, they had what it takes to link shore with shore, land with land, race with race; and all of them with God.

Lo, soul! seest thou not God's purpose from the first?
The earth to be spanned, connected by network,
The peoples to become brothers and sisters,
The races, neighbors . . .
The oceans to be crossed
  The distances brought near,
The lands to be welded together.

Walt Whitman

The most radical division that it is possible to make of
humanity is that which splits it into two classes of

creatures: those who make great demands on themselves,
piling up difficulties and duties; and those who demand
nothing special of themselves, but for whom to live is to
be every moment what they already are, without impos-
ing on themselves any effort toward perfection; mere
buoys that float on the waves.

José Ortega y Gasset

24

NOT EVEN ANDREW CARNEGIE COULD GIVE BOOKS THIS WAY

Let the beauty of the Lord our God be upon us; and establish
Thou the work of our hands, yea, the work of our hands establish Thou it.   PSALM 90:17

If ever a human being was a perfect footnote on a perfect
psalm it was Grace Chapman that whole year through. For the
beauty of the Lord was obviously upon her. And surely He
established the work of her hands, unbelievably. It seems now
as if there must have been special joy in the presence of the
angels of God on each of the 365 days—not only because of the
sinners who repented, but also because of the saints who turned
up at all the proper times and proper places. Beginning with
the proper Bishop sailing on her ship from Australia to India.
For it could so easily have been some other Bishop going some
other place. But no, it was Bishop Azariah, of the Church of
South India! All their sentences clicked satisfactorily, also; but
probably he had to keep his wits about him every moment to
catch up with this contagious creature.

First, the avalanche of questions . . .

When will the big Mass Movement Conference be held, Bishop? I simply must be there, on account of my Gospel Primers; you know them? Oh, you *don't?* But I want to get them adopted all over India! They're only done in Urdu now, and although that's such a tough tongue to tackle, still the story method comes through simply and tenderly. That's why the Mass Movement Conference is what I'm going over for, especially; I want to show that even the most illiterate village woman can learn to read easily. Thrilling, isn't it? But I keep wondering if I will have time to stop off in the Philippines, too, to consult Frank Laubach, he does such superb literary work; on and on and on . . .

You can see why this was the proper Bishop for her to meet: naturally he knew the Mass Movement dates, since he was to be chairman of the conference himself. And she need have no fear about getting on the program, for he would put her there. And as for Urdu, yes, it really was a hard language, for he had never had time to learn it, himself, although it was the official tongue in his district. His own people spoke Telugu. Had she ever translated her Gospel Primers into Telugu?

Her answer was no, not yet. But she had been praying about it for two years, and had been saving money for it—oh, perhaps fifty dollars already for Telugu Primers.

"Fine!" said the Bishop, "you must come to Dornakal and stay with us!" So *that* was settled, too.

"And now let me run down to my stateroom to get an Urdu Primer. Perhaps you might even learn to read Urdu on shipboard, Bishop?"

"Perhaps I might!" he agreed. And that was settled also. For every morning Bishop Azariah took his Urdu lesson, astonished and enchanted by the ease of her Gospel method for teaching a person to read quickly.

Undoubtedly that was the moment when the angels began their rejoicing. For where else would a Bishop ever find time to learn languages except on a leisurely ocean trip? Obviously one of those occasions ordained of God. And with the added virtue of giving Grace Chapman's Primers their perfect sponsor.

Even stopping off in the Philippines proved unnecessary, for the Bishop explained that Dr. Laubach would be in India for this same Mass Movement Conference, and she could meet him there. Which was a godsend, for her trip had been financed by a friend: "This ought to be enough to last a year!" she said. But with such an uncertain itinerary, how could Grace Chapman calculate?

But there always seemed to be a voice directing her what to do next. For even on the train ride from Colombo across India something said: "Get off at Guntur." It was the next stop! The name of the city was familiar because, some years earlier, certain strangers had come to her door to ask for a glass of water. Casual as this was, they had seen her Gospel Primers, and had suggested that if she ever put them into the Telugu tongue, Mr. Bushman of Guntur would be her man. And here was Guntur!

Without any reservation, she arrived at the Travelers' Bungalow. They had been holding the only free room all day for a guest who had not shown up; and now it was 8 P.M.; so the manager let her have it.

Late as it was she was drawn irresistibly toward the Mission House. Then hesitated to knock so late at night. But seeing a young man about to enter, she made an inquiry, and found that he was a divinity student in town for an Adult Education Conference—"a big night for us all, for Frank Laubach will speak!"

So then she knew why she had been led to stop off in this strange town, midway of her trans-India trip: surely much simpler than that extra excursion to Manila. Yet this was only half of the wonder of the thrilling night. For when Mr. Bushman was introduced, he could hardly believe his ears: "Just wait till our Miss Miller meets you!" he gasped.

For it seems that in Dr. Laubach's literacy campaign there was immediate need for a simple primer for beginners, probably an economic theme would be sensible. And Miss Miller had been chosen to write it. But she had been praying that God would not require this of her, since her own dearly-beloved task was evangelism, and it seemed almost wicked to substitute something secular. Yet here came her answer walking in the front door, Primers and all! *Gospel* Primers, too, with which she fell in love at once.

It kept right on being Grace Chapman's year, no matter where she went. And she went 12,000 miles! Into all corners of India! Moreover, her money held out, due to occasional travel refunds. Although the part she loved best about her tentative invitations to visit small stations was the cautious P.S. which asked: "But be sure to tell us exactly how much your coming will cost us." To which she was happy to reply: "Not one penny will be needed!"

She was invited to be Honorary Literacy Secretary for India, Burma and Ceylon; and her Gospel Primers were translated into a number of languages: English, Persian, Hindi, Panjabi, Marathi, Kashmiri, Guzarati, Canarese. Once when she wanted a certain important man to order 200 Primers, he was thoroughly indifferent to them; but she ordered 200 copies in her own name and stored them away. Almost as if she foresaw that exactly three months later he would write ordering 200; she never told him why, instead of waiting to have them printed, she could ship them off at once.

She had the delight of going to Isabella Thoburn College to instruct the students about how illiterates could be taught by her methods. The girls would then adopt whole villages, make charts and go regularly to these groups. Her priceless little Primers, each language in its own gay cover, appealed first to the eye. But it was Grace Chapman's reward to watch new readers plod patiently across the page falling in love with the unfolding story of Jesus Christ, eager to know what happened next, the divine magnetism touching them. A whole caste in Travancore had become Christians: "with the light of the great God upon their faces."

Contented with all this activity nobody was prepared for the doctor's verdict when she had to go to the Mission hospital for a checkup. Quite suddenly, from apparent health, this hopeless case of cancer. With only a few days to set things in order.

But the miracle of spirit over matter was impressive. Everybody remembered how she had once said: "A saint is one who is at leisure from himself and his own affairs, confident that God is bringing out all things well." For now it was plain that she believed every word of it.

In the most natural way she explained: "Last year I felt it was a great year to be alive! This year will be a great year to pass over!"

As beautifully as that. With the work of her hands established.

There is no doubt that not even Andrew Carnegie could give books as she gave them—with a blessing on every page for every reader. But the wonderful side of this story is that now you can be a Mr. Carnegie, yourself! For a special "Indian Village Library" has been prepared recently, to Dr. Laubach's delight— very simple little Christian books for new readers, packed in a portable tin case, complete with a little oil lamp, for night readers. And anybody can bring this benediction to a bookless village by sending twenty-five dollars to The Christian Literature and Literacy Committee, 156 Fifth Avenue, New York 10, N. Y. For this is indeed a great year to be alive!

Yet to live always as though time were a bridge is pre-cisely what the saints do. Their eyes are forever on the Eternal, that Beyond which is also here and now and within, because they have cultivated the art of seeing eternity through that narrow slit—the ever now moment.
The Path of the Saint

WHEN WE SAW THE GLORY OF HIS SUN-SET-TING WE SAID: "IT WILL BE A LOVELY DAY TOMORROW."
Epitaph in an old English churchyard

25

I LOVE LUCIDITY

And when they bring you into the synagogues and unto magistrates, and powers, take ye no thought how or what thing ye shall answer, or what ye shall say. For the Holy Ghost shall teach you in that self-same hour what ye ought to say.   LUKE 12:12

Lucidity might have been Sarah Chakko's middle name. Her family name was more unpronounceable—Mazurancheriparamnath. But the lucidity was quotable all over Amsterdam in World Council circles; and even outside—among *"powers,"* like that Coronation dinner party at the Queen's palace. We all rejoiced beforehand when Wilhelmina invited her; and we were consumed with curiosity afterward: "How did it go?"

"All right. They put me next to the Prince."

"Prince Bernhardt?" we gasped. "But what on earth could you say to him?" For of course we would have been reduced to weather, ourselves: "Do you often have such cold snaps in August?" That sort of insipidity. But Sarah's casual lucidity probably pricked the poor Prince badly. She told us that after her first spoonful of soup, she turned to him and said: "You know, Prince Bernhardt, I wouldn't want to be in your shoes from now on!"

It sounded guileless. So he beamed on her graciously: "But my wife is the real one to be sorry for!" After which he cast around in his mind for something suitable to match her frankness. Finding it when he became conscious of her becoming peacock-blue sari with its broad gold border. (Ah-h! Of course— *India!*) So he turned and said: "I want a lady from India to know how sorry Holland is to find itself at war with the Netherland East Indies."

171

"Yes, I should think you would be sorry, Prince! But just why are you at war, anyhow? I have never really heard, in so many words."

Such lucidity seemed lamentable at a man's own table: "It is, perhaps, too long a story for now!" he reproved her coldly, attacking his fish instead.

"I am sure it is, Prince," she sighed softly, attacking her own fish. But her lucid wits supplied lucid replies: all that rich rubber lying around loose, or almost loose—for what are trees to tap wth enough natives to tap them; and all that oil; all that et cetera, et cetera to fill Dutch purses.

The Prince had been brooding, too. Apparently over her unjust jibe, for he justified his war by explaining: "The trouble over there is—the people aren't educated! If only they had had proper schooling, they would be able to govern themselves."

"How right you are, Prince! But I can't help asking—why aren't they better educated? The Dutch have owned the East Indies for over three hundred years; wouldn't you say that was long enough to educate everybody everywhere?"

Too annoyed to answer, he would have turned to the meek matron on his left when Sarah Chakko went ahead with the conversation as casually as ever: "Speaking of education in the Indies, you probably point with pride to Princess Kartini, don't you, Prince?"

"Pardon! That name once more? Princess—?"

"Raden Adjeng Kartini, of Java. Oh, surely you know about her? Her father was Regent at Djapara; and that 'Raden Adjeng' indicates membership in the nobility."

"No, the name is quite unknown to me."

"But not unknown to the rest of us over in my part of the globe, Prince! For she turned heaven and earth in the Netherland East Indies to bring education to all the illiterates, and especially to women. She was to education what Elizabeth Fry was to prisons, and Florence Nightingale to hospitals. When nobody in Holland lifted a finger, she lifted all ten of hers! With five fingers she wrote letters, and now they are all collected and bound in a book called *From Darkness to Light*. She had plenty of pen-friends here in Holland and she plied them with questions about everything on earth. And although she died fifty years ago, always on April 21 'Kartini Day' is still celebrated in Java. Before she was twenty she had founded a school at Djapara, herself. Quite a girl, Prince!"

"That I can see," he agreed, although probably appalled at this Atlas who carried much more of his particular corner of the planet on her shoulders than he had known existed. Apparently there was to be more: "And nowadays, in her memory, there are literally hundreds of 'Kartinischools' all over your islands. She died before she was twenty-five. In childbirth. Sometimes I am astonished at God, aren't you? To let a rare creature like that slip away. And yet she had done what nobody else had done. She had stirred everyone up to want something badly enough to get it. I suppose that's enough. Like leaven: 'Come on and get up!' But the lump likes being the lump. She was, for all illiterates, what Queen Esther was for the Jews, for I recall part of a sentence Kartini said, around 1900: *Even if I should perish halfway, I shall have helped prepare the way for Indian women.* And she did perish halfway. But that proved far enough. Quite a subject for a Queen!"

"Quite a subject," he agreed. But turned, nonetheless, toward the less lucid lady on his left. So, when Sarah came back to the Krasnapolski Hotel from the palace, she asked us: "Did I do the Prince wrong?"

"The point is, Sarah, did you do him up?" For we always wondered whether he would remember what was said; and why.

A few days later we saw more of Sarah Chakko's flame flare forth. For she presided every afternoon at a three-hour seminar for women delegates on the theme "The Life and Work of Women in the Church." The room was small and overcrowded, and none of us was prepared for the presence of Karl Barth, the Swiss theologian. Slightly dusty as to coat collar. Slightly stooped as to shoulders. Slightly unbrushed as to hair. Slightly prejudiced as to topic. And always very vocal. All in the German language; which meant a long period of translation after each of his speeches, which pivoted around Genesis Two: how first, God made man;

later, God made woman. So, a Rib was bound to be secondary. Q.E.D.! Or, take Christ choosing His twelve disciples—did He choose a woman? No. Or Paul? How about Paul, if you please? This went on and on, for days.

Until late one afternoon when the seminar was over and Dr. Barth was on his way downstairs. Miss Chakko made a point of catching up with him: "Now in regard to Genesis Two, Professor, it is only fair to remember that it happened long ago. And that there were no colleges for women in Eden at the time. A college education was exactly what Eve was in need of!"

"Translate her! What is she saying?"

So everybody stopped halfway down the staircase and tried to get that simple lucidity into all sorts of college German.

Dr. Barth looked untouched: "Try again," he suggested.

But Miss Chakko did not choose to be re-retranslated. She walked down two more steps and stopped there in his path; then turned and looked up at him with laughing brown eyes: "Dr. Barth, I cannot agree! I did not agree with your main speech to the big Assembly, either. You said that we ought to give up every thought that the care of the churches and the care of the world is our care! You called it a *dreadful, godless, ridiculous opinion that man is the Atlas who is destined to bear the world on his shoulders.* Dr. Barth, where does that put Jesus Christ's own picture of the Last Judgment, where everybody was expected to be an Atlas, bearing all the hungry, all the naked, all the prisoners on their shoulders? What made Peter bother with Dorcas, except that here was a Rib who would be useful in clothing the naked? Why did Paul believe in bearing one another's burdens and so fulfilling the law of Christ? As for me—I love Atlas!"

As for us on that staircase, we loved Atlas, too. But we loved lucidity more! Imagine daring to face up to a famous theologian fearlessly! Imagine laughing into his eyes and saying: "Of course, about women—Paul *admired* them! Think what Chloe did for him—diagnosing the divisions in the church at Corinth. Think what Priscilla did for him: 'laying down her neck for my sake.' Think what Phoebe did for him, carrying a letter all the way from Corinth to Rome. Everybody knows you can't trust letters to *men!* As for Jesus, He trusted women with all His big secrets, then later He would say: 'Well, go now and tell the menfolks.' At least, that's the way it was at the well, in Samaria. And in the garden, Easter, with Mary." In a strange sort of fashion Sarah herself became Atlas, bearing all the women in the Bible on her shoulders. We bungled things a little, trying to put all this into our bad German. But Dr. Barth kept right on looking slightly prejudiced, slightly perplexed. As somebody said later: "He was probably one of those anxious babies! I expect a nurse let him down too hard."

Then there was Sarah Chakko's encounter with the Bishop of Australia.

He came strolling into the dining room at the Hotel Krasnapolski, and chose our table. He said he liked sitting across from an American lady. But, of course, his pleasure was doubled when Sarah too came strolling over—in her cerise sari with the wide silver stripe. Who could keep his eyes off her? Not the Bishop. Not at first. Of course, later—well, later he looked away gladly.

"Sarah," we began, "this is the Bishop of Australia."

Without any further introduction she swept aside the bowl of hotel flowers in the center of the table, and leaned over to prop her elbows where the bowl had been: "My, but I'm glad to meet you, Bishop!" she said.

It was hard not to look flattered: "My dear young lady! But why so glad?"

"Because I have been wanting to ask somebody from Australia why your country passed an Exclusion Act to keep India out? Don't you realize that it broke our hearts? That it disillusioned all of us to have a Christian country so callous? Don't you know that half of our three hundred and fifty million people are starving? That half of us go to bed hungry every night? That half of us have only one meal a day? That half of us earn less than thirty dollars a year? Not that any of us *want* to leave India! But we simply have to find some place with room, and God's plenty. You have both. Lots of land. Few people. But no, you said: 'No Indians!' How could you pass that Exclusion Act, Bishop? How could you?"

"Wait a minute! Now wait a minute! My dear young woman, I didn't do it! I didn't have a single thing to do with it!"

"But Bishop! Bishop! Who tells your people every Sunday what to do next week? Who tells them what to think about and care about and pray about? Suppose India had been written on your heart, Bishop, all three hundred and fifty million of us? Wouldn't you have made everybody see how wasteful it is to have Indians dying with a life expectancy of only twenty-seven years? And Australia with enough and to spare!"

The Bishop looked over at us, appalled: "You tell her! Tell her I wouldn't hurt a fly, personally. Tell her that nobody in Australia asks bishops what acts should or shouldn't pass parliament. Tell her we aren't a hardhearted people at all. We are like Americans, really. Big and warmhearted and generous, really. You tell her!"

But something contagious had happened. We came down with an Atlas-aching, also. We came down with a perspective on history. For we said firmly: "But, Bishop, we won't be any comfort to you, since we are very hardhearted in America, ourselves. We passed an Exclusion Act, too, way back in 1924—to keep the Japanese out. There was a quota system, so it would have meant only one hundred Japanese a year. Surely we could have absorbed that number safely. But no, one hundred was one hundred too many. We didn't like the slant of their eyes, or their thrifty ways. But you may have heard how our Exclusion rankled. It literally exploded on December 7, 1941, at Pearl Harbor! Then on December 8 the Tokyo papers had a big headline: Admiral Tojo says we're beginning to get even. Seventy million enemies—getting even! We were scared, Bishop! So although we didn't have to, we rescinded an even older *Chinese* Exclusion Act. Just quietly tore it up! For there are four hundred million Chinese. Too many to offend. Although we have kept offending more than we should, Bishop. Once all our land belonged to the Indians. But we pushed them farther west and farther west from the good red earth out to the barren dry places. We made them 'wards.' But we forget about them, mostly. We didn't choose to stoop to pick our cotton crops. So somebody captured black slaves in Africa and brought them over in ships, against their wills. Not our own immediate families, of course. None of our own families would hurt a fly, either, Bishop. Like Saul—when Stephen was being stoned—we just stood by, consenting. Even a hundred years after we freed our slaves, fifteen million black Americans still can't always tell how free they really are. So I have come over on the side of Atlas, too; I think that everybody's sorrow is my sorrow."

Sarah reached out her hand to hold ours: *"Even if we perish halfway,"* she said, quoting Kartini.

And now that Sarah Chakko herself has perished, midway of her rich career, surely the secret of her lucid language can be seen in this "After Communion" prayer from the Liturgy of Malabar—used always in the ancient Orthodox Syrian Church of Malabar, to which she and her family have belonged for generations:

Strengthen, O Lord, the hands which have been held out to receive Thy holy things, that they may ever serve Thee. Grant that the tongues which have uttered the "Holy, Holy, Holy," may speak the truth; that the eyes which have seen Thy great love may also behold Thy blessed hope; that the feet which have trod Thy house may walk in the region of light; and that we who have received the living Body and Blood of Jesus Christ may be restored with newness of life, through the same Thy Son Jesus Christ our Lord. Amen.

Ancient Liturgy of Malabar; India, fifth century

The Altar fire is born of the rubbed stick.

Hindu proverb

We are on a journey and to us comes God's question, "Adam, where art thou?" And since we represent the youth of the countries from which we come we also have to face the question, "Where is thy brother?" In the spirit we show and the imagination we display depends the fruitfulness of our coming together. Let us not be too

clever in our cleverness nor yet too fearful in our little-
ness. But let us be humble in our ignorance, depending
on "the foolishness of God which is wiser than the wis-
dom of men." Like the Magi let us seek the King with
confidence, bringing as royal gifts the best of body,
mind, soul, and strength. Let us cast aside with courage
our preconceived notion as to where He can be found.
Let us be ready to be sent forth from His presence to
wherever He may send us.

Sarah Chakko, 1905-1954; principal of Isabella Thoburn College, Lucknow, India—to delegates of Third
World Conference of Christian Youth.

> *Above the individual,*
> *Like an ardent flame,*
> *Floats the standard of nationalism.*
> *Above nationalism waves the banner of race;*
> *But, free and untrammeled,*
> *Far above nationalism and race,*
> *Streams the oriflamme of the Spirit,*
> *For the Spirit knows naught of limitations.*

Gabriela Mistral, Chile; from *Women and The Way*,
Friendship Press, used by permission.

26

FAIR WHITE CLOTH

God hath chosen the foolish things of this world to confound the wise . . . and the base things which are despised, hath God chosen, yea, and things which are not, to bring to nought things that are: that no flesh should glory in His presence.

CORINTHIANS 1:27-29

Of all "base" bridges this one seemed by far the most foolish, but unforgettable, as it went soaring over land and sea, binding two unknown churches together, though half a world apart.

It began very simply in the sewing circle of the Woman's Society of the Ashland Avenue Baptist Church in Toledo, Ohio. Word had come from headquarters that, on account of war shortages, the babies on this earth all stood in dire need of diapers. Millions upon millions. So the Ashland Avenue women started their prosaic hemming. And although they must have talked as they sewed, probably nobody said: "This is sheer poetry we handle! This is the stuff that dreams are made of!" That would have sounded foolish and far-fetched. Mirth, maybe! But mystery? No! Who ever heard of such a thing?

Their box of diapers was shipped off to Burma. But, on arriving at the Rangoon dock, fighting was too fierce for freight to figure in anybody's life. For imprisonments and persecutions had upset normal life. And so the diapers waited. New Burmese babies were born . . . were bombed out of house and home . . . were bundled on the backs of parents for terrifying treks toward safety . . . escaped to still further places . . . stayed in hiding . . . escaped again . . . and again; with the box still standing on the dock, undelivered.

But at last the war ended. The enemy withdrew. Families came straggling home to see what was left. And freight started moving. Miss Helen Hunt received the Toledo box of diapers. Not nearly enough to go around among the large new crop of babies, of course, for not a scrap of cloth of any sort was obtainable in Burma. So, how distribute this boxload justly? Miss Hunt decided to divide them among ministers' wives who had—or were expecting—new babies. Only two apiece! And among other expectant mothers, the wife of the Reverend Maung Gale, pastor of Lanmadaw Baptist Church in Rangoon, received her two.

Meanwhile, with church members returning to Rangoon, they had rescued their sanctuary from rubble; someone had made and given a new hand-carved teakwood table to replace the one destroyed by looters, and Lanmadaw Church was now ready to hold its first communion service. As the preacher's wife waited in her pew she noticed how bare the communion table looked, with no fair white cloth to cover the bread and wine. Commonsense whispered: "But where would our good deacons ever hope to buy cloth in Rangoon? Or in all Burma, for that matter?" At which conscience whispered back: "Except in your own house, woman! Except in that little layette you are hoarding!"

It was then that she left her pew to hurry home and take the two new pieces of birdseye from their box. While carrying them in haste to the church she consecrated them: "Lord God, surely it will be well for my unborn child to sacrifice something special from his own comfort for making Thy House more suitable and sacred."

She walked down the middle aisle like a priestess celebrating some holy rite. Both minister and congregation watched her signal to the deacons to lift both the silver cup and the silver bread platter, while she laid one fair white cloth below these Elements, and then spread the other cloth above them. She returned quietly to her pew. But everybody sensed that some difficult decision had been made, and some great gift given to God. For as they looked around, they realized that these were the very walls of the first church Adoniram Judson had built. Everything they saw told of his long years of testing, too, and his triumphant unselfishness. So that all was beautiful and blessed, over in Burma.

But not so, back in Toledo, Ohio. Not when the pastor of the Ashland Avenue Church received an unexpected letter of gratitude from the Lanmadaw Church, thanking the Toledo ladies for their contribution which had made their first Lord's Supper in Rangoon seem like a benediction.

Benediction, indeed!

The Toledo pastor seemed shocked as he read this letter to his congregation. Immediately they were shocked, also. The women sat there, thunderstruck, thinking back to the year they hemmed those ridiculous little rectangles so absent-mindedly, not dreaming they would stir up such a fuss.

"Good gracious!" they groaned.

Their husbands turned to them with amusement: "Not half bad, my dear!" But of course not half good enough, either. It was then that a quickening seemed to spread from pew to pew. For it was obvious just what could be done. Therefore, with the same contagious enthusiasm by which the Lord had stirred up His people back in the days of Moses, He now stirred up the willing-hearted in the days of Herbert Haslam. The following letter tells the rest of the story which has built this unbreakable bridge between Toledo and Rangoon:

From the Ashland Avenue Baptist Church of Toledo, Ohio, to the Lanmadaw Baptist Church of Rangoon, Burma. Fraternal Greetings and Christian Salutations:

As of old worshipers of the One True God brought to tabernacle and temple the fruit of their looms and dedicated it to be used in the sanctuary; so, in lesser measure, worshipers in Ashland Avenue Baptist Church on World Communion Sunday, October the sixth, 1946, by consent of the people, through the hands of the deacons and the voice of the Pastor, dedicated a new linen cloth and used it on their communion table that day.

Now that cloth is being presented to the Lanmadaw Church in appreciation of its faithful witness in time of war and persecution with the hope that it may help to fill the need for beauty and order in the sanctuary of the church built on the foundation laid by Adoniram Judson.

May it be also a lasting symbol of ever-widening Christian fellowship around the world even as in much greater measure the bread and wine on the communion table symbolize the sacrifice of our Lord Jesus Christ who gave His life a ransom for many.

May His blessing rest on both pastor and people in all the years to come.

(Signed) A. Herbert Haslam, Pastor
Marguerita W. Hall
Chairman, Missionary Committee

Stir up, we beseech Thee, O Lord, the wills of Thy faithful people; that they, plenteously bringing forth the fruit of good works, may by Thee be plenteously rewarded; through Jesus Christ our Lord. Amen.

The Book of Common Prayer

Stir me, O stir me, Lord, I care not how,
But stir my heart in passion for the world.
Stir me to give, to go, but most to pray;
Stir till Thy glorious banner be unfurled
O'er lands that still in deepest darkness lie,
O'er deserts where no cross is lifted high . . .
Stir me to give myself so back to Thee
That Thou canst give Thyself again through me.

Bessie Porter Head; used by permission

27

THE CORNER THAT HELD THEM

Yet shall not thy teachers be removed into a corner any more,
but thine eyes shall see thy teachers; and thine ears shall hear a
voice behind thee saying: "This is the way, walk ye in it, when ye
turn to the right hand, and when ye turn to the left."

ISAIAH 30:20-21

There is an exquisite little Gothic chapel on the first floor of the
Metropolitan Museum of Art in New York, set between narrow
walls, dimly lighted, complete with lovely old stained-glass
windows at one end, and a few rush-bottom chairs with kneeling
stools. People pause briefly to look in, hushed and holy; and
someone is sure to whisper wistfully: "Now if I only had a
setting like that . . ."

As if then they would surely seek God in prayer. As if then
He could count on their regular remembrance of Him. As if at
long last their Creator could delight in this picturesque person
lost in prayer.

"Master, see these stones!" the disciples called out one day
in Jerusalem, overwhelmed by the magnificence of the Temple.

But Jesus, inside the Temple, had just said: "Friends, see these
mites!" For the poor widow worshipping was more treasurable
than all the opulence of stone and marble.

"I was ready to be consulted by those who asked me not, I was
ready to be found by those who found me not; I said: 'Here
am I! Here am I!' to a nation that called not upon my name"
(Isaiah 65:1 [Goodspeed]).

For the fact remains that when God is so constantly ready, a
chapel is an unnecessary gem. A chair will do! A Chair for

183

Recollection! Preferably one not used frequently; either because it is too tall, too handsome, perhaps too remote in some corner. Yet perfect for sitting in, daily; corner and all. Quietly turn it around to face this corner; closing your eyes, so that to the casual passerby it seems to be just yourself, resting. Whereas it is yourself in a private chapel of mysterious simplicity. In case this all sounds unlikely, then remember that a well-known writer in England not only did it, himself; but so deeply influenced John Wesley that the seeds of Methodism grew out of William Law's books and ways of worship; and even the famous Samuel Johnson was driven into reading the Bible and William Law's books with fascination.

Tell yourself what a strong and vital personality William Law must have been back in the year 1728 when he was writing *A Serious Call to the Devout and Holy Life.* Perhaps it is enough for you to know that this brilliant scholar had been a private tutor for many years, and then became the center of a small spiritual community at King's Cliffe, where he kept four cows for no other purpose than to furnish milk to certain poor neighbors.

Therefore it might prove persuasive to you, too, to carry certain sentences from William Law with you each time you retire to this corner chapel, letting him train your spirit in private worship. A fourteen-day experiment is given in the remainder of this chapter, together with a provocative Bible verse. If you have grown too accustomed to the crumbs of meditations offered in small daily reading books, here is a fresh approach—for if you still yearn for impossible stained-glass windows, you might try an ecclesiastical touch by cutting large pointed Gothic window shapes from colored construction paper (to be found in any Woolworth store). Then the first few moments in your "Chair for Recollection" could be spent copying one of these William Law's quotations, daily; since this act of writing can engrave his wisdom, word by word, in your memory.

First Day: "If you were to accustom yourself (as far as you can) to pray always in the same place; if you were to reserve that place for devotion, and not allow yourself to do anything common in it; if you were never to be there yourself, but in times of devotion; if any little room, or (if that cannot be) if any particular part of a room was thus used, this kind of consecration of it as a place holy unto God would have an effect upon your mind, and dispose you to such tempers, as would very much assist your devotions. For by having a place thus sacred in your room, it would in some measure resemble a chapel or house of God. This would dispose you to be always in the spirit of religion when you were there; and fill you with wise and holy thoughts when you were by yourself. Your own apartment would raise in your mind such sentiments as you would have near an altar; and you would be afraid of thinking or doing anything that was foolish near that place, which is the place of prayer and holy intercourse with God." (Romans 12:10-12.)

Second Day: "For every day will be a Sunday to thee, and wherever thou goest thou wilt have a priest, a church and an altar along with thee . . . accustom thyself to the holy service of this inward temple . . . and thou wilt have learned to live unto God above time and place." (I Corinthians 3:16, 17.)

Third Day: "As the morning is to you the beginning of a new life; as God has then given you a new enjoyment of yourself, and a fresh approach into the world . . . you have seen all things new created on your account, and can magnify so glorious a Creator." (Psalm 92:1-3.)

Fourth Day: "If you will stop and ask yourself why you are not as pious as the primitive Christians were, your own heart will tell you that it is neither through ignorance nor inability, but purely because you never really intended it." (Galatians 5:7-9.)

Fifth Day: "God Almighty has sent us into the world with very few wants; meat, and drink, and clothing are the only things necessary in life; so the present world is well furnished to supply these needs. If a man had half the world in his power, he can make no more of it than this. . . . The man of pride has a thousand wants, which only his own pride has created; and these render him as troubled as if God had created him with a thousand appetites, without creating anything proper to satisfy them. Envy and ambition have also their endless wants, which disquiet the souls of men, and render them as foolishly miserable as those who want to fly and creep at the same time." (Philippians 4:19.)

Sixth Day: "There is no state of mind so holy, so excellent and so truly perfect as that of thankfulness. . . . A dull, uneasy, complaining spirit is of all tempers the most contrary to religion, for it disowns that God which it pretends to adore. . . . If, therefore, you live in murmurings and complaints, accusing all the accidents of life, it is not because you are a weak, infirm creature, but it is because you lack the first principle of religion, a right belief in God." (Psalm 103:1-5.)

Seventh Day: "Would you know who is the greatest saint in the world? It is not he who prays most or fasts most; it is not he who gives most alms, or is most eminent for temperance, chastity, or justice; but it is he who is always thankful to God, who wills everything God willeth." (Ephesians 5:19-21.)

Eighth Day: "For the spiritual life is as much its own proof as the natural life, and needs no outward or foreign thing to bear witness to it." (I John 3:1-3.)

Ninth Day: "This holy Jesus is already within thee, knocking at the door of thy heart, and wanting nothing but thy own faith and goodwill to have as real a birth in thee as He had in the Virgin Mary." (Galatians 4:19.)

Tenth Day: "There must be some sort of an earthquake within us, something that must rend and shake us to the bottom, before we can be enough sensible either of the state of death we are in, or enough desirous of that Saviour who alone can raise us from it." (Luke 23:5.)

Eleventh Day: "All self-love in every creature is absolutely condemned." (I Corinthians 5:8.)

Twelfth Day: "A Christ not in us, is a Christ not ours." (Colossians 1:27-29.)

Thirteenth Day: "If you should see a man that had a large pond of water, yet living in continual thirst, not suffering himself to drink half a draught, for fear of lessening his pond; if you should see him wasting his time and strength, in fetching more water for his pond; always thirsty, rising early and late to catch drops of rain, gaping at clouds, always studying how to make every ditch empty itself into his pond; and at last end a careful, thirsty life by falling into his own pond; would you not say that such a one was not only the author of his own disquiets, but was foolish enough to be reckoned among idiots and madmen?" (Luke 12:16-21.)

Fourteenth Day: "This mystery of an inward life hidden in man is his most precious treasure. . . . What a miserable mistake it is, therefore, to place religious goodness in outward observances, in notions and opinions which good and bad men can equally receive and practice, and to treat the ready, real power and operation of an inward life of God in the birth of our souls as fanaticism and enthusiasm!" (Ephesians 1:18-19.)

There was once a Leader who decided to demonstrate this Corner, this "Chair for Recollection" and this Worshiper, in order to persuade the members of her church that they too could try such a plan for daily meditation and prayer. In order that everybody in the room might catch the effect, she used fourteen large Gothic "windows," twenty-six inches long at their high-pointed peaks and fourteen inches wide, all cut from cardboard in a shade of ecclesiastical blue. Screens had been arranged on the platform to form a corner, and one interesting highbacked upholstered chair faced the audience. The Worshiper's first act on entering was to turn this chair toward the corner, to insure privacy—all while the opening paragraphs of this chapter were being read aloud. There were two Readers at opposite ends of the platform, one for the readings from William Law; the other for the various Bible verses which have been specially selected to supplement the thoughts.

The Worshiper could be seen writing, one at a time, on the pile of fourteen windows stacked on her (his) knees; as each of the daily readings ended, one of these windows was then fastened on the screens with Scotch Tape and thumbtacks, while the audience sang the Charles Wesley hymn, "Love Divine, All Loves Excelling." When the windows were all in place, seven on each screen, a churchly effect had been created. Twice during the readings various objects were placed on a table in the corner, in such a balanced fashion as not to detract from the chapel atmosphere; e.g., while the *Fifth Day's* reading went on, first a plate of food, cup of tea and folded coat were laid on the table; then a long row of shoes; behind them a long row of hats; then behind them piles of neatly stacked clothes in various colors; a row of colored umbrellas with hooked handles were hung across the front of the table; and lamp, clock, vases, pictures, all placed to produce a balanced sense of plenty. For the *Thirteenth Day*, the Worshiper was offered a glass of water, but held hand upright at arm's length, refusing it.

Up now, slight man! Flee, for a little while, thy occupation; hide thyself, for a time, from thy disturbing thoughts. Cast aside, now, thy burdensome cares, and put away thy toilsome business. Yield room for some little time to God; and rest for a little time with Him. Enter the inner chamber of thy mind; shut out all thoughts save that of God, and such as can aid thee in seeking Him; close thy door and seek Him.

St. Anselm, of Canterbury

And so I come for deeper rest to this still room;
For here the habit of the soul
Feels less the outer world's control,
And from the silence, multiplied
By these still forms on every side,
The world that time and sense have known
Falls off, and leaves us, God, alone.

John Greenleaf Whittier

28

A TENDER TURTLE IS A TENDER TURTLE

The voice of the turtle is heard in our land.

SONG OF SOLOMON 2:12

Although this strange title may sound like something out of Gertrude Stein (she of "Tender Buttons" and "a rose is a rose is a rose" fame), actually the words "tender turtle" antedate Miss Stein by more than sixteen centuries, and come straight from something St. Augustine said. Probably about the Gertrude Steins of his own generation. Or was it about his own character he spoke when he said: *"They that sit at rest while others take pains are tender turtles, and buy their quiet with disgrace"*?

Miss Stein wrote an unusually popular musical drama called *Four Saints in Three Acts,* although it is extremely doubtful whether she knew a single thing about saints, since she said that saints should do nothing: if you were a saint that was enough—a saint existing was everything! Whereas one look at St. Augustine's tender turtles shows us what one saint felt about mere existence and sheer idleness.

It is a temptation, therefore, to turn the tables on Miss Stein and dramatize her life under some such title as *Four Professors in Three Acts,* when it would show up only too plainly how the tender turtle in her character became the tender turtle—

Act One, a Radcliffe College classroom, with the famous Dr. William James conducting a semi-final examination in Philosophy. Outdoors, a charming spring day. Enter Gertrude Stein. She has been at the opera in Boston every night that week. What with weather so lovely outdoors and music still sounding in her ears, it is hard to settle down. But she sits. She glances briefly at the

189

examination paper. She feels an immense boredom sweep over her. Therefore she writes: "Dear Professor James, I am so sorry but I simply do not feel a bit like an examination paper on Philosophy today." Exit Gertrude Stein. Curtain. Then a small brief scene the next morning when she receives the following postal card: "Dear Miss Stein, I understand perfectly how you feel. I often feel like that myself." And underneath this note, William James gives Gertrude Stein the highest mark in all that class! This must have been the moment when she realized how comfortably a turtle can amble through life—mere existence, enough.

Act Two, a Johns Hopkins College laboratory with Gertrude Stein seen enthusiastically dissecting brain tissues in an anatomy class, spellbound by wonder over the inside of a human head, so complicated and intricate and fascinating. Another professor passes her, with excellent marks; so that she reaches the final years in her course at Johns Hopkins where Medicine is the subject to be studied, with real patients in real pain to be treated. And Gertrude Stein is bored stiff at all these weary whining creatures needing pills and other tedious treatment. It is true that in spite of her miserable showing one professor passes her —because of her excellent anatomy record, earlier; but a fourth professor refuses to pass Gertrude Stein, feeling that such an indifferent doctor would be dangerous, professionally, with live patients!

Act Three, therefore, shows Miss Stein turned author instead of physician. Her writing always involved and truncated; sometimes simply sound effects. People quoting sentences like these: In the United States there is more space where nobody is than where somebody is. That makes America what it is. Unquote. A smile goes the rounds: *"That's* pure Gertrude Stein for you!" And once she says, at a college: "I am, because my little dog knows me!" But in the end, when Gertrude Stein lay dying, the emptiness of all such tender turtle living shows up when she rouses from a coma and asks an anxious question: "What is the *answer?"* Then lapses back into unconsciousness. Later still, however, she rouses once more, and asks with even more intensity: "What is the *question?"*

For maybe a tender turtle can by-pass her semi-final examination, and live out her life semi-detached, semi-conscious, semi-serious, semi-frivolous, semi-blind, semi-scientific, semi-pagan, semi-good, semi-social, semi-human. But always in the end that final examination: What is The Question? What is The Answer? Why? Who?

You must have noticed about turtles that their shells seem tough, their gait seems tedious, their necks stick out only from curiosity about their own location and never from friendliness or helpfulness; and in this self-contained, self-centered private world their soft bodies stay huddled under their private roofs to a ripe old age.

This was, indeed, St. Augustine's own life, personified; the reason why he could call a turtle a turtle. He who had been brought up rich and pampered in North Africa—semi-lazy; semi-vain because of his own good looks and his brilliant brain; semi-religious and yet not totally so. For as he himself wrote later in his *Confessions:* "From my tenderest infancy, I had in a manner sucked in with my mother's milk the name of my Saviour, Thy Son; I kept it in the recesses of my heart; and all that presented itself to me without the Divine Name, though it might be elegant, well-written, and even full of truth, did not altogether carry me away."

For Monica, his mother, never stopped praying for this profligate wild son of hers, sinning all the worldly sins, going his own private gait through life. Of this semi-awake period, St. Augustine wrote: "Thus with the baggage of this present world was I held down pleasantly as in sleep: and the thoughts wherein I meditated on Thee were like the efforts of such as would awake, who yet, overcome with a heavy drowsiness, are again drenched therein. And when Thou didst on all sides show me, that what Thou didst say was true, I, convicted by the truth, had nothing to answer, but only those dull and drowsy words: 'Anon! anon!' 'presently!' 'leave me but a little longer!' But 'presently, presently' had no present; and 'my little while' went on for a long while."

This is all so modern that it happened only this morning in each of our lives. Suppose, then, we could hold in our hands one of St. Augustine's turtles and let its voice be heard in our land—what would it quote from this saint of God? Written on each back, so that he who runs may read, would appear such total frankness as this—

"O Lord, Thou in Thyself remainest but I am rolled about in experiments."

"Woe to the rash soul which hopes by forsaking Thee to find something better. It tosses and turns; but the bed is hard; and Thou alone art rest. And lo! Thou art near, and settest free from the misery of wandering and plantest our feet in Thy road, and comfortest us, saying: 'Run, I will carry you, and I will bring you home, and then I will set you free.'"

"It is not by feet, or change of place, that men leave Thee or return to Thee; rather in lustful darkened affections is the true distance from Thy face, O my God."

"Lord, grant me chastity and continence; but do not give them now; not now; not yet!"

"How can God grant what thou dost not truly desire to receive?"

"God wants to give us something, but cannot, because our hands are full."

"This is the very perfection of a man, to find out his own imperfection."

"I was swept up to Thee by Thy beauty, and torn away from Thee by my own weight."

"If in me there dwells a desire for anything superfluous, do Thou purify me, and make me capable of beholding Thee. . . . Man prays to God that he himself may be constructed, not that God may be instructed (*ut ipse construatur, non ut Deus instruatur*)."

"That we pray is a divine gift. There is an interior prayer without ceasing . . . yearning prays continually even though the tongue is silent . . . the goal of all perfection is this, that the spirit is freed from all carnal inclinations and is lifted up into the spiritual until every word and every volition becomes one continuous prayer."

"I am the Food of the full-grown. Grow, and thou shalt feed on me."

"God is the only reality, and we are only real insofar as we are in His order, and He in us."

"Thee, most merciful God, do I now invoke to descend into my soul, which Thou hast prepared for Thy reception by the desire which Thou hast breathed into it. Ere ever I cried to Thee, Thou, most merciful, hadst called and sought me, that I might find Thee, and finding, love Thee. Even so, I sought and found Thee, Lord, and desire to love Thee. Increase my desire. See! I love Thee, but too little! Strengthen my love. When my spirit meditates upon Thy unspeakable goodness, the burden of flesh becomes less heavy, the tumult of thought is stilled, the weight of the body is less oppressive."

"What do I love when I love Thee? Not the beauty of bodies, nor the fair harmony of time, nor the brightness of the light gladdening the eyes, nor the sweet melodies of various songs, nor the fragrant smell of flowers, ointments, spices, nor manna nor honey, nor limbs that carnal love embraces—none of these I love when I love my God. And yet I love a kind of light and melody, of fragrance and meat and embracement when I love my God: the light, melody, fragrance, meat and embracement of the inner man—where there shineth unto my soul what space cannot contain; and there soundeth what time beareth not away; and there tasteth what eating diminishes not; and there clingeth what satiety divorceth not. This is what I love when I love my God."

Moment by moment, therefore, a mother on her knees is praying that the tender turtle life of her son may be given up; and, moment by moment, this son inching his slow way out from under the heavy shell of himself—that hard stubborn core of his brilliant self-sufficiency, into a new relaxed pliability. Until Augustine could write: "Truth unveils itself to him who lives well, prays well, studies well!"

He could write this because one day in a garden in the city of Milan, in Italy, he heard a voice saying: *"Tolle, lege! Take, read!"* And when he opened his Bible he was startled to find himself described on every page! After that he startled other people who might also be in the same tender turtle state, by saying: "Scripture is a long letter sent to us from our eternal country, and we who hope in time to reach its shores should learn what we can about it, and about the conditions of reaching it while we may." He also said: "I have read in Plato and Cicero sayings that are very wise and very beautiful; but I never read in either of them: 'Come unto me, all ye that labor and are heavy laden, and I will give you rest!'" To which he could add that lovely old Latin we always connect with St. Augustine's name: *"Inquietum est cor nostrum donec requiescat in Te: Our heart is restless until it rest in Thee."*

Then, in his practical way, Augustine reminded his self-satisfied tender turtles: "If you believe what you like in the Gospel, and reject what you do not like, it is not the Gospel you believe, but yourselves!" And probably it was at this point that he made two observations about the contents of the Bible: "Because God was God, He heard people thinking. . . . Guard your thoughts, for they are read in heaven!" No wonder he could say of himself that he was "salted with Christ's salt"—for Christianity has never had a theologian more profound, nor one who could combine stern rigorous logic with such a communicative tenderness; so that he speaks straight to the soul of each of us—sixteen centuries later, as we too pray with him:

"O Thou good Omnipotent, who so carest for each of us, as if Thou carest for him alone; and so for all, as if all were one! Blessed is the man who loveth Thee, and his friend in Thee, and his enemy for Thee. I behold how some things pass away, that others may replace them, but Thou dost never depart. O God, my Father, O Thou most supreme, most good, most potent, most omnipotent, most merciful yet most just, most secret yet most present, beauty of all things beautiful, what have I said now, my God, my Life, my holy Joy? Or what says any man when he speaks of Thee? To Thee I entrust whatsoever I have received from Thee, and so shall I lose nothing."

Which sounds like a reminder to the tender turtle never to let its small ego boast: "I am, because my little dog knows me!" but rather to quote the more famous St. Augustine: "I think, therefore God is!" Both question and answer for Gertrude Stein, dying!

"Late have I loved Thee whose fairness is so old and yet so new," St. Augustine confessed. "Late have I loved Thee. And behold, Thou wert within, and I without, and there I sought Thee. Unlovely, I broke upon the loveliness which Thou hast fashioned. Thou wert with me, but I was not with Thee. Long was I held from Thee by those things which, without Thee, are nothing. Thou didst call and cry and burst my deafness. Thou didst gleam and glow and dispel my blindness. Thou didst exhale fragrance. I draw breath, and I pant after Thee. I have tasted, and do hunger and thirst. Thou hast touched me, and I burn for Thy peace."

This is not at all "merely existing," which Miss Stein had felt was all that a saint needed to do; this is not "a tale told by an idiot, full of sound and fury, signifying nothing," which Shakespeare used first in a play but which Gertrude Stein imitated faithfully in the meaningless syllables of *Four Saints in Three Acts*. ("The difference between me and the insane," she said, "is that people go on reading me!")

But to imitate an idiot deliberately is a strange choice even for a tender turtle; who would, of course, take offense if another turtle called him an idiot; and yet, on many a day, having ambled to the end of a dead-end street must have said to himself, in secret: "You idiot! You sweet, dumb, ridiculous idiot, you! Look where you have landed yourself, semi-blindly, semi-consciously!"

All this St. Augustine had learned for himself, and even said to himself, through those long years when he traveled from Africa to Italy, before he heard a child's voice in a garden saying: "Take, read!" But he never forgot that Monica had been praying, as only mothers can pray for prodigal sons. How she had prayed, for instance, that her boy might never get to Rome or Milan, so much more sinful than Carthage. But as St. Augustine wrote later: "What was she praying for, O my God, with all those tears, but that Thou shouldest not allow me to sail? But Thou didst see deeper, and granted the essence of her prayer. Thou didst not do what at that moment she was asking, that Thou mightest make of me the thing she was always asking."

When Monica finally joined Augustine in Milan, it was at a time of bitter religious controversy splitting the Church into

Orthodox and Arian factions. Since Ambrose, Bishop of Milan, was Orthodox, and the Empress Justina was Arian, she used all her power to persecute him—soldiers always surrounding his church. But inside that church, day and night, his faithful flock formed a constant bodyguard around their beloved bishop. In order to help them keep awake during such endless vigils, Ambrose composed hymns for them to sing—at least two of which are still in our Presbyterian, Lutheran and Methodist hymnbooks ("O Splendor of God's Glory Bright," and "O Trinity of Blessed Light.") They also sang the "Te Deum," written somewhat earlier, stating point by point the beliefs which the faithful should accept! It is stirring to think of Monica and Augustine in such vigils. In his *Confessions,* St. Augustine admits: "What tears I shed over the hymns and canticles when the sweet sound of the music of Thy Church thrilled my soul! As the music filled my ears and Thy truth flowed down into my heart, the tide of devotion swelled high within me, and my tears ran down in gladness."

Adding: "If thou art singing a hymn, thou art praising God. . . . Then the hymn comes to an end and it is time for a meal; if thou keepest thyself from overeating, thou wilt be praising God. Dost thou labor as a farmer? Then be sure there are no weeds left in the ground thou art digging, then this too will be an opportunity for praising God. Thus by the innocency of thy labors thou canst praise God all day long."

The tender turtle told to take pains, and not be a "sweet idiot," resting! In this connection two amazing thoughts come to mind —the first: the fact that St Augustine called all the symbols carved on church walls *"libri idiotarum—books of the simple"* So that in a day when few could read or write, he who runs could read the symbols! Therefore he was using the turtle itself as a symbol for idiots. For every dictionary defines "idiot" as a person living in a private world of his own creating, feeling he is some self-important Caesar, Napoleon, Cleopatra, Queen Victoria. Totally deficient in the eyes of everybody else, poor sweet idiot; thoroughly contented to say: I am, because my little dog knows me! As if that were enough.

The second interesting discovery is that St. Augustine was a splendid psychologist, sixteen centuries ago—for, in our own generation, here are Dr. Fritz Künkel and Roy E. Dickerson fitting everybody into one of four categories: Hero, Star, Clinging Vine, Turtle! In their book, *How Character Develops,* you can meet their turtle also: a recluse, a hermit, never coming all the way out of the shell. So that in daring to distribute to you on the backs of turtles these unforgettable sayings of the Church's most unforgettable saint, we too have made *"libri idiotarum,"* to remind you that life is far more than a tale told by an idiot, signifying nothing! For as St. Augustine himself once wrote—

"They came to life again by remembering their proper life which they had forgotten."

"The nature of God is a circle, whose center is everywhere and its circumference nowhere."

"I take the whole Christ for my Saviour; I take the whole Bible for my staff; I take the whole Church for my fellowship."

"The world is a great book of which they who never stir from home read only a page."

"You were ground in the mill of preparation, moistened by Baptism, baked by the fire of the Holy Spirit in confirmation. See how this unity has been brought about and be of one accord, cherishing one another."

"O God, the Light of every heart that sees Thee, the Life of every soul that loves Thee, the Strength of every mind that seeks Thee, grant me ever to continue steadfast in Thy holy love. Be Thou the joy of my heart; take it all to Thyself, and therein abide. The house of my soul is, I confess, too narrow for Thee; do Thou enlarge it, that Thou mayst enter in; it is ruinous, do Thou repair it. It has that within which must offend Thine eyes; I confess and know it; but whose help shall I implore in cleaning it but Thine alone?"

"O Thou who fillest heaven and earth, ever acting, ever at rest; Thou who teachest the heart of the faithful without the din of words, teach us, we pray Thee, through Jesus Christ our Lord. Amen."

[*Note:* It is possible to add depth and imagination to this Meditation in four ways: (1) While the chapter is being read, *Augustine* is seen seated on right side of platform in front of a beautiful altar, containing Cross,

Bread, Chalice; he should wear white Roman toga, and write continuously. (2) *Monica* is seen kneeling in prayer, in front of table with Cross; she should wear royal blue or purple Roman draperies. (3) When reaching Orthodox-Arian controversy, both hymns by Ambrose should be sung to tune *"Wareham"*; or, a recording of the *"Te Deum"* played. (4) Each of the Augustine quotations may be copied on the backs of turtles cut from green construction paper, with diagonal markings on outside in heavy black, together with white numbers; to be arranged, in order, along the edges of the platform, in a processional. One at a time members of the audience should go forward to remove and read aloud their souvenir quotations.]

All virtuous women, like tortoises, carry their house on their heads, their chappel in their hearts, their danger in their eye, their souls in their hands, and God in all their actions.

Jeremy Taylor, 1613-1667

A good conscience is the palace of Christ; the temple of the Holy Spirit; the paradise of delight; the standing Sabbaths of the world.

St. Augustine, 345-430

Give us other mothers, and I will give you another world.
St. Augustine

Watch Thou, dear Lord, with those who wake, or watch, or weep this night, and give Thine angels charge over those who sleep. Tend Thy sick ones, O Lord Christ. Rest Thy weary ones. Bless Thy dying ones. Soothe Thy suffering ones. Pity Thy Afflicted ones. Shield Thy joyous ones. And all for Thy Love's sake. Amen.

St. Augustine

What we need, God, what we finally need is a woman who shall also be a saint.

Charles Péguy, *Jeanne d'Arc*

2 9

TIME TO SPARE FOR GOD

Meditate upon these things; give thyself wholly to them; that thy
profiting may appear to all.   Timothy 4:15

If you could have your way, would you not love to persuade
every congregation in our country to spend at least one evening
together, discovering for themselves the wonderful warmth
wrapped up in the words Thomas à Kempis wrote five hundred
years ago?

Once, in one city, it was possible to re-create for one night
much of this medieval atmosphere. It is true that there was no
cloister in that down-town church. But the meeting place had
the usual four walls which soon seemed like a medieval cloister
as a black-robed choir kept up a continual processional, slow and
reverent, around and around the outer margins of the room—humming an ancient Gregorian chant throughout the service, only
one voice singing at intervals a hymn which Thomas à Kempis
is said to have written. In order to establish even more of a monastery atmosphere, black crepe-paper hoods had been made for
the choir. Before they were put on, however, broad white muslin
bands had been pinned around each forehead. Gold paper crosses
had been pinned on the yokes of their gowns; and each of the
choir carried, held only partly open in both hands, a purple book
which looked like a Missal straight out of the Middle Ages! Actually it was only a folded sheet of purple construction paper, with
two gold crosses on the outside; and inside, the mimeographed
hymn and all the quotations for the following responsive service.
But at the last moment, the Leader felt enough genuine medieval
zeal to cause her to dip her brush in gold paint, adding bright

gold scrolls around the borders of these purple covers. Then they
appeared ancient and authentic to the audience at each passage
of the choir around the room.

The scene on the platform was equally austere but memorable.
On the background of a tall dark screen a large gold paper cross
had been fastened. On the floor in front of this—side view—a
man was seen kneeling, writing at his *prie-dieu:* which was simply
the seat of a high-backed Gothic pulpit chair. He wore the same
sort of robe which the choir wore. Throughout the service he did
nothing but write in this quiet cell; the choir did nothing but pace
their cloister, their Gregorian chant always faintly in the air, a
solo voice occasionally singing. From such simplicity, a spirit
swept over the people as they waited expectantly.

Purple programs, with white crosses chalked on their covers,
were ready to be distributed, containing the quotations; but
these were withheld at first, lest the turning of pages distract
from the Leader's opening words—

It is the year 1441, in Holland. You see Thomas à Kempis in
his cell, writing *The Imitation of Christ.* As far as we know now,
the book itself originated fifty years earlier from the pen of a
man named Gerhard Groote; but Thomas à Kempis edited and
copied these words which he prized so dearly that he wanted
others to share them. Yet little he dreamed in that cell, that his
book would be translated into more than fifty languages, going
into over six thousand editions! Nor did he dream of this room,
now, with mimeographed portions from this beloved Classic soon
to be placed in your hands, together with a hymn the Lutherans
say that he wrote. It was sung in his cloisters to some ancient
Gregorian chant—perhaps the same one you will hear, still printed
in all our hymnals today under the title "Hamburg."

There are several other things to bear in mind as our program
progresses. First of all, remember that, in 1441, there were no
printing presses. Books were few and far between. Moreover,
many Christians could not read nor write. But, as they sat in
their pews, who could not read that great carved crucifix up on
their high altar? Strong and stern and solemn, it spoke to them
as the Plus Sign in their lives, adding a Redeemer to their three

unknown R's. At stated hours, all day long, robed figures paced through cathedral cloisters, singing matchless music—often some old Gregorian chant like our "Hamburg" melody—written in Rome a thousand years earlier, before a single Christian had been won to Christ in Britain or before Thomas à Kempis knelt in his cell to copy.

You will soon see how steeped in the Scriptures this man was. No wonder that he should have said: "Take thou a Book in thine hands as Simeon the Just took the child Jesus into his arms to carry Him and to bless Him."

You will soon see, also, how blunt and penetrating his observations were. It may even surprise you to discover how little human nature has changed in the past five hundred years! And it may amuse you to hear that when Thomas à Kempis visited Rome and saw the priceless treasures collected in the Vatican, the Pope said to him: "You see, my son, the Church can no longer say: 'Silver and gold have I none!'" To which Thomas à Kempis answered severely: "How true, father! But neither can the Church now say: 'Rise up and walk!'"

It was about such rising up and walking that *The Imitation of Christ* was written, copies of which are now being distributed. Please note that the responsive readings will be read by pews, beginning with the front row. No matter where our choir may be in their processional around our cloister walls, occasionally you will hear a verse from the Thomas à Kempis hymn.

Solo (tune: "Hamburg"):
> O love, how deep, how broad, how high,
> O great, O wondrous mystery,
> That God, the Son of God should take
> Our mortal form for mortals' sake.

First Pew (reading in unison): If thou knowest the entire Bible by heart, and the sayings of all the philosophers, what would it profit thee without the love of God, and without grace? At the Day of Judgment we shall be examined, not on what we have read, but on what we have done.

Second Pew: Extol not thyself for the height of thy stature, or beauty of thy person, which could be disfigured and destroyed by a little illness. Take not pleasure in thy natural gifts, or thy wit, lest thereby thou displease God, whose is all the good, whatsoever thou hast by nature.

Third Pew: If there be any good in thee, believe better things of others, that so thou preserve humility. It doth no hurt to thee to set thyself lower than all men, but it hurteth thee exceedingly if thou set thyself above even one man.

Fourth Pew: If every year we would root out one vice, we should soon become perfect men. But now oftentimes we perceive it goeth contrary, and that we were better and purer at the beginning of our entrance into religious life . . . it is accounted a great matter if a man can retain but some part of his first zeal.

Fifth Pew: Endeavor to be patient in bearing with the defects and infirmities of others; for that thou hast also many failings which must be borne by others. If thou canst not make thyself such a one as thou wouldest, how wilt thou be able to have another in all things to thy liking?

Sixth Pew: For occasions do not make a man frail, but they show of what stuff he is made.

Seventh Pew: Why doth a little matter spoken against thee make thee sad? Even although it had been much more, thou oughtest not to have been moved. But now let it pass; it is not the first that has happened, nor is it anything new; neither shall it be the last, if thou live long. . . . Put it out of thy heart the best thou canst. . . . Bear it at least patiently, if thou canst not joyfully.

Eighth Pew: All is not lost, although thou do feel thyself very often afflicted or grievously tempted. Thou art a man, and not God; thou art flesh not an Angel.

Leader: Let us pray—also in the words of Thomas à Kempis: Grant me, O most sweet and loving Jesus, to rest in Thee above every creature, above all health and beauty, above all glory and honor, above all power and dignity, above all knowledge and subtlety, above all riches and arts, above all joy and gladness, above all fame and praise . . . above all

mirth and exuberation that the mind can receive or feel.
... Because Thou, O Lord my God, art above all things the
best; Thou alone most noble and glorious above all things,
in whom all things together both perfectly are, and ever
have been, and shall be. And therefore it is too small and
unsatisfying, whatsoever Thou bestowest on me besides Thyself. For surely my heart cannot truly rest, unless it rest in
Thee. Amen.

Solo: He sent no angel to our race,
Of higher or of lower place,
But He Himself to this world came
And wore the robe of human frame.

First Pew: By two wings a man is lifted up from things earthly,
namely, by Simplicity and Purity. Simplicity ought to be in
our intention; Purity in our affection.

Second Pew: If thy heart were right, then every creature would
be unto thee a looking glass of life, and a book of holy doc-
trine. There is no creature so small and mean, that it doth
not set forth the goodness of God. If thou wert inwardly
good and pure, then thou wouldest be able to see and understand all things well without hindrance.

Third Pew: Count not of great importance who is for thee, or
against thee; but let this be thy aim and care, that God be
with thee in every thing thou doest. Thou art not the more
holy when thou art praised; nor the more worthless when
thou art found fault with.

Fourth Pew: My son, be not curious, nor trouble thyself with idle
anxieties. *Follow thou Me.* For what is it to thee, whether
the man be such or such, or whether this man do or speak
this or that? Thou shalt not need to answer for others, but
only give account of thyself. Why therefore dost thou en-
tangle thyself?

Fifth Pew: We ask how much a man hath done; but from what
degree of virtue he acteth is not so carefully weighed. We
inquire whether he hath been courageous, rich, handsome,
skillful, a good writer, a good singer, or a good laborer; but

how poor he is in spirit, how patient, how devout, on this most men hold their peace.

Sixth Pew: For what are words, but words? They fly through the air, but a stone they cannot hurt. If thou art guilty, think thou wouldest gladly amend thyself. . . . And why do such small matters go to thy heart? It is because thou art afraid of being despised that thou art unwilling to be reproved for thy faults, and seekest the overshadowing of excuses.

Seventh Pew: But hear My word, and thou shalt not care for ten thousand words of men. Behold, if all should be spoken against thee that could be maliciously invented, what would it hurt thee, if thou shouldest suffer it to pass entirely away, and make no more reckoning of it than of a mote? Could it pluck so much as one hair from thy head?

Eighth Pew: Some carry their devotion only in books, some in pictures, some in outward signs and figures. . . . He who listens to the Divine Voice is saved from many unnecessary notions.

Leader: Groan and lament that thou art yet so carnal and worldly . . . so unwatchful over thy outward senses, so often entangled with many vain imaginations; so much inclined to outward things, so negligent in things inward; so lightly moved to laughter and unbridled mirth, so hardly to tears and contrition; so curious to hear what is new, and to see what is beautiful, so slack to embrace what is humble and mean; so covetous of abundance, so niggardly in giving, so close in keeping; so inconsiderate in speech, so reluctant to keep silence; so unruly in manners, so fretful in conduct; so eager about food, so deaf to the word of God; so swift to take rest, so slow to labor; so wakeful after gossiping tales, so drowsy at the sacred Services at night; so careless in prayer, so lukewarm at Communion; so joyful at prosperity, so weak in adversity.

Solo: For us He prayed, for us He taught
For us His every work He wrought,
By words, and signs, and actions, thus
Still seeking not Himself, but us.

First Pew: Love is a great thing, yea, altogether a great good; by itself it maketh light everything that is heavy, and it beareth evenly everything that is uneven.

Second Pew: Nothing is sweeter than Love, nothing stronger, nothing higher, nothing wider, nothing more pleasant, nothing fuller nor better in Heaven and earth.

Third Pew: A lover flieth, runneth and rejoiceth; he is free, he is not holden.

Fourth Pew: He giveth all for all, and hath all in all; because he resteth in One Highest above all things.

Fifth Pew: Love is watchful, and sleeping slumbereth not. Though wearied is not tired; though alarmed is not confounded.

Sixth Pew: Love is swift, sincere, affectionate, pleasant and delightsome; brave, patient, faithful, prudent, long-suffering, never seeking itself.

Seventh Pew: Love is circumspect, humble and upright; not yielding to softness, or to lightness; nor attending to vain things; it is sober, chaste, firm, quiet . . . and without sorrow none liveth in love.

Eighth Pew: Without the Way there is no going.

Without the Truth there is no knowing.

Without the Life there is no living.

Leader: Thomas à Kempis wrote of the Saints, about God, their eternal Lover—I am he who made all the Saints; I gave them Grace; I bestowed on them Glory. I know what every one hath deserved; I have kept them from evil with the blessings of My goodness. I foreknew My beloved ones before the ages, I chose them out of the world, they chose not Me first. I called them by grace, I drew them by mercy, I led them safe through sundry temptations. . . . I made both the small and the great. . . . Nothing can turn them back, or press them down; for being full of the eternal Truth, they burn with the fire of unquenchable charity.

Solo: For us to wicked men betrayed,

Scourged, mocked, in crown of thorns arrayed;

For us He bore the Cross's death,

For us at length gave up His breath.

First Pew: Jesus hath now many lovers of His heavenly Kingdom, but few bearers of His Cross. Many He hath that are desirous of consolation, but few of tribulation.

Second Pew: Many He findeth that share His table, but few His fasting. All desire to rejoice with Him, few are willing to endure anything for Him. Many reverence His miracles, few follow the shame of His Cross.

Third Pew: Thou canst not escape the Cross whithersoever thou runnest; for wheresoever thou goest thou carriest thyself with thee, and ever shalt find thyself.

Fourth Pew: Turn thee above, turn thee below, turn thee without, turn thee within, and in all these places thou shalt find the Cross.

Fifth Pew: If thou bear thy Cross cheerfully, it will bear thee, and lead thee to the desired end, to wit, where there shall be no more suffering.

Sixth Pew: If thou bear it unwillingly, thou makest for thyself a load, and burdenest thyself the more.

Seventh Pew: If thou cast away one Cross, without doubt thou shalt find another and perhaps a heavier one.

Eighth Pew: Thinkest thou to escape that which no mortal man could ever avoid? Which of the Saints in the world was without Cross and tribulation?

Leader: I offer up unto Thee my prayers and intercessions for those especially who have in any matter hurt, grieved, or found fault with me, or who have done me any damage or displeasure.

For all those whom, at any time, I may have vexed, troubled, burdened and scandalized, by words or deeds, knowingly or in ignorance; that Thou grant us all equal pardon for our sins, and for our offenses against each other. Take away from our hearts, O Lord, all suspiciousness, indignation, wrath and contention, and whatsoever may hurt charity and lessen brotherly love.

Solo: For us He rose from death again,
For us He went on high to reign,
For us He sent His Spirit here
To guide, to strengthen, and to cheer.

First Pew: O God, grant me to begin perfectly this day to serve Thee, for what I have done hitherto is as nothing.

Second Pew: One of the best means to acquire humility is to engrave in our minds the maxim that each one is really only what he is in the sight of God and none other.

Third Pew: Blessed is the man who is glad to have time to spare for God.

Fourth Pew: Blessed is the soul which heareth the Lord speaking within her, and receiveth from his mouth the word of consolation.

Fifth Pew: Blessed are the ears that catch the pulses of the divine whisper, and give no heed to the whisperings of this world.

Sixth Pew: Blessed indeed are those ears which listen not after the voice which is sounding without, but for the Truth, teaching inwardly.

Seventh Pew: Blessed are they that enter far into things within, and endeavor to prepare themselves more and more, by daily exercises, for the receiving of heavenly secrets. Blessed are they who are glad to have time to spare for God.

Eighth Pew: Why wilt thou defer thy good purpose from day to day? Arise and begin this very moment, and say: Now is the time to be doing! Now is the time to be striving! Now is the fit time to amend myself.

Prayer (in unison): O merciful Lord, who hast made of one Blood and redeemed by one Ransom all Nations of Men, let me never harden my heart against any that partake of the same nature and redemption with me; but grant me a universal charity toward all men. Give me, O Thou Father of compassion, such a tenderness and meltingness of heart that I may be deeply affected with all the miseries and calamities, outward or inward, of my brethren, and diligently keep them in love. Amen.

Benediction Solo:

O love, how deep, how broad, how high
O great, O wondrous mystery,
That God, the Son of God, should take
Our mortal form for mortals' sake. *Amen.*

God be in myn hede
And in myn vnderstandynge.
God be in myn eyen
And in myn lokynge.
God be in myn mouth
And in myn spekynge.
God be in myn herte
And in myn thynkynge.
God be at myn ende
And at myn departynge.
                    Sarum Primer, 1529

3 0

IN THE CHOICEST KIND OF KITCHEN

But Martha was cumbered with much serving.   LUKE 10:40

Any advertisement of a new kind of kitchen could catch Martha's eye. Instantly she could see herself in the middle of it, just as the copy man had dreamed she might: every latest little item within immediate reach; every gleaming new gadget gay with color, almost too glamorous for everyday use. Every box and bin brought up to waist level, with no more backbreaking bending. "Somebody," Martha would always think, "somebody has surely shown imagination! Inventors certainly think up everything these days—like that automatic oven which roasts the meat while I'm in church, without half the old worry about its burning."

But the inventors never think up quite enough, she knows. Never enough to "temper my spirit, O Lord!" And it might bother Martha that Brother Lawrence could temper his. And even say:

It is not necessary for being with God to be always at church; we may make an oratory of our hearts, wherein to retire from time to time, to converse with Him in meekness, humility and love. Everyone is capable of such familiar conversation with God, some more, some less. He knows what we can do. Let us begin, then!

Right in the middle of the most old-fashioned kitchen imaginable, he began. Right in the thick of traffic with a lot of other Brothers making tracks all over his newly-washed floor. Right with everybody bustling around in the very places where Brother Lawrence should have been if monastery meals were to land on refectory tables on time. Nothing was ever within reach. It was tramp here for the kettles, tramp there for the keys to the cooling cellar, tramp down for milk, tramp up for raisins drying on the roof. Nothing had a color scheme to carry him right out of this world. And yet he was carried right out of this world. Right up into the presence of God. Moment by moment practicing this presence. Deliberately! Delightedly! Even describing the bliss of such busyness by saying: "The time of business and the time of prayer are no different with me."

Where Martha would be all dusty with Duty, Brother Lawrence would be all silent with Spirit. Where Martha would go to bed grumbling that a woman's work was never done, Brother Lawrence would climb to his monastery cot saying: "Those who feel the gale of the Holy Spirit go forward even in sleep! If the vessel of our soul is still tossed with winds and storms, then let us wake the Lord, who rests in it, and He will quickly calm our sea."

The disturbing thing for Martha to have remembered just then would be the fact that this very same Lord had eaten a meal under her own roof, and had tried in vain to calm her sea, by saying: "Martha, Martha! You are careful and troubled with too much serving; only one thing is needful; and Mary has chosen this better part which can never be taken away from her. See, sitting here listening, while I am in the house. Tomorrow she will do her share of the work, as usual."

For all the world like Brother Lawrence himself! Except that he had learned the harder recipe for listening-and-cooking-and-praying, all at the same time.

Not that he was a born cook. Far from it. He had detested cooking at first. For he was not an indoor man, either. No, he had been a soldier. But the Carmelites in Paris had made this Nicholas Herman a lay Brother and their monastery servant. Cribbed, cabined and confined to K.P. duty, as it were, for forty years! His work never done! In a dark centuries-old kitchen! And yet he kept thinking and saying so many quiet sentences that men began writing him letters and he began answering. Nobody threw away a single scrap of paper received from him. Later, they were brought together in a little book. It must have literally named itself from the phrase most often on his lips: "PRACTICING THE PRESENCE OF GOD." And although this was nearly three hundred years ago, the small volume has been a beloved classic for centuries; indeed, it has made over many a modern Martha—in her own kitchen. For in its own beautiful invisible fashion it can redecorate the whole place, actually.

Just as Brother Lawrence began very simply redecorating his own interior living.

Did you know that his whole remarkable story began with a tree? A *dead tree?* In winter? He wrote about it in this impersonal way:

Seeing a tree stripped of its leaves and considering that in a little time the leaves would be renewed, and after that the flowers and fruits appear, he received a high view of the Providence and power of God which has never been effaced from his soul. This view had set him perfectly loose from the world, and kindled in him such a love for God that he could not tell whether it had increased in the forty years that he had lived since.

To be set perfectly loose from the world was one-half his secret; the Spirit of God was the other half. Martha might bear this in mind. That all the tumult and war in the world cannot stop God's spring from coming. Either outdoors, in trees. Or indoors, in kitchens. Eternal verities wrapped up in every sight from a kitchen window: "immortal tidings in your mortal hands" in that smallest sprig of parsley. Brother Lawrence continued his story by writing:

This made me resolve to give my all for the All; so, after having given myself wholly to God, I renounced, for the love of Him, everything that was not He; and I began to live as if there were none but He and I in the world. . . . And I make it my business to persevere in practicing the presence of God. . . . One way to recollect the mind easily in time of prayer, and preserve it more in tranquility, is not to let it wander too far at other times.

Even for Brother Lawrence this was very hard indeed. That was when he began the charming device of interior decorating, as it were:

Sometimes I considered myself before Him as a poor criminal at the feet of his judge; at other times I beheld Him in my heart as my Father, as my God. . . . Sometimes I consider myself there as a stone before a carver, wherefrom he is to carve a statue; presenting myself thus before God, I ask Him to form His perfect image in my soul, and make me entirely like Himself.

When he failed in his duty, he simply confessed his faults, saying to God: "I shall never do otherwise, if Thou leavest me to myself; it is Thou must hinder me from falling, and mend what is amiss." After this he gave himself no further uneasiness about it.

Here, too, a modern Martha might welcome such common sense. For when she begins to get a meal and the meal gets her instead, then—no post-mortems! *One thing is needful.* Choose this better part: go and sit at His feet. Confess the tantrum. And begin again, moment by moment. Someone has said that the trouble with housework is its deadly "dailiness." For this Brother Lawrence had his recipe, too:

He lays no great burden on you—a little recollection from time to time—a little adoration—sometimes to pray for His grace—sometimes to offer Him your sorrows—sometimes to offer Him thanks for the blessings He has given you, and still gives you in the midst of your troubles—He asks you to console yourself with Him the oftenest that you can. You need not cry very loud. He is nearer than you think!

[Note: This chapter has been effectively presented as a meditation for a midweek evening program by four persons—*two stood at the rear of the room*, a woman on the left side read aloud all the paragraphs about Martha; a man on the right side read aloud the Brother Lawrence paragraphs. *Two other persons, on the platform, acted in quiet pantomime*—on extreme left side, a woman wearing kitchen apron stood behind modern red kitchen table, covered with colored mixing bowls, egg beater, eggs, canned goods. She read advertisements, stirred food impatiently, nervously wiped forehead with back of hand, frequently consulted watch: ill at ease, etc.; on extreme right, a man wearing long plain brown or black robe with rope girdle, stood behind wide carved oak table, with two or three immense black pots and a large copper kettle in all of which he kept stirring. Occasionally facing right, in silhouette, head bent, chin resting on hands; this he did between certain of "his" quotations, at which times a man's voice—unaccompanied— was heard at the rear of the room singing one verse each time of the following ancient ninth-century Latin hymn often used in monasteries, to the haunting medieval Plainsong "Iam Lucis": No. 58 in *Methodist Hymnal*; No. 164 in *Episcopal Hymnal*:]

O come, Creative Spirit, come
And make within ourselves Thy home
Supply the grace and heavenly aid,
To fill the hearts that Thou hast made.

O gift of God, most high, Thy name
Is Comforter; whom we acclaim
The fount of life, the fire of love,
The soul's anointing from above.

The seven-fold gift of grace is Thine,
Thou finger of the hand divine.
The Father's promise true to teach
Our earthly tongues Thy heavenly speech.

Drive far away our spirit's foe,
Thine own abiding peace bestow;
If Thou dost go before as Guide
No evil can our steps betide.

Through Thee may we our Father learn,
And know the Son, and Thee discern,
Who art of both; and thus adore
In perfect peace forevermore.

Amen.

To give our Lord the perfect service, Mary and Martha must combine. The Lord, when you are busy in the kitchen, is beside you; He walks among the pots and pans.   St. Teresa of Avila, 1515-1582

It comforts me to hear the hours strike, for I feel that I have drawn a little nearer to God.
                                        St. Teresa of Avila

Quiet minds cannot be perplexed or frightened, but go on in fortune or misfortune at their own private pace like the ticking of a clock during a thunderstorm.
                                    Robert Louis Stevenson

31

CENTERING DOWN

Jesus stood in the midst . . . and breathed on them, and saith: "Receive ye the Holy Ghost."   JOHN 20:19, 22

No Quaker would ever dream of telling the life of Thomas Kelly this way. But then, no Quaker would need to! Since he is born knowing what "centering down" means: how—without rising or moving or speaking or singing—there is an Inner Light *in the midst.* Quakers and mystics and poets know this. But how can a roomful of matter-of-fact Christians discover an inmost center?

Or conduct a book review of Thomas Kelly's *A Testament of Devotion* which can live on in the memory and touch the imagination?

That is why a circular table, surrounded by a ring of chairs several feet away, might be a simple way to start. Especially for persons more accustomed to sitting in straight rows, facing a platform. The middle of this table can then become the resting place for certain graphic symbols: little in themselves, but catching up the beauty of Thomas Kelly's words.

Suppose, therefore, that such a service could begin by lifting from the middle of this round table a circular piece of paper, bearing a call to worship:

> Truth is within ourselves; it takes no rise
> From outward things, whate'er you may believe.
> There is an inmost center in us all
> Where truth abides in fullness; and around,
> Wall upon wall, the gross flesh hems it in,
> This baffling and perverting carnal mesh
> Binds it, and makes all error; and, to know,
> Rather consists in opening out a way
> Whence the imprisoned splendor may escape,
> Than in effecting entry for a light
> Supposed to be without.
>
> ROBERT BROWNING

It would have meaning to follow this by our Lord's own prayer to His Father: John 17:11-21. After which a small Bible could be placed in the center of the table by another speaker, who could say: "Have you never wondered what the poet meant by 'imprisoned splendor'? Perhaps this is what St. Luke meant when he wrote of the Boy Jesus sitting *in the midst of* the doctors, both hearing and asking them questions with such a deep wonder on His face that these men were astonished at His understanding. Nobody knows exactly what He asked, of course. But He could easily have wondered how a boy of twelve could live in The Secret Place of the Most High. Exquisite, exciting words! But *how? how?* And how has God been our dwelling place in all generations? And has any child ever yet been born whose name has been Wonderful, Counsellor, the Mighty God, the Everlasting Father, the Prince of Peace? For the thoughts of youth are long, long thoughts. And when the Holy Scriptures lie at very center of a boy's home, how natural to think on these things! This was true in the life of Thomas Kelly, in our own generation—born into a Quaker family in Ohio, in the year 1893." (With other details from the Introduction, in his book.)

The next speaker could place a very small seed in the center of the table, telling more about Thomas Kelly's life, and his remark to Rufus Jones at the end of his first day of teaching philosophy at Haverford College: "I am going to make my life a miracle!" That he could succeed is due in large part to his being part of the "nucleus" built around this tiny seed—a nucleus of earlier great souls of whom Rufus Jones once said: "It was Jesus' faith that, if you get in the world, anywhere, a seed of the Kingdom, a nucleus of persons who exhibit the blessed life, who are dedicated to expanding goodness, who rely implicitly on love and sympathy, who try in meek patience the slow method that is right, who still feel clasping hands of love even when they go through pain and trial and loss, this seed-spirit will spread, this nucleus will enlarge and create a society."

You will see that this was exactly what Jesus had promised: "Where two or three are gathered together in my name, there am I *in the midst of them.*" And Thomas Kelly's book tells about the spreading of this seed-spirit: "The Society of Friends arose as a rediscovery of the ever-open inward springs of revelation. George Fox and the Quakers found a principle within men, a Shekinah of the soul, a Light Within. . . . Dedicating themselves utterly and completely to attendance upon this Inward Living Christ, they were quickened into a new and bold tenderness toward the blindness of the leaders of Christian living. . . . John Woolman, the Quaker tailor of Mt. Holly, New Jersey, resolved so to order his business burdens that nothing, absolutely nothing would crowd out his prime attendance upon the Inward Principle. And in this sensitizing before the inward altar of his soul, he was quickened to see and attack effectively the evils of slaveholding, of money-lending, and of wars upon the Indians. . . . A

practicing Christian must above all be one who practices the
personal return of the soul into the inner sanctuary, who brings
the world into its light and rejudges it, who brings the light into
the world with all its turmoil and its fitfulness, and re-creates
it. . . . "

The way George Fox re-created men and women in England,
when he wrote: "Wee made ym tremble att ye Word of God";
saying of himself that he was "baptized into a sense of the conditions and needs of all men"; adding: "One man, raised by God's
power to stand and live in the same spirit the prophets and
apostles were in, can shake the country ten miles around." (Evi-
dences of such actual "shaking," in England and in Boston, are
given in our chapter entitled "Plimsoll Mark.")

Thomas Kelly continued his argument: "Such men are not
found merely among the canonized Saints of the Church. They
are the John Woolmans of today. They are housewives and hand
workers, plumbers and teachers, learned and unlettered, black
and white, poor and perchance even rich. . . . They may not be
widely known, nor serve on boards of trustees, or preach in
pulpits. . . . They have found the secret of the Nazarene."

The next speaker could place a lighted candle in the center of
the table, telling how Jesus still stands *in the midst of* His disciples, saying: "Receive ye the Holy Spirit!" Thomas Kelly thought
of this inmost center as light, for he said: "Deep within us all is
an amazing inner sanctuary of the soul, a holy place, a Divine
Center, a speaking Voice, to which we can continuously return.
Eternity is at our hearts, pressing upon our time-torn lives, warming us with intimations of an astounding destiny, calling us home
unto Itself. . . . It is a Light Within which illumines the face of
God and casts new shadows and new glories upon the face of
men. It is a seed stirring, if we do not choke it. It is the Shekinah
of the soul, the Presence in the midst. . . . The basic response of
the soul to the Light is internal adoration and joy, thanksgiving
and worship, self-surrender and listening. The secret places of the
heart cease to be our noisy workshop. They become a holy sanctuary of adoration, if our minds are stayed on Him. . . . Power-
fully are the springs of our will moved to an abandon of singing

love toward God. . . . In this Center of Creation all things are ours, and we are Christ's and Christ is God's. . . . This practice is the heart of religion. It is the secret, I am persuaded, of the inner life of the Master of Galilee. He expected this secret to be freshly discovered in everyone who would be His follower. It creates an amazing fellowship, the church catholic and invisible, and institutes group living at a new level, a society grounded in reverence, history rooted in eternity, colonies of heaven. . . . It is the living Center of Reference for all Christian souls and Christian groups who seriously mean to dwell in the secret place of the Most High. . . .

"Begin now, as you read these words, as you sit in your chair, to offer your whole selves, utterly and in joyful abandon, in quiet glad surrender to Him who is within. In secret ejaculations of praise, turn in humble wonder to the Light. . . . Formulate them spontaneously: 'Thine only, Thine only'? Or seize upon a fragment of the Psalms: 'So panteth my soul after Thee, O God.' Repeat them inwardly, over and over again. . . . All we can say is, Prayer is taking place, and I am given to be in the orbit. In holy hush we bow in Eternity, and know the Divine Concern tenderly enwrapping us and all things within His persuading love."

After each of these speakers a period of silent meditation should follow—perhaps with eyes on the Bible, or the seed, or the candle at the center. Following such silence, the entire circle could hum the tune *"Louvan"* very softly, while someone sings as a quiet prayer:

> Lord of all being, throned afar,
> Thy glory flames in sun and star;
> Center and soul of every sphere,
> Yet to each loving heart how near!

For such repetition could emphasize the idea of the true "Center" of Christian living. The next speaker, however, should place a small globe in the middle of the table, quoting from Paul's letter to the Philippians: "That ye may be blameless and harmless, the sons of God without rebuke, *in the midst of* a crooked and perverse generation among whom ye shine as lights in the world." Undoubtedly it is wholesome to notice what worldly ambitions Thomas Kelly himself had felt, before telling Rufus Jones that he intended to become a "miracle"! Both in universities at Harvard, Earlham and Hawaii, seeking recognition which did not seem to come—"dreams of fame," "acute fever," "a love of trinkets," a desire for "little cushions," "a whole committee of selves"; these are all mentioned on pages 48, 53, 63, 69 and 114 of his *Testament of Devotion.* Yet later in that same book, he wrote of the Inner Light: "He plucks the world out of our hearts, loosing the chains of attachment. And he hurls the world into our hearts, where we and He together carry it in infinitely tender love. . . . Positions of prominence, eminences of social recognition which we once meant to attain—how puny and trifling they become! Our old ambitious and heroic dreams—what years we have wasted in feeding our own insatiable self-pride, when only His will truly matters! . . . Placed in coveted surroundings, recipients of honors, we count them as refuse, as nothing, utterly nothing. Placed in the shadows, we are happy to pick up a straw for the love of God. No task is so small as to distress us, no honor so great as to turn our heads."

The last person to speak should place a small toy house in the center of the table, quoting Longfellow: "Each man's chimney is his golden milestone, the central point from which he measures every distance through gateways to the world around him . . . his own hearth, the axis of the earth."

But what terror that word "axis" strikes; remembering the Axis which once ran out of Germany through Italy into Japan! A Christian needs some higher focus for his gaze than his own chimney corner; yet such is the miracle of language that the word "focus" itself once meant "*hearth*"! This must be what Pascal meant when he said that "all the mischief in the world is done by one thing: the inability to remain at rest within one's own room"— focusing on the True Light which lighteth every man who comes into the world; centering down on the imprisoned splendor, the real home of our spirits. For the dwelling place of God is with man. And Thomas Kelly lived all his life in that beautiful room.

Whether at home in America, teaching; or abroad, helping German refugees after the war; or now, in the Divine Presence.

Therefore, as we too "center down" in this church-which-is-in-our-house, we replace around it this Book of Life, this Seed of the Word, this Light of the World. May the beauty of the Lord our God come upon us.

Let us then labor for an inward stillness
An inward stillness and an inward healing,
That perfect silence where the lips and heart
Are still, and we no longer entertain
Our own imperfect thought and vain opinions,
But God alone speaks in us, and we wait
In singleness of heart, that we may know
His will, and in the silence of our spirits,
That we may do His will, and do that only!
                    Henry Wadsworth Longfellow

You go to your saint and find God working and mani-
fest in him. He got near to God by some saint of his that
went before him, or that stood beside him, in whom he
saw the Divine Presence. That saint again lighted his
fire at some flame before him; and so the power of the
sainthoods animates and fills the world.
                              Phillips Brooks

3 2

BEHIND OUR WALL, LOOKING THROUGH
OUR WINDOW

Behold, he standeth behind our wall, he looketh forth of the
windows.   SONG OF SOLOMON 2:9

The oak in an acorn, the bird in an egg, each provided with every
element needed for growth—it was for providence like this that
Helen Keller once thanked God because He had put so much of
His Word into raised type out of doors that the blind might
read. Turning back to the chapter in this book on the bee, the
butterfly, the breeze, the bird, the sunflower, we trace more of
this Word; yet as Job suggested: "These are but the outskirts of
His ways; how small a whisper do we hear of Him!"

The other half of the same whisper is like an echo from old walls
and windows and steeples. Things carved or painted or woven to
remind God and one another how much we too have loved and
remembered and understood Him. Shorthand, really! Notes on all
the sermons Jesus preached when He was here among men. So
that our stained-glass windows jot down in their margins purple
grapes, golden grain, a green tree growing, a sower sowing, a
sparrow falling, a lily outglamorizing Solomon, a lamb safe in
the Shepherd's arms.

Not that people in the pew knew enough to carve or paint or
weave of their own accord, at first. But just as it was in the days
when Solomon was carving lily-work on the capitals of his pillars,
people "whose hearts stirred them up" began weaving blue and
purple and scarlet hangings for the temple. And this stirring has
never stopped. In his day St. Augustine called symbols "*libri idiotarum: books of the simple*"; and in the sixth century Gregory

could say: "Those who do not know letters may be taught from the pictures on the walls what they cannot learn from books." It was almost a case of letting your conversation be known in heaven, for Ruskin said of them: "The builders have died, but they have left us their adoration."

Even the simplest of us can see each Gothic arch like a pair of hands lifted in silent prayer. Sermons, in stained glass. The whole Gospel, digested into the Creed. Memos, in hymnals. A spire, beckoning heavenward. A cock on that spire to remind everybody of Peter. A bell to summon the hungry at mealtime. With the middle aisle a path to the never-failing Feast. Down this path the bride and groom come for a wedding, the child for a christening, the dead for a funeral, and all of us for the Lord's Supper, to partake of the Bread broken for us, the Vine crushed for us. It is then we see Him looking through our windows— through the purple of those grapes, the whiteness of that wheat. Yet many are too blind to read even this raised type.

The way it has been in Denmark for many centuries, where a Protestant congregation in Jutland had the strange custom of nodding to the wall when they entered. To the blank wall! Nobody knew why, but the custom had been passed on from father to son, from mother to daughter, through many generations. Then a Copenhagen architect, restoring the old church, removed the whitewash of four centuries and discovered a picture of the Virgin Mary, painted back in the days when all Denmark had been Catholic and not Lutheran.

Precisely this same old racial unconsciousness may account for something significant woven into the beautiful blue hangings on one wide wall of the Security Council Chamber in the United Nations; for in this fabric of Scandinavian origin are figures in silver and gold, representing anchors, hearts, sprays of wheat, and three parallel lines. When the artist had been located in New York, he was totally unaware he had used ancient Christian symbols—they had seemed exquisite, and so he had woven them in, with no meaning at all. Moreover, on the door of this same room, a brass Cross shaped like a dagger had been inlaid. But this, too, had no particular significance, he said.

Yet in the Middle Ages in Europe, when the Guild of Carpenters was formed, and wanted a symbol to represent the great Carpenter forerunner in their trade, these simple artisans—who could not read, themselves—chose a door. Then, in order to tell even more of the Carpenter's story, toward the top of their door they hollowed out two squares, and two longer rectangular cutouts beneath, until the raised central portion stood out clearly—a Cross. But millions of Christians across the centuries since then have sat in their pews facing such doors, with no least idea of the significance. As Carlyle said in his *French Revolution*: "What the parish needs, what every parish needs, is a man who knows God at more than second hand." Someone aware of what the family's walls and windows are telling him, and accepting it gratefully from the past into his present. Someone whose heart loses a beat when he reads on a brass plate in St. Paul's Cathedral in London what happened around the year 179: BE HIT KNOWN TO AL MEN THAT THE YEERYS OF OUR LORD GOD, CLXXIX, LUCUS, THE FYRST CHRISTIAN KING OF THIS LAND, THEN CALLED BRYTAYNE, FOWNDYD THE FYRST CHYRCH IN LONDON, APON CORNHYL, AND HE FOWNDYD THER AN ARCHBISHOPPYS SEE, AND MAD THAT CHYRCH THE METROPOLITANT, AND SO ENDURYD THE SPACE OF CCCC YEERYS AND MORE, UNTO THE COMYNG OF SENT AUSTEN, AN APOSTYL OF ENGLAND, THE WHYCH WAS SENT INTO THE LAND BY SENT GREGORY, IN THE TYM OF KING ETHELBERT, AND THEN WAS THE ARCHBISHOPPYS SEE REMOVYD FROM THE AFORESEYD CHYRCH APON CORNHYL UNTO WHAT NOW YS CALLED CANTERBURY, AND THER YT REMEYNETH TO THIS DAY.

Think how this simple plate restores England's long Christian past—a building with walls still standing, a Table where Bread and Wine had been given the Lord's family for seventeen centuries. It is the same continuity we feel in seeing "The Angelus": a sense of the sacred in those bowed heads and praying hands—a renewal of strength, standing in the hush of that Holy Air, on that Holy Earth, after planting the Holy Seed, and knowing the Holy Water will descend from heaven, and the HOLY SUN will release life.

John Donne wrote: "One of the most convenient Hieroglyphicks of God is a Circle: and a Circle is endless; whom God loves, He loves to the end; and not only to their own end, to their death, but to His end, and His end is that He might love them still." For eight centuries the circle was almost all that was widely used, it was so inescapably revealing! St. Patrick picked up the idea when he let the shamrock with its three little circles stand for Father, Son and Holy Spirit. Three interlocked circles on all church walls have always stood for the Trinity; and yet, on thousands of buses Christians ride to Communion facing the car cards of Ballantine's Ale, with the same trade mark of three interlocked circles, and hardly a Christian knows enough of his heritage to realize that this is sheer sacrilege! Worse than the Danish Protestants bowing to a blank wall for four hundred years without knowing why; for this is not knowing there is something to bow to! And speaking of *"Trinity"*—has anybody written to ask the scientists why they ever named their first successful bomb experiment with that Divine title?

Any study of "threes" in religious symbolism is rewarding. Underneath the symbol of Peter's fishing boat, on the walls of the Catacombs, there are three waves—Father, Son and Holy Spirit. And in a beautifully wider universal fashion, Japanese flower arrangements, with flower stems cut in three lengths, arranged at three levels, match this mystical mood, since they stand for body, mind and spirit. The Chinese numeral three catches this same symbolism; three short horizontal lines (like our equal sign, with a third line added), the top line to represent *yang*, the heaven father; the lowest one *yin*, the earth mother; the middle one *jen*, man.

That was a wise old Eskimo deacon who said to his missionary after a sermon which had struggled to explain "Trinity" to such an illiterate flock: "But, Teacher, we really know all about three-in-one perfectly! You see, there is snow, there is ice, there is water, wherever we look; and one is the other, at different times!"

The Christian sits in his own church, therefore, and notices that there are three steps up from the nave to the chancel, and three steps on the Cross on the altar—in one case the Trinity; in the other Faith, Hope and Love.

John Calvin permitted the gratification of the ear through

music and poetry, but denied the gratification of the eye—quite overlooking the glorious statement in Genesis which says so plainly that God saw everything He had made, and said: "It is good!" It is still so good that perhaps the listless unobservant Christian might adopt St. Augustine's word *"hilaritas"* to learn a deeper delight in the beauty and the meaning at the heart of life. When Martin Luther finished reading the eighth chapter of Romans, he looked up from verse twenty-one toward his little dog: "Ja! thou too shalt have a little golden tail!" That would seem to be a good first step in recapturing delight over creatures great and small; but there is even better therapy in repeating daily this old German carol from the year 1623, half the value lying in the restoration of St. Augustine's word. *"Duke Street"* is simply splendid for it, because of the lift in the alternate lines where the Latin occurs—

> The whole bright world rejoices now,
> *Hilariter, hilariter;*
> The birds do sing on every bough,
> *Alleluya, Alleluya.*
>
> Then shout beneath the racing skies,
> *Hilariter, hilariter;*
> To Him who rose that we might rise,
> *Alleluya, Alleluya.*
>
> And all you living things make praise,
> *Hilariter, hilariter;*
> He guideth you on all your ways,
> *Alleluya, Alleluya.*
>
> He, Father, Son and Holy Ghost,
> *Hilariter, hilariter;*
> Our God most high, our joy and boast,
> *Alleluya, Alleluya.*

It was quite literally on this exhilarating, exuberant note that a marvelous old cathedral like the one at Chartres was built. The entire countryside—nobles, peasants, priests, artisans—swarmed out to the quarries, chiseled loose the great blocks of stone, harnessed themselves to carts and dragged the stones to the place where their cathedral was to be. They sang just such lusty canticles of praise as this old carol, they chanted litanies, they recited together the long Latin prayers of Mother Church as they panted and pulled their precious load uphill, they lived purely, and worked in a kind of creative rapture. Overflowing with gladness himself, each man went ahead to his own taste and humor. So that to this day the tourist rounds some dark corner and finds little laughing flowers, merry saints, gentle angels looking from behind old walls and through those sapphire windows.

In the end, years later, when this ecstasy was over, the citizens of Chartres complained that the cathedral made their city look too small! It sounds as if they had lapsed into illiteracy—sitting dull and proper and formal in that lovely place.

> The hand that rounded Peter's dome
> And groined the aisles of Christian Rome,
> Wrought in a sad sincerity;
> Himself from God he could not free;
> He builded better than he knew—
> The conscious stone to beauty grew.
> These temples grew as grows the grass;
> Art might obey but not surpass.
> The passive master lent his hand
> To the vast soul that o'er him planned . . .
> One accent of the Holy Ghost
> The heedless world hath never lost.

Emerson here spoke for the whole world as it worshiped. For Gandhi, who would say of God: "He is the most exacting Personage in the world and in the world to come"—for God was always getting Gandhi into trouble in India; until the symbol of his simple spinning wheel was woven into the flag of the new India he helped to free, and his final gesture after being shot was a bringing together of his hands in an ancient symbolic Hindu greeting to his assassin: "The spirit of God in me greets the spirit of God in thee!" God who was always giving rest in India: for along the roadsides there are provided high shelves called *suma-tanga*, where travelers carrying heavy burdens on their backs may drop such loads without stooping, and sit on the seat below. One Indian pilgrim, who had just heard of Christ, exclaimed with delight: "Why, He must be my *suma-tanga!*"

It is in the discovery of such fresh symbols that the Church renews itself around the earth. Exactly as the great Japanese sculptor, Nobumichi Inoye, was remade when he received a commission to carve a four-foot Crucifix for a Christian church. He began studying the passion scenes in the Gospels, and as the pity of those thorns, those nails, that spear in the side took hold of him, he bowed both his heart and his chisel in obeisance, becoming a Christian. It is really Chartres all over again, a glad rendering up of all skill to retell the world's most beloved story.

So that the Cathedral Church at Zanzibar is built over the old slave market there—as if to show jubilantly what Christ can do in a place which was once so tragic. In Madagascar this same recognition of the power of God is seen in the steppingstone into the cathedral, the very rock from which ten thousand earlier Christians had been hurled down the steep precipice to death, during twenty-five years of persecution there. But now, Christ saying to new Peters: "On this rock I will build my Church, and the gates of hell shall not prevail against it!"

The common Chinese sailor used to paint an eye on his ship: a prayer for safety, that the boat might see its way to the harbor. But in the days of an uncommon sailor like Christopher Columbus, all ships were prayers! The sails prayed with great red crosses woven into the cloth; the mast prayed, with its yard arms forming another Cross; and even the reef points on the sails prayed, for they were marked AVMGP—*Ave Virgo Maria Gratia Pleno.*

"Take with you words and turn to the Lord"! Much as Coleridge and Wordsworth made an agreement that the former would treat the supernatural and make it credible, and the latter would present the commonplace and make it wonderful. So the name of Jesus is not so much written as plowed into the history of men; standing behind our walls; looking through our windows. Until the very Sanctuary Knocker of the old cathedral in Durham could speak volumes—rewriting the entire history of all seven of the ancient Hebrew "cities of refuge, set on a hill." For no matter

what his crime, any Englishman was safe from all his pursuers if he could only reach that front door and grasp that Knocker! For thirty-seven days Durham had to give him food and lodging; and then, if no pardon had been obtained, he had to be allowed to make his escape from the country: "Forgive us our trespasses, even as we forgive . . . " And on the high altar at Durham, the priests laid boughs of mistletoe throughout Advent, symbol that all men were safe in memory of the Child whose name was Wonderful . . . the Prince of Peace. On earth! In Durham!

"Hope is the mark of all whom God would make His friends," Dante wrote. So we carve this hope in old symbols on old walls not only for aesthetic enjoyment, but to keep us in closer touch moment by moment with the Eternal Goodness: to lift us up from our ignorance into an awareness that there is more in this than meets the eye.

Precisely what certain blunt Buffalo laymen wrote in the bulletin of their First Reformed Church, the year they were pastorless: "Suppose membership in the Church were good for one year, and re-election depended on the good you had done in Church during that time, would you be re-elected?"

We are like dwarfs seated on the shoulders of giants; we see more things than the ancients and things more distant, but this is due neither to the sharpness of our own sight, nor to the greatness of our own stature, but because we are raised and borne aloft on that giant mass. . . . It is the duty of a religious man to weep. Cities must be to him as prisons, and solitude his paradise.
                                    Bernard of Clairvaux, 1091-1153

I have gone the whole round of Creation: I saw and I spoke!
I, a work of God's hand for that purpose, received in my brain

And pronounced on the rest of His handwork—returned
    Him again
His creation's approval or censure. I spoke as I saw . . .
Do I task any faculty highest, to image success?
I but open my eyes—and perfection, no more and no less,
In the kind I imagined, full-fronts me, and God is seen
    God
In the star, in the stone, in the flesh, in the clod.
And thus within and around me I ever renew
(With that stoop of the soul which in bending upraises
    it too)
The submission of man's nothing-perfect to God's all-
    complete,
As by each new obeisance in spirit I climb to His feet!
                                        Robert Browning

3 3

I AM A STAINED-GLASS WINDOW

For now we see through a glass, darkly; but then face to face;
now I know in part; but then shall I know even as also I am
known.   1 CORINTHIANS 13:12

Tourists make terrible parents for an eight-year-old in Europe.
Interminable museums, art galleries, cathedrals! what on earth
could grownups see in all those stuffy buildings? Daytimes, with
noses buried in Baedeker; nighttimes, writing it up in diaries.
About nothing whatever. *Nothing!* But he was a wise father. And
he made her see something in a stained-glass window.

She had dragged her feet despairingly indoors. But when her

parents started to inspect some three-starred tomb, she let herself be fascinated by finding on the cathedral floor a brilliant chessboard of colors reflecting the windows above. She was dancing with hops, skips and jumps from the red to the green to the blue, when a verger came up behind her and tapped her lightly on the shoulder with his finger.

She hurried over to her parents with the news: "That man in the long black robe almost hit me. Not quite! Just sort of."

"No more than you deserved, dancing in church! The idea!" her father said, taking her by the hand and leading her back to the chessboard.

"But David did it! It says so in the Bible. He danced before the Lord!"

"I know, my darling, but David knew why he danced. Not a game; but gratitude! Back in the days when people did lovely dramatic things like that to tell God something. In fact, I never saw a better picture of the Bible than this outline on the floor, right now. You'll like it—come on!"

So, hand in hand, they walked sedately to the gorgeous sunshine on the great stone floor, and stood together on a big blue patch.

"This is exactly like the Bible, dear! As long as you live, never let anybody anywhere upset you about the Bible. Never let them say it is full of disagreeable blue people who complain a lot, and grumble a lot, and forgot all about God. Always try pretending you stand in their shoes, just to be sure how it feels. And half the time you will discover that they simply adored God, too, and wanted Him above anything else on earth. Why don't we let this big blue patch be David for a while. Yes, he danced before the Lord when he had had a fabulous victory. But often and often he was blue as indigo, and wrote the bluest Psalms about the way he felt about himself and God. Listen—'all Thy waves and Thy billows have gone over me.' 'I looked on my right hand, and beheld, but there was no man that would know me: refuge failed me; no man cared for my soul. Attend unto my cry, for I am brought very low: deliver me from my persecutors, for they are stronger than I!' 'My enemies have compassed me about, like a lion that is greedy for his prey—as a young lion lurking in secret places. Arise, O Lord, disappoint him and cast him down; deliver my soul from the wicked.' That sort of thing. Pretty blue, wasn't it?"

"My goodness!" the child said, her eyes looking curiously at the blue stone floor. "Even our shoes are blue, Daddy."

"Of course they are; because we are standing in blue. An emperor in Rome years ago, named Marcus Aurelius, said that the soul is dyed the color of its secret thoughts. But there's this about the Bible: You will find the same blue people stepping over into a brighter light and saying that 'God is my refuge and strength— of whom shall I be afraid?' And that was exactly why God sent Jesus Christ. To be everybody's hope and cheer. People who met Him always got better, if they wanted to get better. Can you think of a terribly blue father who wanted his daughter to get better?"

"Jairus!"

"Splendid. And plenty of others. Blue because they were lame. Or blind. Or lepers. Or lonely. Or blue because they were blue! The Bible is brimful of blueness and cheerfulness. You can go to it and find what you need, even when you get to be an old-old lady you can find it! Even if you are a poor-*poor* old-old lady, the Bible is the Book for blue people. Well, what color shall we stand on next?"

"Red! Will it be jolly?" she asked hopefully, after the above dose.

"Not jolly at all," he sighed. "In fact, worse than the blue. For red is all blood and battles and hatreds. Never forget about the Bible that it is full of rough and dreadful people, doing rough and dreadful things. Half the time you will find them saying that God wanted them to do some awful thing. The rest of the time it was frankly their own idea! Like Cain killing Abel. Or David secretly getting Uriah put in the front row of troops to be shot down. The Old Testament is red with such stories of hatred. So it was high time for God to send the Lord Jesus on earth. And He sent His angels to sing two perfectly wonderful white shining words to the shepherds. I know you know them by heart?"

"Peace and goodwill?"

"Of course! And don't they sound safe? Yet even the twelve

men who went wherever Jesus went, even *they* saw red much too often! Like James and John, the Sons of Thunder, who wanted to call down fire from heaven to burn up a town that didn't want Jesus to speak there. Then there was Judas who brought soldiers with spears into a garden to arrest Jesus. Spears! Into a garden where Jesus had been praying, my darling. The Prince of Peace— praying. And one of his own friends betraying Him with a kiss. Although from time out of mind everybody has always known that kissing is only for people who love each other dearly. Perhaps we shouldn't forget Peter in that same garden. For he saw red, too. So angry over having Jesus in trouble that he pulled his sword and cut off the ear of the high priest's servant. The whole New Testament has these red patches—Pilate letting his soldiers scourge Jesus, and slap that lovely face again and again. As for the crucifixion, it is very red and very, very ugly. But, three days later, *Easter!* White and shining and wonderful!"

"Good!" the child cried, "and I just hope it stays that way!" She tried to leave the old disagreeable red color, but her father held her back.

"Just a moment! Not so quick—for it did *not* stay that way: people went on killing people, often because of Jesus Christ. Paul was beaten and stoned just the same way he used to beat and stone people. You must always remember about the Bible that the red dreadful pages are filled with simply superb bravery, too. And ever since then, other Christians in other places have been just as magnificent. One of the exciting things in Europe, on this trip, has been discovering that new pages of the Bible are still being written. You have thought that it was a big nuisance for me to keep copying down things from old manuscripts and old inscriptions. But, my darling, how else will you ever know that, before you, there lived marvelous mortals, and that you must match their spirit? Listen to this, written way back in the year 290, in Rome, when the Emperor Diocletian threatened to torture a Christian named Hermas. See how he expected even his little sons and daughters to go right on living the Bible, for he said to the Emperor: 'Though thou shouldest take from our hand all our writings, Dread Inquisitor, so that there should appear no traces at all of this true tradition anywhere in the whole world, yet our descendants, taking thought for the memory of their fathers and for their own souls, will compose and write greater volumes, and will teach yet more strenuously the fear that we ought to pay to Christ.' Isn't that a wonderful thing to have copied down when we were in Italy? And here is a brave, brave thing which Martin Luther said in Germany when certain Christians were trying to threaten him; the Cardinal legate thundered at him: 'The pope's little finger is stronger than all Germany. Do you expect your princes to take up arms to defend you—a wretched worm like you! I tell you, No! And where will you be then? Tell me that—where will you be then?' To which Martin Luther answered quietly: 'Then, as now, in the hands of Almighty God!' Just think—you have stood where he stood. As we are standing now, in this red dangerous color."

The little girl looked properly impressed: "I'd just as soon stand somewhere else, though," and started to move.

"Of course you would. That was a strong dose! Let's do the royal purple patch next, to think about kings and queens in the Bible. How many can you remember?"

She had rather a limited list of four: King Herod, and "We three kings of Orient are." So they lingered over David, Solomon, the Queen of Sheba, Jezebel, Belshazzar, Caesar Augustus, Agrippa, Bernice—who did, and who didn't, help or hinder?

"The Bible is really nicer than I thought," she confided as they stepped over to a vivid yellow streak.

"Cowardice!" her father sighed. "Let's think about Peter and that nasty girl who pestered him into denying that he ever knew Jesus."

Green was last: Saul so jealous of David that he threw his javelin at him; the mother of Zebedee's sons so jealous of the other disciples, that she wanted one of her sons to sit on the right hand of our Lord when He became King, the other son on His left hand. The little girl saw how human it was; and on their way out of the cathedral they looked up at the window itself, much more exciting and gorgeous than the mere reflection on the floor, its clear central Figure luminous because of His dazzling seamless robe: "Whitened as no fuller could whiten it," her father quoted as they walked out, looking back over their shoulders.

So that evening in the hotel, the child began drawing a stained-glass window with colored crayons. But by bedtime she said forlornly: "Look at my photograph, Daddy! See, I'm a stained-glass window all right, for I'm bluer than blue here, and terribly red here—but what's wrong with me? Somehow I haven't turned out pretty, like the one in church this morning."

"In church this morning don't you remember how our Lord stood in the center of the window, just the way we saw Him standing in the Bible? With everybody's face turned toward His face, to catch some of His glow? But this is just you! Just colors!"

"But do I know enough to draw Jesus properly?"

"Nobody has ever done it quite right yet, dear. But that's all a Christian is for—to keep drawing that face, and drawing that face, and drawing that face. Until at last the Christian falls asleep drawing it. And then he wakes up some morning to find that his own face looks like the Lord's face. Because enough light shines through! Learning all this takes a lifetime, my darling."

But she was not discouraged: "I'll start tomorrow morning," she promised.

And so to bed.

Take thou a book in thine hands as Simeon the just took the Child Jesus into his arms to carry Him and to bless Him.   Thomas à Kempis

Correct the portrait by the living Face, man's God by God's God in the mind of man.   Robert Browning

The Bible is alive, it speaks to me; it has feet, it runs after me; it has hands, it lays hold on me.
          Martin Luther

If in the Old Testament you see nothing but history, and read that Adam was made out of mud, that his wife

was unobtrusively taken from his side while he slept;
that the serpent tempted her with forbidden fruit; that
God walked in the cool of the evening, and that a guard
was placed at the gates of Paradise to keep the fugitives
from returning—would you not fancy that the whole
thing was a fable from Homer's work shop? But under
those wrappings . . . Good heavens! What splendid wis-
dom lies concealed!　　　　　Desiderius Erasmus, 1515

34

ST. BARTHOLOMEW IS ALWAYS WITH US

God hath set some in the church, first apostles, secondarily prophets, thirdly teachers, after that miracles, then gifts of healing,
helps. . . .　　　　　　　　　　　　　1 CORINTHIANS 12:28

Bartholomew was just a name on the early church roll. He was
called; and he followed. Whenever Matthew, Mark or Luke
mention him at all, their record reads: "Philip and Bartholomew."
With Philip always first. So nobody knows to this day what Bartholomew ever said or did or thought. Almost, but not quite,
"Anon": obviously an "average" Christian. Inarticulate? Unemployed? Illiterate? For the poor man was even present at Pentecost, we read in the first chapter of Acts; but even after that tre-
mendous renewal—no extra signs and wonders connected with
his name.

This may not have embarrassed Bartholomew at all, since
going around with Philip probably gave him plenty to do. But it
really has embarrassed all the later writers who compiled lives
of the saints; it seemed only right to fix something more definite

to his memory, so they gave him a father who was a prince, and let him get to India to preach, and even be painfully martyred there—his symbol is an unusually cruel-looking butcher knife. And, of course, a date to remember him on—August 24.

In honor of his memory, we, the average church members, have a rendezvous with the history of all the church that day. Because we went around with Philip, we Bartholomews, we could and we did gather up a thousand and one loose ends: carrying luggage; distributing hymnbooks; tacking up notices; taking them down for use tomorrow, elsewhere; buying supplies; writing letters; posting the same. And, best of all, we were *there*. David complained in one of his Psalms: "I looked, and there was no man to help me." But Philip always had Bartholomew; even in print in the Bible there they go, between semicolons; "Philip and Bartholomew"; it may not seem much; but actually it is everything.

For although all our pastors wish we were not so abysmally average, still—we are the ones who are there; we come and sit; we stand and sing; we put our tithe in the envelope; we close our eyes to pray and open them to watch the man of God preaching. We sing a hymn and go out. But—we come back. And between Sundays we never beat our wife, or kill our neighbor, or steal from our boss. We are on time at our job. And we quit on time, too. If it sounds dreadfully dull, it is also decent and dependable. We go to bed tired out. Philip is the one excitement in our day, and he surely takes the starch out of us. The way it was on the road to Gaza the day the queen's eunuch came riding along in his chariot, reading Isaiah. The Spirit of God said to Philip: "Go and join that man!" *And Philip ran.* So that was the last seen of him all day. But what to do about that other errand we had been headed toward doing? Just go and do it ourselves, of course. We could only do it so-so, perhaps. But, anyhow, it tired us out. That's what comes of being *there*, however; moment by moment, day in and day out.

Preachers get so provoked at us in public conventions: "The average Christian never thinks for himself!" he complains. But, pastor! pastor! we do think. We think enough to keep coming back for more; we think the church is good for our children; we think the wife does a mighty fine job in her woman's society, working all over the map; we think it safe and sure to belong to something as sacred as the Kingdom of God on earth. We have even been willing to die for it!

Just take August 24, pastor. The wife's folks are French; Huguenots, from way back. And on St. Bartholomew's Day in France, three centuries ago, they murdered 40,000 Huguenots as heretics! Nobody knows their names, pastor. Average folks, like my wife's family. But 40,000 average French Christians believed enough in the Protestant church to be slaughtered right there in their pews, that August. Nameless, now. But doesn't the good Book make the Good Shepherd say: "I know my sheep *by name*"?

The pastor took Paul's survey of the total membership for his next Sunday sermon: "God hath set some in the Church, first apostles, secondarily prophets, thirdly, teachers, after that miracles, gifts of healing, HELPS!"

Which is why we dare to celebrate the Bartholomew in ourselves this August, as we go around with Philip—helping.

All who speak truth to me commissioned are;
All who love God are in my Church embraced.
Not that I have no sense of preference,
None deeper, but I rather love to draw,
Even here on earth, on toward that perfect law,
And heaven's fine etiquette, where "Who?" and
    "Whence?"
May not be asked, but at the Wedding Feast
North may sit down with South, and West with East.

                                        Robert Browning

One moment in a man's life is a fact so stupendous as
to take the lustre out of all fiction.

                                        Ralph Waldo Emerson

ACKNOWLEDGMENTS

For permission to reprint certain of her own stories, the author is grateful to the Methodist Board of Education and Publication (for "Just What God Had Been Waiting For" and "Diminuendo"); and to the David C. Cook Publishing Company (for "All My Heart This Night Rejoices" and "This Watch Chain Is Never to Be Sold"). Also to Harper & Brothers, for permission to quote extensively from *A Testament of Devotion*, by Thomas Kelly.